transcending CSS

the fine art of web design

andy clarke

edited and with a foreword by *molly e. holzschlag*

preface by *dave shea*

New Riders | VOICES THAT MATTER™

Transcending CSS
The Fine Art of Web Design

Andy Clarke

New Riders
1249 Eighth Street
Berkeley, CA 94710
510/524-2178
800/283-9444
510/524-2221 (fax)

Find us on the World Wide Web at: www.newriders.com
To report errors, please send a note to errata@peachpit.com

New Riders is an imprint of Peachpit, a division of Pearson Education

Editor: Karyn Johnson
Developmental Editor: Molly E. Holzschlag
Production Editor: Kate Reber
Technical/Design Editors: Aaron Gustafson, Mark Boulton
Interior Design: Charlene Charles-Will, Kim Scott
Compositor: Kim Scott
Copyeditor: Kim Wimpsett
Proofreader: Jessica McCarty
Indexer: Emily Glossbrenner
Cover Design: Mimi Heft

ISBN 0-321-41097-1

9 8 7 6 5 4 3 2

Printed and bound in the United States of America

To my nana, born the year that the Titanic sailed.

And to my son, Alex; you make me very proud.

Andy Clarke has been working on the Web for almost ten years. He is a visual Web designer based in the UK, and he started his design consultancy, Stuff and Nonsense (www.stuffand-nonsense.co.uk), in 1998.

As lead designer and creative director, he works with clients that include local and national businesses, charities, and government bodies. In addition, he has designed for the British Heart Foundation, Disney Store UK, Save the Children, and WWF UK.

Andy is a member of the Web Standards Project where he redesigned the organization's Web site in 2006. He is also an invited expert to the W3C's CSS Working Group where he represents the needs of working Web designers and developers. Andy regularly educates Web designers in the practical and creative applications of Web standards and in how to create beautiful, accessible Web sites, and he speaks at workshops and conference events worldwide.

Outside his studio, Andy annoys his neighbors and anyone else within earshot with his collection of mod and ska music and dreams of having Paul Weller 'round for tea.

Acknowledgments

When I started working on the Web in 1997, I knew little about the stuff that makes the Web work. In 2000, when I discovered Web standards, I learned from the hard work and knowledge of so many people that it would be impossible to list them all here. My love, respect, and deepest thanks go to all of those who have shared their knowledge.

Writing this book has been one of the hardest but, at the same time, the most rewarding challenges in my life, and I can't thank the Peachpit/New Riders team enough for their patience and understanding. Karyn Johnson, my editor at Peachpit/New Riders, and Kim Wimpsett, my copy editor, not only read every word and provided edits but also heaped on advice and encouragement to keep me going during the difficult times. (Karyn, start up that bike—I'm coming for a ride.) Kim Scott, Charlene Charles-Will, and Kate Reber turned my designs into a reality that I could not have imagined. My everlasting respect goes to Nancy Aldrich-Ruenzel for the faith she has shown me—I hope you are as proud as I am.

It has been a pleasure to work with technical editors Aaron Gustafson and Mark Boulton, and Molly E. Holzschlag, who introduced me to New Riders and helped to shape my ideas into the book you are now reading by acting as my development editor. I might wear the parka, but these guys steered the scooter.

Thanks also to César Acebal and the folks at the University of Oviedo, Spain, for their groundbreaking work on the CSS3 Advanced Layout prototype scripts that round off this book in style.

Without Flickr, surely the next wonder of the world, I would not have found the many talented artists and photographers whose work graces many of these pages. Thank you to everyone who published work under a Creative Commons license. In particular, thanks to Ron Huxley whose painting for the cover is everything I could have wished for, to Lara Ferroni and Eric Fung whose food photography makes my mouth water on every page, and to Dave Shea and Molly E. Holzschlag who let me cherry-pick from their wonderful images. My special thanks to the super-talented Patrick Lauke for the portrait and for making me look cooler than I deserve to look.

Finally, my love always to my wife Sue for her endless support and patience, and for being there when the tough got going.

To all those who have taught, inspired, and supported me. This book could never have happened without you.

adactio.com	mezzoblue.com
airbagindustries.com	mikeindustries.com
allinthehead.com	molly.com
andybudd.com	rachelandrew.co.uk
boxofchocolates.ca	simplebits.com
brothercake.com	shauninman.com
brucelawson.co.uk	sidesh0w.com
cameronmoll.com	simon.incutio.com
clagnut.com	splintered.co.uk
collylogic.com	stopdesign.com
dean.edwards.name	subtraction.com
hicksdesign.co.uk	tantek.com
ian-lloyd.com	themaninblue.com
jasonsantamaria.com	veen.com/jeff
joeclark.org	veerle.duoh.com
joshuaink.com	vivabit.co.uk
markboulton.co.uk	westciv.typepad.com
meyerweb.com	zeldman.com

Foreword

One of the greatest challenges Web designers and developers face is to bridge the communication gap between highly visual and highly linear thinkers. It's only the rare individual who has been able to show a balance between sophisticated, innovative design and progressive, complex technical issues. People such as Jeffrey Zeldman, Douglas Bowman, and Dave Shea have each made significant contributions to the industry for precisely this reason: They've been able to not only work on both sides of that gap but also to articulate to others a means of getting to that point.

Some years ago I published a book with New Riders called *Integrated Web Design* in which I attempted to address this very concern. How do we get designers thinking in terms of semantics and structure? How do we get the more programmatic, analytical thinkers to appreciate and understand aesthetics? Add to that the greater complexities in communicating with management, marketing, and other areas of our field, and we have significant challenges to face in order to create truly strong platforms for effective workflow, strong technology, fantastic design, and ongoing innovation and excellence in our profession.

That brings me to Andy Clarke. Andy's work first came to my attention several years ago via his blog, where he was writing about naming conventions in markup and CSS, a topic that had long interested me. As I began to dig deeper through his articles and his design work, it became clear that here was a person who was actively bridging the divide with practical and passionate ideas. We met personally at the SXSW conference during the famous "Britpack Invasion" of 2005, and we started talking about these issues. Within several months we began to develop a series of popular workshops including "CSS for Designers" and "CSS for Developers," geared to educate and inspire our peers through our complementary skills and experiences.

When the idea for a book inevitably entered the conversation, I was extremely enthusiastic and introduced Andy to Nancy Aldrich-Ruenzel, the publisher of Peachpit and New Riders. I knew that if any imprint could grasp what Andy wanted to do, it would be within the New Riders' *Voices That Matter* series. The three of us met in San Francisco, and readers who know me will find it amusing that I never got three words in edgewise during their excited conversation. Clearly, a match was made. We determined that the book would be a natural fit, particularly in light of the success of *The Zen of CSS Design* by Dave Shea and myself. I would edit the book, working with Andy to shape its vision and content, and Dave would also be involved, writing the preface, and connecting the books in spirit as resources for anyone seeking to become better designers and developers.

The book's development did not come without its challenges. You see, as technical as Andy can be, he is and will always be a visual fellow. And as much aesthetic and formal training I might have in the design field, I am a linear, logical person. Andy, like many visual thinkers, lives mostly in a world of imagination and creativity, whereas I like order, communication, and process. Ironically, many of the challenges we had to face and solve in the process of writing this book had to do with the kinds of problems that typically exist in our field between these types of personalities.

That this book, with its incredible beauty, solid technology, and true vision, ultimately is everything we originally envisioned it to be is just more proof that when people are committed to bridging those difficult gaps, true innovation can occur. It is with great pride, respect, confidence, and honor that I am today able to share the results of this experience with you, the people working so hard to transcend the challenges within our profession. May *Transcending CSS: The Fine Art of Web Design* serve you well in our shared desire to make the Web everything we have ever wanted and can imagine it to be.

Molly E. Holzschlag
London, October 2006

Preface

In order to introduce this book, I invite you to stop reading it. Take a minute first to *look* at it.

Hopefully in a precursory flipping through the pages, you have already picked up some sense of its design style. The art direction is fantastic, isn't it? Photography and screen shots abound. Points are cleverly made using images rather than boring line after line of markup and CSS. Real world examples are pulled in to demonstrate Web-specific topics. Books about code really have no right to look this good.

And that's what I'd like to impress upon you. As you may have deduced from the title, *Transcending CSS* is not just another code book; it's about far more than that. It's about design and code playing together nicely. It's about the way code is meant to support design considerations. It's about breaking the chains that sometimes keep us far too grounded in reality.

As you'll learn within these pages, very large online spaces like Yahoo have started using techniques that provide backwards-compatibility for older browsers but, more importantly, companies are starting to deliver new features to users with new browsers able to take advantage of them. These are techniques all of us need to begin experimenting with and putting into effect in our own projects; Andy Clarke shows us how.

In a sense, this book reminds me quite a lot of one that came out in early 2005. Perhaps you've read *The Zen of CSS Design*, a book I had the pleasure of co-authoring with Molly Holzschlag, who is the editor of *Transcending CSS*.

In our book, we set out to discuss CSS not just in a structured code-oriented manner, but also with the goal of combining design theory with well-designed examples to explain, illustrate, and inspire. *Transcendent CSS* strikes me as a very good next step—

you've finished *Zen*, now what? Mr. Clarke has come along and given all of us that answer.

We learned in *Zen* that CSS-based design doesn't have to be ugly, that the possibilities are wide open when placed in the hands of strong visual designers. Now we learn in *Transcendent CSS* that the current state of the Web is simply a starting point, and it's time to look to the future.

And that's important to understand. This book is not simply a guide that covers ground well-trodden by other more technical manuals; you are meant to be challenged by its concepts and inspired to take the current state of the Web to new heights.

The entire concept of *Transcendent CSS* is not so much of a how-to as it is a manifesto: *Transcend the Web of today*. Don't keep your mind focused on the past, turn your head around and start looking to the future. Mr. Clarke is here to show you how.

Dave Shea
October 2006

CONTENTS

2

Inspiration

3

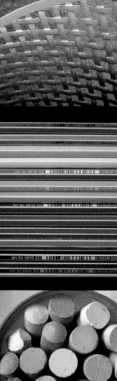

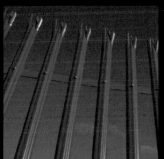

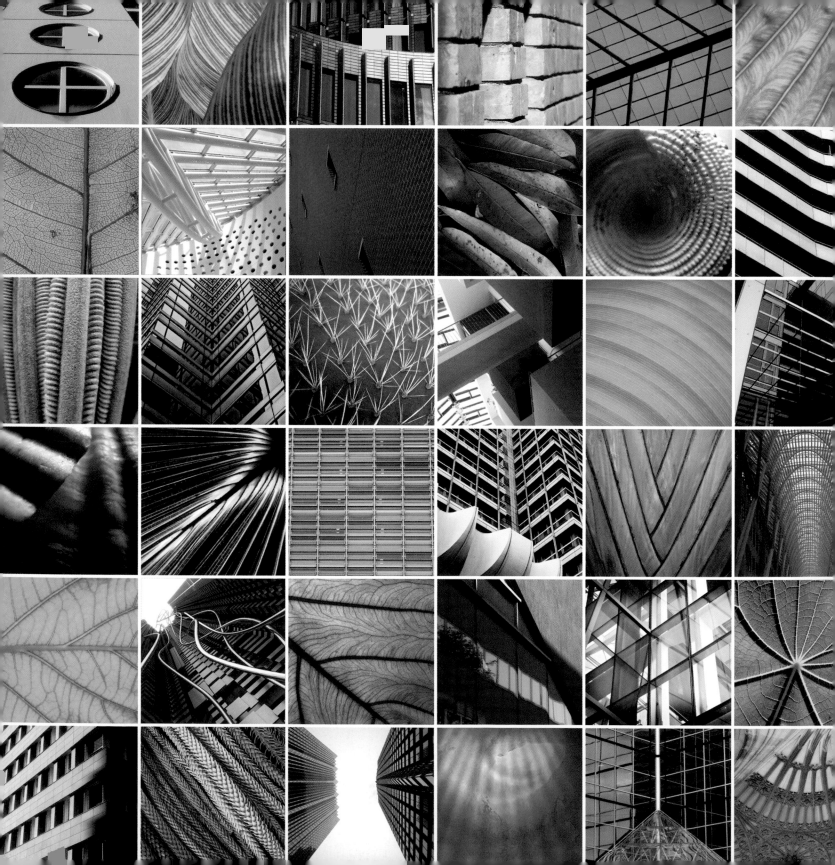

1

Discovery

Think differently about the Web design process.

See how to improve the design workflow.

Look forward to exciting possibilities.

Introducing Transcendent CSS

Transcendent CSS is more than a plea to use the latest, coolest CSS. It's a quest to use the lessons you're learning in CSS as a means to becoming the finest artist and designer you can be. Transcendent CSS asks you to embrace the new rather than the old and to stimulate new ways to find inspiration, create more agile and appropriate workflows for Web design, and encourage yourself to constantly learn more about both the design and the technical issues with which you work.

Which tools do you need to get started?

Which tools do you need to adopt the Transcendent CSS approach and to work along with the principles explained in this book? You don't need anything more than you are probably using already. Don't worry, you won't need a spanner or a monkey wrench. You won't even need special software or new server configurations.

This book is not aimed at beginners; I assume you already have a good, working knowledge of XHTML (eXtensible HTML) markup and CSS and you understand the core concepts of Web standards. If you are still at the stage of using tables for layout, this book won't teach you about the basics of selectors or common CSS properties; many other fantastic references are already available that will do just that.

But if you are a newcomer to CSS, I hope you will find the concepts and examples found in this book inspiring and that you will want to grab hold of the handlebars and learn as much as you can about CSS. No matter how long you have been working with CSS, you'll find new places to go and new things to learn.

This book also assumes you have an open mind. Although not everything discussed will be 100 percent relevant to you or the work you're doing for your organization, studio, or clients, I encourage you to take on new ideas. You can then adapt them to suit you better and in ways that I could not have imagined. Most important though, I want you to have a real desire for looking toward future methods and thereby creating fresh and exciting work for the Web.

Why do you need Transcendent CSS?

I'm a designer. I like to design stuff. Some days I wish I designed iconic stuff such as classic cars or maybe the Apple iPod—stuff that people love and that makes me piles of cash...enough cash to buy as many classic scooters and 1960s Minis as I can fit in my garage. But you see, for one, I don't have a garage, and for another I enjoy what I design too much. Call me Mr. Obsessed if you like, but I just love designing for the Web.

I haven't always enjoyed the Web so much. Many times in my design career I could have cheerfully put down my computer after days of frustration and gone to do something completely different. Sometimes after struggling with one problem or another, the thought of spending hours in a garden shed with nothing but an old radio for company and growing gigantic leeks seemed appealing indeed. But rather than talking to vegetables, I stuck to talking to myself, and before too long, it was "problem solved." My passion for the Web was back. Funny, though—I never expected Web design would be so challenging; I mean, it's not like climbing Mount Everest. People don't choose to do it just "because it's there."

But many parts of the Web design process can be challenging for designers like me who are visual thinkers. Every day we use visual tools such as Adobe Photoshop, Macromedia

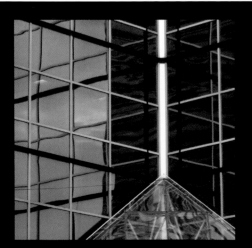

Fireworks, and others to move pixels around a screen to achieve our design goals. Some of the more technical aspects of the stuff that makes Web sites work today, particularly writing meaningful markup and CSS, can be unfamiliar or even seem counterintuitive.

CSS is not designer friendly

One factor is that as a technology built to help solve design problems, CSS is not very designer friendly largely because it was created for designers by technologists rather than by other designers.

Although the basic principles are simple enough, as you can see here:

```
p { color : #000; }
body { background-color : #fff; }
```

for some designers, terms such as *the cascade* and *inheritance* are more difficult to understand. Add to this discussion talk of *positioning*, *collapsing margins*, or the *box model*, and you might see one of the many reasons why designers have taken a reasonably long time to adopt CSS.

For the longest period of time after CSS was launched, it was very much the domain of technologists. Their big brains were better equipped to understand concepts such as *specificity* as well as the myriad of largely unintelligible CSS hacks that were necessary to implement a design more or less consistently across different browsers.

These difficulties have done little to reduce the knowledge gaps that have always existed between visual designers and the technical developers who work to implement designs using code, and they have often left designers feeling frustrated with CSS.

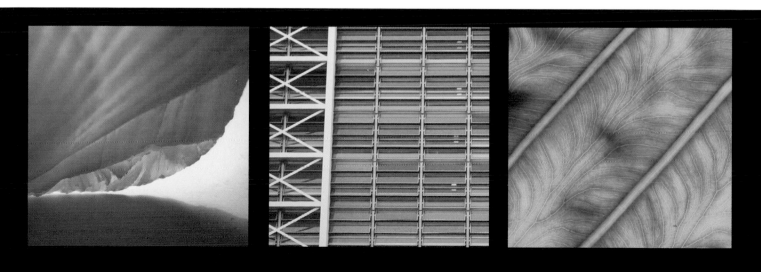

Web browsers' rendering inabilities have stifled progress

And then of course Web browsers challenge us. From the earliest implementations of
CSS in Microsoft Internet Explorer 3 (the first mainstream browser to support any CSS),
working with CSS has often been exasperating. Browser bugs, rendering errors, or just the
plain stupidity of certain browser behaviors all made our lives more difficult.

This situation did get better over time; Netscape 4.*x* was better than Internet Explorer 3,
and Internet Explorer 5 for the Mac showed for the first time that CSS could "work."
Internet Explorer 6 had the best CSS support of any browser when it was released, despite
its now well-known catalog of colorfully named bugs.

I imagine my fourteen-year-old son, now taking his first steps into Web design, might
look back in years to come and laugh when he reads about the "double-margin float" or
the "peekaboo bug." He also might wonder whether the "3px jog" was how designers today
exercised before they ate breakfast.

Never underestimate the power of the individual

Still, a way was found; largely because of the dedication of developers including Tantek
Çelik, Todd Fahrner, and Eric Meyer whose work then made it possible for designers such
as Douglas Bowman and Dave Shea to show that working with CSS was not only desirable
but a practical reality. Throughout the years since the first CSS specification was released,
dedicated people like this all over the world have battled with and found workarounds for
almost all the problems designers working with CSS face on a daily basis.

It is also important not to forget that by working on liaisons with browser vendors and
software developers and also working in education, members of the grassroots Web
Standards Project—including Rachel Andrew, Molly E. Holzschlag, and Dori Smith—have
all played major roles in raising awareness of the importance of standards.

Without these individuals working separately in small groups, CSS use would never have
been the powerful Web design tool it is today.

Relatively speaking, today we have it easy when compared to the pioneering early days of
CSS. Many new Web designers will never have experienced working with table-based layouts
or the frustrations of getting CSS layouts to work in what we think of now as ancient
browsers such as Netscape 4.

Some accessibility sites are downright ugly,

but the problem lies with those sites' designers

and not with accessibility, which carries

no visual penalty. The same is true for Web

standards, even if the look and feel of the W3C

Web site is unlikely to motivate designers to

get busy learning about XML or CSS2.

—JEFFREY ZELDMAN
Designing With Web Standards. First Edition, May 2003

Expanding the creative possibilities

Now that Web browsers have reached a certain level of maturity in their support for standards such as CSS, they provide us with a firmer foundation on which to develop our designs. It is time to move forward, not stand still.

The mechanics of table-based layouts confined our designs to a rigid grid and reinforced time after time the conventions of the typical two- or three-column layout still seen on countless Web sites. CSS offers new creative possibilities by using floats and different forms of positioning, it offers layering in the form of the z-index, and it gives you the power to style any element through the CSS box model. These opportunities for creativity were not possible with table-based layouts (**Figure 1.1**).

Designs that adapt beyond the screen

Two years before the publication of the first CSS specification and a full six months before Netscape launched its first Web browser, Chris Lilley, who would become the chairman of the W3C (World Wide Web Consortium) CSS Working Group, essentially predicted what would happen to the Web during the rest of that decade:

> *If style sheets or similar information are not added to HTML, the inevitable price will be documents that only look good on a particular browser, at a particular window size, with the default fonts, etc.*
>
> —Chris Lilley (former chairman of the CSS Working Group, at the time snappily called the Style and Formatting Properties Working Group), May 1994

After many years of hard work, the Web has now finally made its way onto mobile phones, gaming devices, and televisions; in the future, this will include all manner of other portable devices that haven't been invented yet.

Hold that download for a moment; I'm going into a tunnel

The truth of the matter is that we simply do not know where the Web will crop up next. In years to come, my son will laugh at the idea that the Web was ever "hardwired" to the desktop, just as I laugh at the memory of my first mobile phone that came with a battery pack the size of a house brick and weighed just about the same.

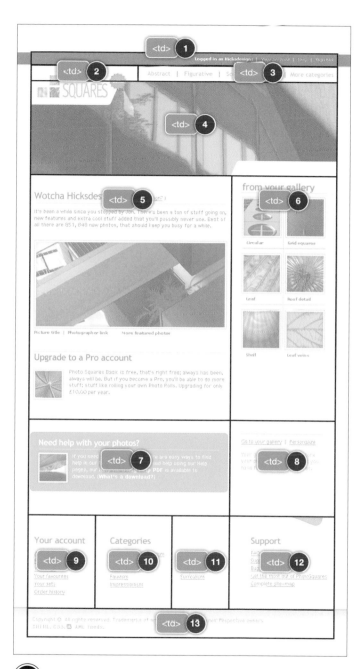

1.1 Transitioning to CSS-based layouts does not always mean better structured or ordered code. Left: The presentational content order of a table-based layout. Right: The tables have been replaced by `<div>`s without reordering the content.

In such a rapidly changing medium, Lilley's words now ring truer than perhaps they did when he first wrote them. Today's designers should at least be aware that their designs will have to adapt to the many needs of these different environments. Lightweight, meaningful documents and CSS are key factors in successfully transitioning a design from the desktop to other devices, be those devices printers, small-screen handheld computers, or personal media players or mobile phones (**Figure 1.2**).

Accessibility is design, not a feature

Good information architecture, usability, and accessibility have rightly become areas of concern for professional designers and developers. In particular, ensuring the widest possible accessibility is not only an ethical issue but also a commercial one. However, many designers, developers, and other specialists in the accessibility realm have wrongly limited conversations about accessibility to merely serving the needs of people with disabilities.

Accessibility is a matter of usability

Much of what has been written about accessibility has focused on ensuring that sites are accessible to people who are blind or visibly impaired. Much more has been written about ensuring that sites comply with accessibility guidelines or in some cases laws. However, most of this simply misses the point.

Although serving the needs of people with disabilities should of course be a concern, the far wider issue—that accessibility is a matter of usability—has rarely been discussed. As designer professionals, we should be designing our content so it is globally accessible and meets the needs of as many people as is possible and practical given our specific circumstances, regardless of their abilities or the type of device they choose to access the Web.

For the traveling businessman, whether he can successfully log on to his company's intranet to check sales figures on a handheld computer is both a usability and an accessibility issue, as is that many movie sites offering branded goodies for your mobile phone do not offer you the ability to access those pages using a mobile phone. It's important to realize that it is through good design that you can remove as many barriers to access for as many people as possible.

Opera Mini™ simulator

1.2 Using CSS everywhere

Wearing badges is not enough in days like these

Unfortunately, many designers still view accessibility concerns as limitations on their creativity, guidelines they should comply with, or laws they should obey rather than as an everyday part of the job of a designer. Accessibility has too often been viewed as an external factor with sites tested after completion to ensure that they meet one standard or another:

> *If you look at accessibility as a feature, you'll probably leave it out. Most developers are gonna leave it out anyway; most developers don't know the first thing about accessibility or even that it's important.*
>
> —Joe Clark (http://joeclark.org/ice/iceweb2006-notes.html)

It is sad that much of the work involved in ensuring that content and services are accessible at best currently takes place late in the design and development processes and at worst is an afterthought that requires a refit. When given the choice between the latest exciting Ajax interface and accessibility, many companies will choose the dynamic interface and may plan accessibility testing or features as part of a future release.

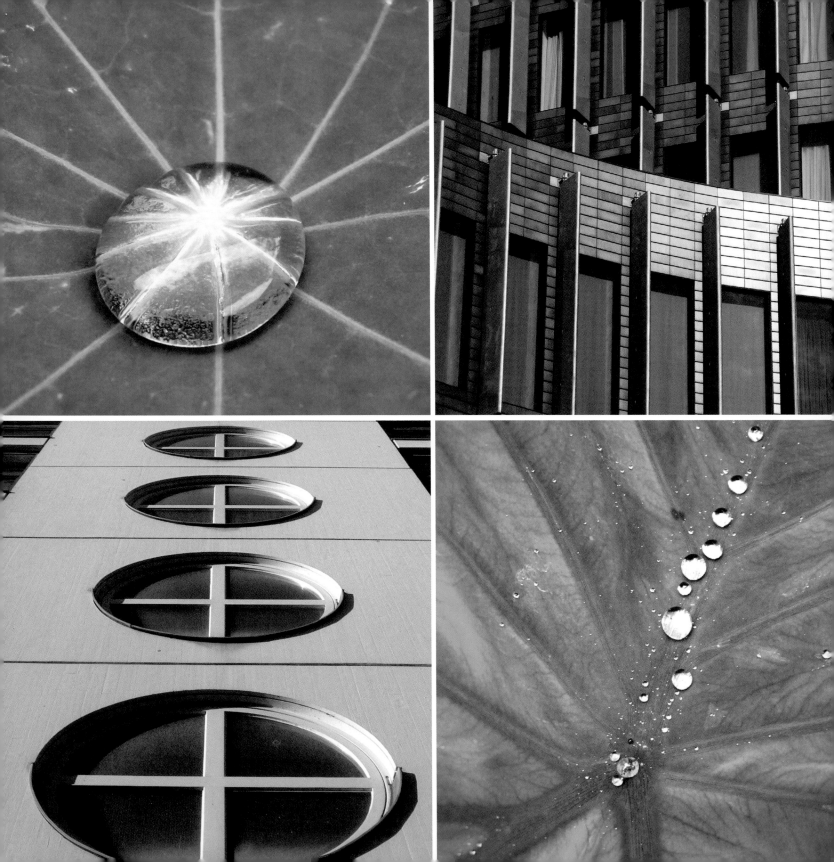

Explaining Transcendent CSS to your clients

Many designers have been itching to use the full power of CSS in their work but have been held back because they believe their clients will expect their designs will appear the same across all browsers.

It is true that many clients, companies, and hiring organizations do expect it is part of a designer's job to ensure such cross-browser compatibility. Although it rarely should be a designer's job to educate a client, some simple analogies can help you explain in broad terms the concepts of Transcendent CSS to your clients.

In many other areas of design and technology, the concept that the functionality or user experience of a product is the same regardless of the age or competence of a technology is ridiculous. Consumers not only expect that technologies will improve over time, but they also want to know they have bought the most up-to-date product.

You can easily explain to a client that you design for the most modern browsers using the latest coding techniques, but you still provide a good experience for people who use outdated browsers.

HIGH-DEFINITION TV

HDTV (high-definition television) offers a far-higher-resolution picture and better-quality sound than conventional television for people using HDTVs and receivers. High-definition broadcast television has been available in the United States for far longer than it has been in the United Kingdom. Since the first satellite broadcasters announced they were beginning high-definition broadcasts in the United Kingdom in 2006, electrical retailers and makers of televisions have been clambering to jump aboard the "HD-ready" bandwagon.

If you choose not to upgrade your equipment to HDTV or not to pay an additional subscription to view in high-definition, you are not excluded from watching your favorite soap, cop show, or football game; you simply see a slightly inferior but perfectly acceptable picture quality because your hardware is less up-to-date.

THE IPOD FACTOR

When Apple first launched its iPod portable music player, the player had fewer features and a different user experience than buyers of more recent models now enjoy. In a highly competitive marketplace, Apple has maintained its lead by providing new features with almost every release, such as the capability to store album art and play music videos or TV shows downloaded from its iTunes Store.

Older versions of the iPod still provide the same functionality they did when they were first unboxed. Consumers would never expect that an older player would offer the same facilities as a newer model, and they accept that to gain access to the new features they must upgrade.

PERPETUALLY UPGRADING YOUR SOFTWARE

The software industry has typically been littered with buggy, unstable software releases and operating systems that would freeze or crash on an almost daily basis. Yet despite these failings, consumers accept that a newer, better version will be just around the corner and are prepared to upgrade.

As well as being people who commission designers to develop Web sites, clients are also consumers who are exposed to changing technologies almost daily, and as such they can easily understand that people using more modern browsers will get an enhanced user experience or design.

In June 2005, I expanded on my opinion that in order for the needs of people with disabilities to be better served on the Web, government-sponsored laws and regulations were counterproductive. "Accessibility and a society of control" sparked many interesting comments about how best to move the cause of Web accessibility forward (www.stuffandnonsense.co.uk/archives/accessibility_and_a_society_of_control.html).

However, when you work from the content out, using well-ordered and meaningful markup to provide the content and structure and using CSS for visual styling, you can build accessibility directly into the design process from the start. This will benefit everyone, including the designer who will be less challenged by accessibility issues, the client who will ultimately save money on retrofitting and have happier customers, and, most important, the visitors to those sites who will more easily get the stuff done that they need to get done.

Moving toward Transcendent CSS

Compared to the freedom enjoyed by print and multimedia designers, those of us who choose to work with markup and CSS have always suffered from factors limiting our designs; these factors are often beyond our control.

Since the first CSS specification was published, our creative potential has been hampered by the limited performance of browsers—unless, that is, we are prepared to sacrifice the purity of our documents by using presentational markup or choose to work solely in Flash.

Browser makers have mostly continued to improve their support for Web standards, particularly CSS and the W3C DOM (Document Object Model), but Microsoft's prior decision to allow development of its Internet Explorer browser to stagnate at version 6, plus the widespread, though thankfully now, reduced usage of its older versions has led to designers being hesitant about using some of the more advanced aspects of CSS.

When competing browsers such as Mozilla Firefox, Mozilla Camino, Apple Safari, and Opera began to shave percentage points off Internet Explorer's market share (**Table 1.1**), forward-thinking designers began to investigate ways to reward users of these more modern browsers by giving them an extra layer of design finesse. This technique became known as *progressive* or *MOSe enhancement*.

Table 1.1 Browser usage in July 2004–2006

	Internet Explorer 7 (beta)	Internet Explorer 6	Internet Explorer 5	Firefox	Mozilla	Netscape	Opera
2006	1.9%	57.8%	4.2%	25.0%	2.2%	0.4%	1.4%
2005	–	67.9%	5.9%	19.8%	2.6%	0.5%	1.2%
2004	–	67.2%	13.2%	–	12.6%	1.8%	2.0%

Source: W3 Schools (www.w3schools.com/browsers/browsers_stats.asp), August 2006

MOSe enhancements

Way back in 2003, Dave Shea, the Canadian designer, author, and creator of the CSS Zen Garden, wrote about a compelling new approach to the problem of creating designs for the differing capabilities of competing Web browsers; he coined this approach MOSe (Mozilla, Opera, Safari enhancement).

With MOSe, Shea claimed it was acceptable for designers to exploit Internet Explorer 6's (and earlier edition's) lack of support for certain CSS selectors (among them child, adjacent sibling, and attribute selectors) to provide an enhanced design for users of modern browsers that was layered on top of a standard design that was visible to all.

In theory, Shea's suggestion was no more complicated than the @import at-rule technique. This widely used technique exploited that Netscape 4 could not interpret @import and prevented the aging browser from CSS that it either could not understand or bungled, but this technique has one important difference. When Shea wrote his article, Internet Explorer 6 was, despite its many flaws, a browser capable of supporting most of the CSS specification. It was the most widely used browser in circulation, so any attempt to design away from it had to be a subtle one.

Working around Netscape 4.*x*

Netscape 4.*x* had some CSS support. In an attempt to shield CSS styles that Netscape 4.*x* could not interpret, many designers chose to hide all but the most basic styles by using the @import at-rule.

This is a basic style sheet visible to all browsers including Netscape 4.*x*:

```
<link rel="stylesheet"
type="text/css" href="simple.
css" />
```

This is a more advanced style sheet for browsers with more explicit CSS support:

```
@import "modern.css";
```

All browsers will load simple.css; however, only browsers that understand the @import at-rule will load modern.css. Since modern.css is imported after simple.css, its rules will override those in simple.css unless those rules are more specific.

The key to the MOSe method is somewhat similar to how NN4 (Netscape Navigator 4.x) page design developed as CSS became more prevalent. After creating a basic, functioning page in IE, you add extra functionality with these selectors.

—DAVE SHEA
www.mezzoblue.com/archives/2003/06/25/mose/

FROM THE CSS ZEN GARDEN

Building on the MOSe approach, This Is Cereal, Shaun Inman's CSS Zen Garden design, used the CSS selectors that weren't supported in Internet Explorer to provide visitors using modern browsers with a richer experience. Inman transformed unordered lists of links into subtle drop-down menus with alpha-transparent PNG images. Although he was not the first designer to use this technique, his results were inspirational.

Visitors using older browsers see styled but plainer unordered lists and are not aware that an alternative version exists. Subtle MOSe enhancements such as this have since become a common feature in many of CSS Zen Garden's designs (**Figure 1.3**).

1.3 Featuring MOSe enhancements on CSS Zen Garden

AND ALL THAT MALARKEY

Inspired by Inman, for my personal Web site I created two distinct designs: one full-color design inspired by the British mod(ernist) music movement of the 1960s and one black-and-white 20ld design that was inspired by the stark two-tone imagery made famous by the British ska record label 2Tone.

Because ska music came before mod, I made the ska design available only to legacy versions of Internet Explorer. I implemented the mod design using CSS2.1 selectors that are understood only by mod(ern) browsers, which was a fun way to highlight the different capabilities of browsers.

Note: My decision to "punish" visitors using Internet Explorer by depriving them of the full mod design was not altogether well received, as you can see for yourself at www.stuffand nonsense.co.uk/archives/and_all_that_design_malarkey.html.

Progressive Enhancement

Several months after Shea's MOSe article appeared, another was published in *Triangle TechJournal* that further explained the concept of progressive enhancement:

> *Progressive Enhancement presents a viable approach by enabling the delivery of information as demanded by the users, while embracing accessibility, future compatibility, and determining user experience based on the capabilities of new devices.*

> —Debra Chandra and Steve Champeon (http://hesketh.com/publications/ progressive_enhancement_paving_way_for_future.html)

But fully adopting the methods of progressive enhancement has been difficult for designers to achieve in commercial projects until now. This difficulty stemmed not only from the commanding market share of Internet Explorer 6 but also from the belief that it is correct to set a design benchmark based on the most popular browser, even if that browser is less capable and less advanced in its support for modern standards than its competitors.

For such a young and dynamic medium as the Web, the notion that designers should not push design boundaries forward because of only one browser, even when that browser is the market leader, seems incompatible with progress.

Both MOSe and progressive enhancement were ideas intended to encourage designers to use all the tools made available to them in the CSS2.1 specification for browsers that supported these selectors and rules. Even today, several years later, these CSS rules are often described as *advanced* or *cutting edge* despite that they were invented only a few years after the birth of the commercial Web.

MOSe and progressive enhancement have been used on personal portfolios and blogs; you can rarely find them on mainstream, commercial projects. As a result, progressive Web design has largely stalled and, if left much longer, will begin to go stale.

My question is, can progressive enhancement still be called *progressive* three years after the term was first coined? The answer must be no, so it is time to move forward.

The Principles of Transcendent CSS

This brings us to the subject of this book. The principles of Transcendent CSS allow Web designers to focus on their creative goals without being preoccupied with technical constraints. These principles allow Web designers to look to the future without being compromised by the limitations of the past.

1. **Not all browsers see the same design.**

2. **Use all available CSS selectors.**

3. **Use CSS3 where possible to look to the future.**

4. **Use JavaScript and the DOM to plug the holes in CSS.**

5. **Avoid using hacks and filters.**

6. **Use semantic naming conventions and microformats.**

7. **Share your ideas, and collaborate with others.**

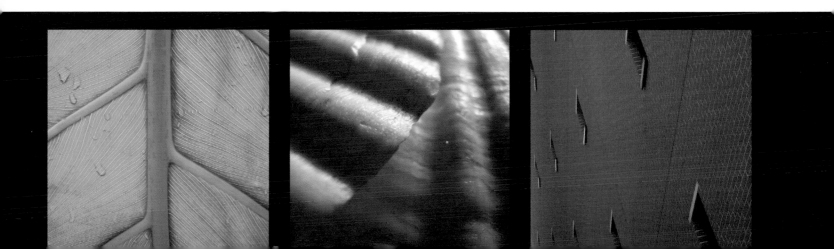

1.4 Sending different designs to different browsers at All That Malarkey

① *Not all browsers see the same design*

Whereas progressive enhancement begins with less capable browsers such as Internet Explorer 6 and then uses CSS selectors to add functionality, Transcendent CSS abandons the notion that a less-capable browser is the benchmark.

Transcendent CSS reverses the Progressive Enhancement approach that creates a design that can be rendered by all browsers but is limited to the capabilities of the lowest common denominator.

Transcendent CSS sets that benchmark squarely where it belongs today, with the CSS2.1 specification and those browsers that support it. It uses all the available CSS2.1 features, not to add visual enhancements but to accomplish the best design for the most, standards-capable browsers (**Figure 1.4**).

In practice, this approach will result in some visitors seeing a reduced design—how much of a reduced design of course depends on your preferences and the specific needs of the audiences using the sites you create.

② *Use all available CSS selectors*

Transcendent CSS uses all CSS2.1 selectors plus other CSS features including pseudo-elements and dynamic pseudo-classes. These selector types include the following:

Attribute selectors

Attribute selectors are amazingly powerful; they offer ways to style an element either based on whether an element has an attribute name such as `href` or based on the attribute value such as `"http://www.stuffandnonsense.co.uk"`.

In the following examples, all images that contain an `alt` attribute will have a gray border (**Figure 1.5**):

```
img[alt] {
border : 1px dotted #999;
}
```

```
<img src="http://www.hicksdesign.co.uk/images/love/bp.gif"
alt="Brit Pack: A proud member" />
```

1.5 Outlining images with an `alt` attribute

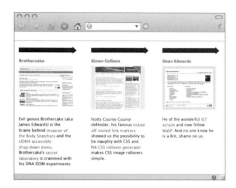

1.6 Highlighting anchor with `title` attributes

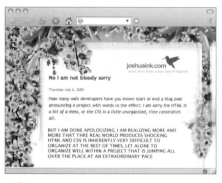

1.7 Styling a class rant

1.8 Floating a main content division

And all anchors that contain a `title` attribute will be red (**Figure 1.6**):

```
a[title]  {
color : #c00;
}
```

```
<a href="http://www.collylogic.com/" title="Simon Collison">
Former Notts County Defender
</a>
```

You can also apply styles to an element based on the content of its attributes (**Figure 1.7**):

```
p[class="rant"]  {
font-weight : bold;
text-transform : uppercase;
}
```

```
<p class="rant">
But I am done apologizing. I am realizing more and more that the real world
produces shocking HTML and CSS is inherently very difficult to organize at the
best of times, let alone to organize well within a project that is jumping all
over the place at an extraordinary pace.
</p>
```

(**Figure 1.8**)

```
div[id="content_main"]  {
float : left;
}
```

```
<div id="content_main">
<blockquote>
<p>I hope that things will change. I hope that some young guns will take up
the challenge, stop following the crowd, and really push CSS to its fullest
potential.</p>
<p>Jeremy Keith</p>
<blockquote>
</div >
```

With pattern matching, you can style an element based on only part of its attribute, in this case the base URL of the quotation's citation (**Figure 1.9**):

```css
q[cite*="http://www.andybudd.com/"]   {
padding-left : 100px;
background : url(images/budd.jpg) no-repeat left top;
}
```

```html
<q cite="http://www.andybudd.com/archives/2006/07/layout_grid_bookmarklet/">
Inspired by Khoi Vinh's post about using a background image of a grid for
layout, I decided to knock up a quick Photoshop style Layout Grid Bookmarklet
</q>
```

You will learn much more about attribute selectors and their practical applications in
Part 4, "Transcendence."

Child selectors

A *child selector* targets a direct child of a given element. For example, this gives you the
potential to style anchors that are direct children of list items differently from other anchors
on a page. Child selectors consist of two or more selectors separated by the > combinator.

> **Note:** *Combinators* separate two or more selectors that make up a *combined* selector.
> Available combinators include white space, >, and + as well as a comma or a colon.

This rule will style all anchors that are children of a <div> element:

```css
div > a {
text-indent : -9999px;
}
```

This rule affects only <a> elements that are direct children (not other descendants) of
<div> elements. If any other elements appear between the <div> and the anchor—for
example, a <ul> element—the selector will not match, and the text-indent style will
not be applied (**Figure 1.10**):

```html
<div>
<a href="#content">Skip to content</a>
<ul>
<li><a href="http://www.andybudd.com">Andy Budd</a>
<li><a href="http://www.adactio.com">Jeremy Keith</a>
<li><a href="http://www.clagnut.com">Richard Rutter</a>
</ul>
</div>
```

1.9 Adding a background image to a quotation

1.10 Hiding a "skip to content" link

Adjacent sibling selectors

An adjacent sibling selector consists of selectors separated by the + combinator. It matches an element that is the next sibling to the first element. Elements must have the same parent, and the first must immediately precede the second:

```
h2 + p {
font-size : 110%
border-bottom : 1px solid #666;
}
```

When applied in the following example, the previous rule will affect only the first paragraph (**Figure 1.11**):

```
<h2>Hicksdesign</h2>
<p>Hicksdesign was started by Jon Hicks in 2002, after 8 years working
as a designer with charities, government bodies and publishers.</p>
<p>You won't hear jargon or pretentious designer talk, we have built
a reputation for being friendly and easy to work with.</p>
```

1.11 Sibling selectors

Pseudo-classes and pseudo-elements

You can use pseudo-classes and pseudo-elements to style elements based on information that is not available in the DOM. For example, it is often desirable to style the first line of a paragraph or the first letter of a heading.

PSEUDO-CLASSES

Pseudo-class style elements are based on characteristics other than their identifier, attributes, or content.

This `:first-child` pseudo-class matches an element that is the first *child* of another element. Imagine you want to give the first paragraph of a news article more visual prominence. If the article appears in a `<div>` element with a class name of `news`, the following rule styles the first `<p>` element in each article (**Figure 1.12**):

```
div.news p:first-child {
font-size : 110%;
font-weight : bold;
}
```

1.12 First-child pseudo-class

```
<div class="news">
<p>We are really pleased that this years d.Construct sold out in under 36hrs.
If you were lucky enough to secure a ticket, we look forward to seeing you in
sunny Brighton.</p>

<p>Brighton is a popular little spot and hotels yet booked up early.</p>
</div>
```

A subset of pseudo-classes is the *dynamic* pseudo-class. These are pseudo-classes that have some dynamic feature. You can use dynamic pseudo-classes to style elements depending on certain actions that a site visitor might perform.

`:focus` applies while an element has the *focus*, such as when a visitor either clicks within a form or tabs to a form input (**Figure 1.13**):

```
input[type=text]:focus {
color . #000;
background-color : #ffc;
}
```

You can use the `:lang` language pseudo-class to style elements where content is in a particular language, perhaps a language that differs from the main language of the document. For example, the following rule applies a small German flag icon to any `<blockquote>` in the German language (**Figure 1.14**):

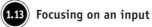
1.13 Focusing on an input

```
blockquote:lang(de) {
padding-right : 30px;
background: url(images/de.png) no-repeat right top;
}
```

```
<blockquote lang="de">
<p>Die Webkrauts setzen sich dafür ein, die Vorteile der Webstandards auch
im deutschsprachigen Raum stärker zur Geltung zu bringen. Wir leisten
Aufklärungsarbeit durch Veröffentlichungen im Netz und in anderen Medien.</p>
</blockquote>
```

PSEUDO-ELEMENTS

Pseudo-elements also allow you to style parts of the document that are not available as nodes in the DOM.

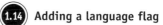
1.14 Adding a language flag

The `:first-line` pseudo-element targets the first line of a paragraph of text. The number of words in any first line will vary according to the scaling of the text size in the browser.

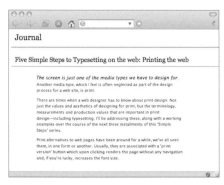

1.15 Styling the first line

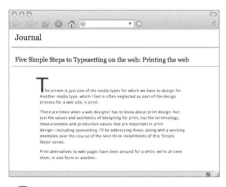

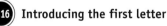

1.16 Introducing the first letter

The following rule applies to the first line of text in any paragraph on a page (**Figure 1.15**):

```
p:first-line {
font-size : 120%;
font-style : italic;
}
```

The :**first-letter** pseudo-element allows you to target the first letter or digit of an element. The next rule applies to the first character in a <p> element with a class name of introduction (**Figure 1.16**):

```
p.introduction:first-letter {
font-size :400%;
font-weight : bold;
}
```

③ Use CSS3 where possible to look to the future

Although CSS2.1 is, at the time of this writing, still not yet a final recommendation and the W3C's CSS Working Group has much to do before completing its work on all aspects of the CSS3 draft modules, evolving browsers such as Firefox already support some of these new technologies. When practical, Transcendent CSS makes it possible to use some of the already implemented CSS3 features. These include parts of the CSS3 multicolumn module that is already supported by Firefox or multiple background images that are currently enabled in Safari.

Although it is too early to rely heavily on CSS3 features in everyday design, it is important to use what is practical today as a way of understanding the creative opportunities of what will be possible tomorrow. You will see many of the exciting possibilities of CSS3 in Part 4, "Transcendence."

④ Use JavaScript and the DOM to plug the holes in CSS

One of the ways designers and developers can work around the limitations of browsers is by using JavaScript and the DOM to plug some of the holes in CSS support. This technique has been made popular by JavaScript developers including Cameron Adams and Dean Edwards (see Part 4).

⑤ *Avoid using CSS hacks and filters*

Hacking and filtering CSS has been a necessary evil since the earliest days of CSS layouts. From the first media HTML filter that was used to hide CSS from Netscape 4.*x* to the (in)famous box model hack, using hacks and filters has become an almost everyday necessity with which to handle the inconsistencies in some browsers' treatment of CSS.

Just like your markup, hacks should be valid

In 2002, Tantek Çelik's box model hack, in all its ugly glory, made CSS layouts consistent across all browsers. It did this by working around the fact that, at the time of its invention, Internet Explorer for Windows still incorrectly calculated the width and height of a box:

```
div#content {
width : 400px;
voice-family : "\"}\"";
voice-family :inherit;
width : 300px;
}
```

These unfamiliar voice-family properties hid the second, correct width of a content area from Internet Explorer for Windows by giving it an incorrect width and then confusing it with valid declarations that it could not interpret. Browsers that supported the voice-family property then implemented the correct CSS width. CSS layouts were, as a result, finally practical.

Despite its unfamiliar syntax, the box model hack contains valid CSS, one of the key principles in a transcendent approach to using CSS hacks or filters.

Toward the end of 2005, Çelik wrote a seminal article, "Pandora's Box (Model) of CSS Hacks and Other Good Intentions," that recapped the history of CSS hacking and recommended best practices. Çelik's article forms the basis of the Transcendent CSS approach to using CSS hacks—that you should avoid using them at all except as a last resort.

If hack use is unavoidable in any given situation, hacks should target either only those browsers that have been abandoned, such as Internet Explorer for the Mac, or browsers frozen in their development but still in wider circulation. This now includes Internet Explorer 6 for Windows. You should always avoid using hacks that target a current version of any browser.

Generated content using :before and :after

The benefit of generated content is often debated between designers and developers who believe CSS should only style content on a page and not add content to it and those who believe it has a rightful place in CSS.

You can use the :before and :after pseudo-elements to insert generated content either before or after an element's content. For example, you can display the href attribute of a link using this:

```
a:link:after {
content : " (" attr(href) ") ";
}
```

The next rule applies to every second-level heading and inserts a decorative image before the content:

```
h2:before {
content : "";
display : block;
height : 20px;
width : 20px;
background : url(target.png)
no-repeat 0 0;
margin-right : 20px;
}
```

CSS-generated content is supported by standards-aware browsers but will not be supported by Internet Explorer 7 or perhaps even future versions of Internet Explorer.

Two popular DOM scripting plugs

Two very popular DOM scripting plugs are Cameron Adams's resolution-dependent layouts and Shaun Inman's position clearing.

Resolution-dependent layouts:

In early 2006, Adams published an experimental technique that uses JavaScript to detect the width of a browser window and load different CSS rules according to that width. This made it possible for designers to provide a slightly modified page layout for visitors using lower screen resolutions than for visitors using higher resolutions such as 1024x800 pixels. You can find out more about the resolution-dependent layout technique at www.themaninblue.com/writing/perspective/2006/01/19/.

Inman position clearing: To solve the problem of footers not "clearing" absolutely positioned columns, Shaun Inman developed an ingenious JavaScript and CSS solution to force footers to drop below absolutely positioned content. You will be using Inman's solution in Part 2, "Process," and you can find out more about Inman position clearing at www.shauninman.com/plete/2006/05/clearance-position-inline-absolute.

Note: Tantek Çelik and Molly E. Holzschlag, among others, have written two excellent articles on how to manage hacks and filters. Çelik's "Pandora's Box (Model) of CSS Hacks and Other Good Intentions" provides a fascinating history of CSS hacks at http://tantek.com/log/2005/11.html, and Holzschlag offers sound advice in "Strategies for Long-Term CSS Hack Management" at www.informit.com/articles/article.asp?p=170511&rl=1.

The demise of CSS hacks and broken pages

In late 2005 with the beta version of the long-awaited Internet Explorer 7 browser released, Internet Explorer's Program Manager for Layout and CSS, Markus Mielke, asked designers and developers to abandon their use of CSS hacks altogether and switch instead to using Microsoft's proprietary conditional comments:

> We ask that you please update your pages to not use these CSS hacks. If you want to target IE or bypass IE, you can use conditional comments.

—Markus Mielke (http://blogs.msdn.com/ie/archive/2005/10/12/480242.aspx)

Supported only by Internet Explorer for Windows, conditional comments make it simple to either target or bypass different versions of Internet Explorer by placing comments in the <head> portion of your XHTML document.

For example, to provide a common set of rules to all browsers but only a specific set of rules to all versions of Internet Explorer for Windows, you can use this:

```
<link rel="stylesheet" type="text/css" href="standards.css" />
<!--[if IE]>
<link rel="stylesheet" type="text/css" href="ie.css" />
<![endif]-->
```

Alternatively, you may need to target a specific version of Internet Explorer, in this example, version 5:

```
<!--[if IE 5]>
<link rel="stylesheet" type="text/css" href="ie5.css" />
<![endif]-->
```

With Internet Explorer 7, providing far better CSS support than version 6 or its older siblings, perhaps the most useful conditional comment targets only Internet Explorer version 6 and older:

```
<!--[if lte IE 6 ]>
<link rel="stylesheet" type="text/css" href="ielegacy.css" />
<![endif]-->
```

Since conditional comments can be used only in the markup layer, not from within CSS, and are proprietary only to Microsoft browsers, many designers prefer to avoid using them. They rely instead on hacks such as the `* html` hack that exploits a bug in earlier versions of Internet Explorer's CSS rendering.

With many such bugs and errors now corrected in Internet Explorer 7 and with conditional comments valid in XHTML, conditional comments are gaining more popularity. I now use conditional comments in all my projects.

⑥ Use semantic naming conventions and microformats

Unless you've been away for a while sewing mailbags at Her Majesty's pleasure, you will already know that the semantic naming of elements and attributes has been a hot topic for designers and developers.

Where once you might not have thought twice about labeling a paragraph with `class="big-black-text"`, it is now more widely accepted that presentational names such as `header`, `left`, or `red` that describe an element's look or position are poor choices.

Some examples of presentational versus nonpresentational naming include the following (**Figure 1.17**):

Presentational name	Meaningful equivalent
#header	#branding
#sidebar	#content_sub
#footer	#site_info

To date, little consistency exists in the names that designers have chosen for their attributes. That's not surprising because it is part of a designer's job to come up with cool new stuff. The idea of using the same names repeatedly isn't something designers like to do; in addition, the idea that they would use the same as other designers doesn't have much appeal either.

Note

You can find out more about Internet Explorer's conditional comments and how to target specific versions of that browser at http://msdn.microsoft.com/library/default.asp?url=/workshop/author/dhtml/overview/ccomment_ovw.asp.

Note

The universal (*) selector targets all children of a given element; for example, `body * { padding : 0 20px; }`. However, because HTML is the *root* element in a document, it can have no *ancestors*.

Note

Former CSS Samurai John Allsopp has long advocated for the adoption of standardized element naming and has created WebPatterns, a site where you can contribute your own ideas on the subject of naming conventions (www.webpatterns.org).

Thinking of element names is one area of Web design where designers should try hard to fit in with their peers, though. Designs won't suffer from it, and it makes working within teams and even across companies a lot more intuitive.

Developers also appreciate naming conventions because they enable them to develop applications that can scrape content such as calendars or contact information from pages to create relationships between sites.

Developing naming conventions

It was again in 2005 that I first turned my thoughts to the subject of the names that designers were choosing to label their elements. Andy Budd wrote an article about this topic:

> You'll wrap a div or a span around another element to act as a hook for your style. By doing this you're adding meaningless markup to your code for display reasons. This makes you feel bad, so you'll try to give these hooks some meaning. You'll put all your branding code inside a div called branding and your main content inside a div imaginatively called mainContent. The question that springs to my mind is, does it matter?
>
> —Andy Budd (www.andybudd.com/archives/2004/05/semantic_coding)

Andy Budd's article and the readers' comments it inspired made me think about what the benefits of establishing conventions for element names might be. I soon realized such conventions do matter; in fact, they matter a lot.

I began by surveying the sites of forty designers and bloggers. I thought that if they worked similarly to the way I did, the names they had chosen for their personal sites would be reflected in their client work.

The result of these late nights of study revealed that at the time, attribute naming included wide variations, even for something as straightforward as the humble page container `<div>`. I found everything from the obvious `page` to `wrap` to Ethan Marcotte's wonderful `going-to-hell`.

When I wrote about this exercise on my Web site, it sparked several conversations elsewhere about why we should adopt common naming and whom it would ultimately benefit.

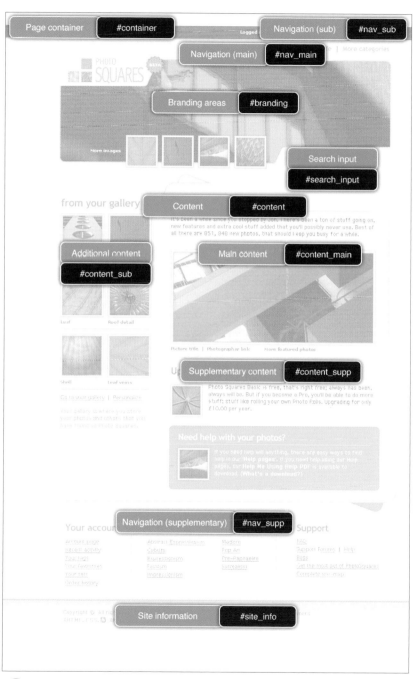

1.17 Using semantic naming

Note

You can read the results of my naming conventions survey at www.stuffandnonsense.co.uk/archives/naming_conventions_table.html.

Eric Meyer suggested in "Elemental Nomenclature," that should a convention be established, he would implement those attribute names on his own site in combination with his CSS *signatures* to give his visitors more control over his site layout and design.

Naming conventions help in teams

In team design and development environments, naming conventions can save your working and thinking time, because they leave you free to design rather than sit around wondering "Now what should I call this thing?"

Naming conventions can also help different people working on any one project to relate to each other, because they can more easily understand the many different elements and how those elements relate to their neighbors and to the wider Web.

When different people are working on a site at any one time, conventions make it simpler to understand the markup that has been written by another designer or developer. Conventional naming practices reduce the time it takes to mentally deconstruct a document and reduce the margins and costs of error.

Even if you work on your own rather than in a team environment, using naming conventions will help you, particularly when you return to a project after a period of time. I'm sure I'm not the only person who has opened a CSS file I wrote months earlier only to sit scratching my head while I wondered, "Umm `clear:left`; what does *that* relate to?" I'm sure you have done something similar.

In team-based work environments, you can extend your naming conventions from markup to other elements including CSS background images. In this instance, you can also use the name of an element for the filename of its background image. Rather than name an image file according to how it looks or what it contains, you can name it according to the element to which it relates. For example: `brighton_pier.jpg` might become `branding.jpg`, and `flowers.jpg` might become `body.jpg` because the new names relate directly to their context and not to their appearance.

Naming conventions can make for hours of geeky fun

Designers Douglas Bowman and Dave Shea made many geeks smile on April Fools' Day 2004 when they swapped their style sheets and stole each other's site designs. Although their swap was intended to be fun, Bowman and Shea were inadvertently making a serious point.

here so visitors can restyle my site consistently

with others that use the same nomenclature.

This is, it seems to me, the least I can do.

—ERIC MEYER, June 2004
http://meyerweb.com/eric/thoughts/2004/06/18/elemental-nomenclature

Note

You can read more about how they swapped designs at Dave Shea's Mezzoblue (www.mezzoblue.com /archives/2004/04/02/poisson_ davr) and Douglas Bowman's Stop Design (www.stopdesign.com/ log/2004/04/02/return.html) articles.

Note

You can find the bastard offspring of the CSS Love Child at http:// themaninblue.com/experiment/ CSSLoveChild.

Much of the effort that was involved in swapping designs was a direct result of the different `class` and `id` attribute names that each had chosen for their own site. Shea's page container `<div>` was labeled `container` while Bowman had chosen a `class` labeled `container`. The names for their side columns were also different, with Bowman's `sidecol` being incompatible with Shea's `sidebar`.

Had they chosen the same names, swapping their designs would have been far simpler. In the absence of common names, both were left with little choice but to edit the markup of each of their sites to make the swap possible (**Figure 1.18**).

SWAPPING STYLES WITH THE CSS LOVE CHILD

As well as being an entertaining example of the chaos that can ensue when you mix one person's markup with another's CSS, Cameron Adams's CSS Love Child demonstration highlights the tremendous benefits that could be achieved if designers chose the same element names as their peers.

TAKE YOUR VITAMINS

What if you love the content of *Vitamin* but prefer the typographical touches of *A List Apart* so you want to combine the two? By choosing the same element names, the designers of both these sites could allow a visitor to apply the *A List Apart* style sheet to *Vitamin*, putting them firmly in control (**Figure 1.19**).

1.18 **Swapping designs**

In an era where the social aspect of integrating content from many different sites is a key part of the Web 2.0 buzz, many more visitors would benefit enormously if designers and developers adhered to common naming.

> **Note:** At the time of this writing, both Vitamin and A List Apart use attributes on their <body> elements, but neither gives visitors the control that either CSS signatures or common naming would provide.

> A List Apart surprisingly uses an empty class placeholder, potentially a sleep-deprived oversight or an erroneous CMS artifact, while Vitamin limits its visitors by using a site-specific homepage body attribute. It would be far more helpful to visitors if both sites adopted both common naming and CSS signatures.

Common naming gives visitors extra control

Establishing these types of conventions has benefits not only for designers and developers but, most important, for visitors to the sites you create, giving them extra degrees of control over the sites they read on a regular basis.

What? Give visitors control over your pages? Yes, that's exactly what I mean, and it's sometimes a difficult concept for designers to grasp. After all, you're the designer, right? You know your Bézier curves from your CMYK conversions, so why should you let *them* tinker with your carefully crafted designs? The truth is that designing for the Web is unlike designing for other media. The Web is the first medium that gives people the option to change the way in which content is presented to them.

Do you enjoy the content of the *Times* but prefer the typography and layout of another newspaper? I'm sorry, but you have little choice but to stick with the *Times'* more traditional feel. The Web is a very different medium than newsprint, and designers must realize they are not designing sites for themselves but for the folks at home. You should make that experience as pleasant as you can by ensuring it is easy for your visitors to change something about your designs they may not like.

Sometimes a visitor might need only to increase a site's default text size. It would be far more convenient if Web designers made it easy for visitors to attach their own user style sheets to override particular styles by tapping in to a site's CSS signature. In reality, you rarely know what people are thinking about your sites, so you should provide them with the tools to display your content in any way they choose.

Barbie's biggest fan sells her 4,000 dolls

By

FOUR thousand Barbie dolls which were collected by a fan over four decades are to be auctioned next month.

The dolls – most in pristine condition because they were never played with – were amassed by a fashion designer in Holland. They went on display at Christie's yesterday.

They range from Barbie No 1 (1959) – black pony tail, black and white swimsuit, pale and with heavy make-up – to Tango (2002), a box set of Barbie and "boyfriend" Ken dancing together. Ietje Raebel bought her first Barbie in the early 1960s for her daughter Marina but kept it for herself after realising the child would rather play with baby-like dolls.

By the time she finished collecting four decades later the dolls had filled three rooms of her home.

Christie's says the dolls give a fascinating insight into the changing style of

among those who attend the London auction on Sept 26. The lots, priced from £70 to £1,200, are expected to fetch more than £100,000.

Mattel, the toy manufacturer, began selling Barbie dolls in 1959.

Mrs Raebel mostly bought them new and stored them in cabinets, wardrobes and the attic of her home.

Plantation Belle Barbie (1960s), Campus Sweetheart Barbie (1965), Fashion Luncheon Barbie (1966) and Sorbonne Barbie (1967) are among the lots being sold.

Twiggy Barbie (1967) is expected to attract fierce bidding, especially as the model has recently made a comeback with her poster and television campaign for Marks and Spencer.

The 'networked generation' finds TV is a turn-off

By
Consumer Affairs Editor

YOUNG adults are watching less television than they were four years ago, according to research published yesterday.

The lure of the internet, mobile phones and computer games means that those aged between 16 and 24 watch an hour and half less television

mobile phones far more than average, making 27 calls a week and sending 70 text messages. The typical Briton makes 20 calls and sends 28 texts.

They are also far more likely to listen to iPods and other portable music players, play games consoles and watch television on their computers than older people.

◼ Digest

Saying sorry to escape jail
The "geeky" son of a millionaire who sexually assaulted a sleeping student was spared jail after agreeing to write a letter of apology to his victim. **P8**

Maybe there is something to global warming

SWITCH-OFF YOUTH FOR SIGNALS OF THE

M Night Shyamalan's new movie is the work of a filmmaker who has simply lost the plot

FILM*on*Frid.

LAST NIGHT ON TELEVISION

Some people love taking on the world. In **Fat Beauty Contest** (C4) size-18 model Charlotte Coyle was determined to "prove to people that being curvy is equally as beautiful as being really slim". To which one could only say: go girl. To do so, she had "agreed" (with whom we were never told but a cynic might suspect a middle when she put a couple

contests are all the rage in America so they should be here, too.

"People think beyond a certain size you're not allowed to be happy," said Charlotte. Certainly that seemed to be the case with many of the women who answered her call for contestants, some of whom mistook the audition for a tearful therapy session. (It *was* a tad insensitive to refer to the fifty or so women who turned up as a "stampede".) Many had suffered under the yoke of sizeism all their lives and were determined to cast it off. But even Charlotte wasn't immune to blind spots of body fascism. She got into trouble when she got into a

for "plus-size" women. According to Charlotte such some kind of criminal offence.

"You've hurt my feelings," responded Charlotte with exquisite model-logic. But wounded as she was, she had to relent – leaving the two contestants in the curious position of being barred for being too thin.

This was a show crammed with contradictions anyway. If you think it is wrong, superficial or unfair to judge beauty on the basis of physique, what's the point of merely changing the goalposts – making them wider, so to speak? You're still playing the same game. And it's all about freedom and self-

"She's got a flat stomach," complained her chubby assistant Zoe, as if it were some kind of criminal offence.

Introducing microformats

HTML markup was always intended by its inventors to add structure and meaning to Web documents. That's cool, because that's exactly what it does. The trouble is that only about forty elements are available for you to describe the meaning of your content. Headers, paragraphs, and tables of data aren't that much of a problem; after all, that's what most of the boffins who invented the Web needed to describe. But on today's Web, forty elements just aren't enough.

Sure, you have ordered lists, unordered lists, and definition lists, but where are the elements to fully describe a book title, a review, or maybe a conversation about whether a book is any good? Microformats extends XHTML and combines all the benefits of precise meaning with greater opportunities for designers to style content using CSS. See the sidebar on page 43 for more details on microformats.

⑦ *Share your ideas, and collaborate with others*

Since the early days of CSS collaboration, sharing knowledge and ideas has helped moved the Web forward. Yes, I know the notion of sharing is all very "happy hippy," but it is true that most, if not all, the techniques designers now use on a daily basis have been developed by individuals who then shared that knowledge freely with the wider community.

Many of these techniques were not designed to be experimental but to help solve the common problems that designers face every day when implementing their designs with CSS.

From the earliest days of CSS layout, designers Rob Chandanais of the BlueRobot Layout Reservoir and Owen Briggs's Box Lessons shared their knowledge and their techniques. Todd Fahrner shared his findings on different browsers' rendering of font size keywords, and later A List Apart Magazine published an article by Douglas Bowman, "Sliding Doors of CSS," about transforming simple unordered lists into tabbed-style navigation.

But this was not the end of designers sharing their knowledge and experiences of CSS. Since CSS began, there have been hundreds, perhaps thousands, of designers who have contribute their knowledge freely on Web sites such as A List Apart Magazine, on dedicated forums, and on their personal sites.

Whether what you share is useful for anyone but yourself rarely matters; it is the process of sharing that is valuable, and you will always get so much more from sharing an idea or

continues on page 45

Note

An interesting use for an `id` attribute placed either on the `<html>` or on the `<body>` element is referred to as *CSS signatures*.

These CSS signatures allow visitors to make changes to the style of an individual site by adding rules to their browser's user style sheet. You can read more about CSS signatures, developed by Eric Meyer and Mark Trons, at http://archivist.incutio.com/viewlist/css-discuss/13291.

Understanding microformats

Independent designers and developers have been hard at work squeezing new meaning from XHTML. Currently, the most well known of these initiatives is *microformats*. Microformats extend existing XHTML rather than create a new language, and as such they are easy to learn and easy to implement. You need only add a set of attribute values to your markup to start using them. Let's take the rudimentary example of my business contact information. This contains a `mailto:` link, and my name will be hyperlinked to my Web site:

Andy Clarke
Principal and Lead Designer
Stuff and Nonsense Ltd.
tcss@malarkey.co.uk

You already have an `<address>` element that most appropriately describes that information, but what about elements that explicitly describe my name, my title, or the company I founded?

You can look all you want through the XHTML specifications, but I'll save you the effort. There aren't any...no name, job, or company elements—nothing. XHTML was designed to be extensible, and microformats are among the first set of extensions to be commonly adopted. Microformats use `class` and other attributes to give such precise meaning to your content.

Need an organization element? Add `class="org"`, and you have one. Need to mark up a family name and can't find an element precise enough? Add `class="family-name"`, and you just created one.

If you need to mark up any contact information so it can easily be extracted and saved in a format that can be imported into Apple iCal or Microsoft Outlook, you simply add `class="vcard"` to your `address`, and you have a simple card format that is meaningful and useful to both people and machines:

```
<address class="vcard">
<a class="url fn n" href="http://www.stuffandnonsense.
co.uk/">
<span class="given-name">Andy</span>
<span class="family-name">Clarke</span>
</a>
<span class="title">Principal and Lead Designer</span>
<a class="org" href="http://www.stuffandnonsense.co.uk/
">Stuff and Nonsense Ltd.</a>
<a class="e-mail" mailto="tcss@malarkey.co.uk"> tcss@
malarkey.co.uk</a>
</address>
```

This development is exciting. Microformats combine all the benefits of precise meaning with greater opportunities for designers to style content using CSS.

> **Note:** You can find out more about the latest microformats and contribute to their development on the microformats wiki (http://microformats.org/wiki).

The microformats community has already released a number of new formats, with more being continually developed and proposed. New applications for microformats have already emerged, and software vendors including Microsoft are advocating for them. While being interviewed by Tim O'Reilly at Microsoft's MIX06 conference, Bill Gates said, "We need microformats."

If the Internet teaches us anything, it is that

great value comes from leaving core resources

in a commons, where they're free for people

to build upon as they see fit.

—LAWRENCE LESSIG
www.lessig.org

technique than you will from keeping it to yourself. For example, I created a simple chart to help me understand specificity in CSS. To help me remember what can sometimes be a complex concept I used characters from the *Star Wars* movies. This chart was intended for my own use, but the article explaining it has since been translated into four languages. I got more satisfaction from the knowledge that the chart was useful to others than I did from making it.

Without this explosion of free and open knowledge of techniques and best practices, the use of CSS may never have grown to the level it has reached today.

Updated and better practices are being developed and shared all the time, and although CSS now has fewer technical trouble spots, new techniques are still being published that can teach you new ways to use CSS.

In October 2005, nine years after the release of the first CSS specification, "In Search Of The One True Layout" described a new method for making columns that were independent of their order in the HTML.

Although the solution is far from perfect, mostly because of browser inconsistencies and not CSS, it came as a surprise to many seasoned CSS experts. The technique clearly demonstrated we could learn new ways to use CSS, and it showed how constructive collaboration could produce an even better solution.

It has not only been caring and sharing, soft-centered individuals who have been committed to sharing their knowledge. Major corporations such as Yahoo and others have been publishing their internal libraries for public use.

The Yahoo Developer Network's UI Library of CSS tools features CSS grid templates that can make more than one hundred page layouts from a single CSS file. This sharing benefits not only the CSS design community but also those people who are sharing those ideas with others.

Despite that designers today have a much greater understanding of what CSS can do, in the future you'll see new ideas for its use and better solutions to older problems that designers haven't yet discovered.

As the last few years have shown, collaboration and sharing can be highly effective in improving our knowledge of what CSS can do. As CSS3 develops and more browsers implement parts of the many CSS3 modules, we will always have more to learn and many more opportunities to collaborate with others to create better solutions.

Note

CSS Specificity Wars is available for you to download at www.stuffandnonsense.co.uk/archives/css_specificity_wars.html

Note

Alex Robinson's "In Search of the One True Layout" is published along with many other inspiring CSS layout techniques at Position Is Everything (www.positioniseverything.net/).

Note

Many CSS templates and tools are freely available on the Yahoo Developer Network's UI Library for you to explore and implement in your own projects (http://developer.yahoo.com/yui/). There is even a blog updated regularly by Yahoo developers for you to keep up with their latest ideas (www.yuiblog.com/).

What Makes Transcendent CSS Possible Now?

For many designers who are new to CSS, it might be difficult to imagine a time when creatively designed sites implemented with CSS were in the minority.

Although sites implemented with meaningful markup and CSS still occupy only a small percentage of the total number of sites launched each year, I hope we have passed the point where there can be any doubt that using CSS is not only highly desirable but also highly practical.

> *As soon as images were allowed inline in HTML documents, the Web became a new graphical design medium. Some people will just want to put out text, but some will want to apply graphical design skills and make a document. These people are, at least, a sizeable minority and there should be a means for them to achieve their ends.*
>
> —Chris Lilley (http://lists.w3.org/Archives/Public/www-html/1994May/0010.html), May 1994

In May 2003, the CSS Zen Garden's experimental playground proved that when designers work with CSS, they can create any number of exciting and inspirational designs from a single XHTML document. Outside the walls of the CSS Zen Garden, the world was slowly changing, and designers were finding new techniques to use CSS in more and more creative ways.

Note: A forerunner to the CSS Zen Garden perhaps, Microsoft's CSS Gallery (developed for Internet Explorer 3 no less) includes "Same Content, Different Style" and demonstrates just how creative CSS designers have become. Explore the CSS Gallery at www.microsoft.com/typography/css/gallery/entrance.htm.

During the earliest days of CSS when many of the solutions to everyday design problems had yet to be invented, CSS designs were thought to be boxy and boring. Thanks largely to the success of the CSS Zen Garden in appealing directly to designers, you can now visit thousands of creative CSS-based sites from the smallest of small businesses to the largest, high-profile commercial companies.

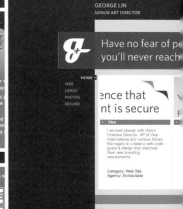

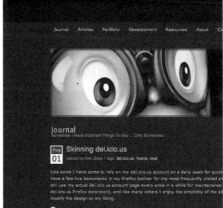

The walls of inspiring CSS galleries such as CSS Beauty and StyleGala are now full of site designs from all corners of the world and all corners of society and commerce. Regular redesign events, including CSS Reboot, encourage designers to reveal their latest redesigns on the same day, which attracts hundreds of designers, including some of the industry's best-known names (**Figure 1.20**).

Unexpected uses for CSS

Over the past few years, CSS has been cropping up in all manner of unexpected places, from instant messaging to everyday applications, such as Web browsers and e-mail clients, right down to the desktop.

In fact, Adium (http://adiumx.com) is an alternative chat client to iChat AV for Mac users that offers them the ability to choose between hundreds of interface themes, all download-able from its Adium Xtras site. Whether you prefer your chat windows to look like metal, look like shiny plastic, or perhaps even resemble a terminal window (if you want to feel really hardcore), the options should keep you entertained for hours.

But the fun doesn't stop there, because beneath the surface of Adium is a chat window made from XHTML and message themes that are styled using—guess what?—CSS. So if you, like me, can't live without a chat window emblazoned with targets, arrows, and the Union Flag, you can easily create new themes and pass them around to your friends. I'm sure they will all love you for it.

CSS is also a key component in the look and feel of Mozilla applications, including the Thunderbird mail client and the Firefox browser. In these applications, you can style but-tons, windows, pages, menus, and sliders all using CSS and images.

The Apple Dashboard Widgets are also created using a combination of XHTML, JavaScript, and CSS as well as some proprietary Apple Script. This simple mix of Web technologies makes it easier to develop new Dashboard Widgets or to edit the thousands of others that have already been developed.

 Achieving camaraderie in the CSS community

Support does not mean that everybody gets the same thing. Expecting two users using different browser software to have an identical experience fails to embrace or acknowledge the heterogeneous essence of the Web. In fact, requiring the same experience for all users creates a barrier to participation. Availability and accessibility of content should be our key priority.

—NATE KOECHLEY
http://developer.yahoo.com/yui/articles/gbs/gbs.html

Graded browser support

Until 2006, MOSe and progressive enhancement were topics largely discussed only in relation to blogs or experimental designs and never in relation to large-scale, commercial Web sites. Many designers thought the approach was too risky while the majority of Web users still browsed using Internet Explorer 6 for Windows.

Surprisingly, affirmation that the techniques central to the Transcendent CSS approach are practical on large-scale commercial projects came not from discussions on designer forums or blogs, but from one of the Web's true giants—Yahoo.

In February 2006, Yahoo standards evangelist Nate Koechley published a Yahoo Developer Network document called "Graded Browser Support."

What exactly does support mean?

Koechley's article makes it clear that it is neither possible nor desirable for people accessing Web content using different browsing technologies or devices to expect to receive exactly the same design. After all, a person will have a different experience browsing the Web using a large desktop monitor than someone using the small screen of a handheld PDA (personal digital assistant) or mobile phone. Extending that notion to browser versions is only a small step.

Graded browser support does not exclude users of older browsers from accessing content; it simply acknowledges that not all visitors will see the same levels of visual design. Koechley explains the concept:

> *An appropriate support strategy allows every user to consume as much visual and interactive richness as their environment can support. This approach builds a rich experience on top of an accessible core, without compromising that core.*

> —Nate Koechley, (http://developer.yahoo.com/yui/articles/gbs/gbs.html)

Note

Although it is now clearly showing its age, the BBC Browser Support Standards table, available at www.bbc.co.uk/guidelines/newmedia/technical/browser_support.shtml, is still an interesting read.

Browser grading

In the past, the widespread adoption of "advanced" CSS has been stymied by the view that a design should look the same across all browsers and platforms. To help solve this problem, Yahoo grouped browsers into three "grades": C-grade, A-grade, and X-grade.

Table 1.2 Yahoo-Graded Browser Matrix

Browser grades	Description
C-grade	Visitors using "incapable, antiquated, and rare" C-grade browsers experience a basic level that consists of core content and functionality. The content and experience is "highly accessible, unenhanced by decoration or advanced functionality." Layers of style and behavior are omitted.
A-grade	Visitors using A-grade browsers can take full advantage of their browser's "powerful capabilities of modern Web standards; the A-grade experience provides advanced functionality and visual fidelity."
X-grade	X-grade browsers include "fringe or rare browsers." Browsers receiving X-grade support are assumed to be capable and not "choke on modern methodologies."

Yahoo browser grading charts are updated approximately every quarter. This chart is as of August 2006.

Browser support standards

The idea of compiling a table of supported browsers is of course not new with Yahoo!. Many large organizations and content providers such as the BBC long ago developed what have often been called *browser matrixes*, and guidelines, for their developers in relation to "target," "supported," and "unsupported" browsers. However, the BBC's approach still harks back to the notion that the most popular browser of the day should be the target browser irrespective of its capabilities.

What is different about the approaches taken by BBC and Yahoo! is Yahoo!'s commitment to the notion that it is acceptable to provide different levels of design experience for modern rather than older browsers and that a target browser need not necessarily be the most popular. In taking this transcendent approach, Yahoo! has demonstrated and stated publicly that Transcendent CSS use is not only possible but required if the Web is to move forward quickly, not stagnate or move at the pace of the slowest browser.

Thousands of designers and developers from all over the world have adopted Web standards. This is great news for anyone who is either creating or consuming Web content. Finally, it is possible to use a Transcendent CSS approach with confidence and know you are in good company.

Discovery, process, inspiration, and transcendence

Transcendent CSS is part of a larger process that involves the following:

- Evaluating how you think about and use markup and CSS
- Thinking about the way you work and how you collaborate with others
- Reconsidering old-fashioned ideas about cross-browser compatibility
- Positioning meaningful, semantic markup at the center of everything you create

Knowing this, it's now time for you to put on your parka, kick start your scooter, and move off. In this book, you will ride pillion through all the important facets of Transcendent CSS. Don't worry, you don't need to put your arms around me; we don't know each other well enough yet!

You will start at the beginning with the **discovery** of the *content-out* approach to using markup, and you'll learn how you should always structure and order markup meaningfully rather than according to how it looks or its visual layout.

Then, in Part 2, you will learn to take a new perspective on the **process** of Web design, finding out more about the meaning-based workflow. You will see how to combine visual design and meaningful markup earlier in your design process by working with standards-based prototyping. If by then you want to get your hands dirty, you will get to build a standards-based prototype using XHTML, CSS, and a little JavaScript.

You will then look for design **inspiration** (Part 3), paying attention to grids and how they have been used in Web design. You will learn how you can derive alternative types of layouts from grids that have been inspired from other media. It is here that you'll learn to look around you for more unusual forms of inspiration to bring home to your designs.

Finally, you will learn how all this fits together in **transcendence** (Part 4) by working through examples that show you how to accomplish Transcendent CSS techniques. You will work with all kinds of positioning, floats, and other layout techniques; learn new techniques for using advanced CSS2.1 selectors; and look at working with different media types.

And if that isn't enough, you will finish by learning about CSS3, which is the next version of CSS, and the many exciting creative opportunities it will offer. You will even get to see the CSS3 Advanced Layout Module and can download all the example files to see it working in action.

Designing from the Content Out

Way back in the mists of 1997, typographer David Siegel changed the Web, as we knew it, when he wrote about an emerging technique for laying out Web pages. Somewhere in the dim light of a laboratory, an HIML <table> element had been stitched together with a spacer GIF and then flooded with 10,000 volts of electricity. This gave life to the idea of using <table> markup as a means for visually laying out pages.

Designers rejoiced that they had found a way to reproduce some of traditional print media's layout conventions on the Web, caring little, if they even realized, that the inventor of the <table>, Dave Raggett, had originally intended his creation to present tabular information.

But while Web designers partied like it was 1997, Siegel soon recognized he had unleashed a monster. Not long after, he wrote "The Web Is Ruined and I Ruined It":

> Some people say I've ruined the Web, and to them it's true. [...] I ruined the
> Web by mixing chocolate and peanut butter so they could never become unmixed.
> I committed the hangable offence of mixing structure with presentation.
>
> —David Siegel (www.xml.com/pub/a/w3j/s1.people.html)

Not only did Siegel's monster go on to spawn several "killer" sequels and millions of Web pages that mixed up their content, structure, and presentation, it also reinforced the thinking that content and structure should depend on visual layout in the minds of Web designers. This notion has stayed in the minds of Web designers ever since to the detriment of flexibility, semantic meaning, and accessibility.

Whereas we understand now that it is always preferable that content and structure be independent from visual presentation, table-based layouts impose *their* order on the content of a document to achieve a specific visual result.

The content order of a table-based design may make perfect sense to a visitor who can see the visual layout, but taking away that visual presentation and that order can make the content incomprehensible (**Figure 1.21**).

Therefore, many people, including Siegel, soon advocated against using tables for layout. But in the absence of a viable, working alternative, the monster was left free to roam.

1.21 Left: View of the Web site. Right: The source order of table-based sites is presentational, not meaningful.

Fortunately, we now have CSS to hunt down and destroy the beast. But even though CSS layouts are now possible in almost every situation, designers continue to find it hard to move away from presentational thinking about the structure and order of their content.

The content-out approach

Peel back the skin of many modern CSS layouts, and you will find that presentational markup and content order still remain. CSS-styled pages are often still constructed in a "top-to-bottom, left-to-right" order that has been designed to satisfy the cravings of the visual design. But this time they use <div> elements rather than a <table> element.

The HTML Working Group at the W3C originally intended the <div> element to be used for the semantic grouping of areas with related content. But many designers now use them in the same way they used tables, to achieve a visual layout, without paying much attention to their divisions' semantic value.

Simply replacing <table> cells with <div> elements will not help you gain the full benefits of using Web standards or CSS. Unless you have carefully considered the meaning of each division, <div> elements are little better than using tables, particularly when they are nested several levels deep. Unfortunately, although they have continued to improve the quality of the code they output, visual Web editors such as Dreamweaver continue to create code that contains an abundance of nested divisions. By adding more <div> elements than are absolutely necessary, not only do you increase the size of your documents, but you also increase the likelihood of errors creeping in during your development.

You should always start writing a document by first using only structural elements such as headers, paragraphs, lists, and quotations. You should then work out in circles, a little like an onionskin, adding any divisions only to group related areas of content into meaningful containers (**Figure 1.22**).

Of course, the world is not a perfect place, and CSS is not a perfect technology. Occasionally, you will need to use extra divisions to accomplish your design, and when you are creating pages for either a smaller-scale site or templates that can be used within a content management system for a larger-scale site, you should aim to add divisions incrementally until achieving your design.

 Starting with the content

A typical, nonoptimized CSS layout

Consider the content order of a simple but typical page that has been styled with CSS (**Figure 1.23**). This document contains branding, two sets of navigation links, two related areas of content, and an area holding site-related information.

1.23 Examining the typical content order of a CSS layout

Note

The Linearize Page feature of the Web Developer extension for Firefox (https://addons.mozilla .org/firefox/60) is a valuable tool for showing the order of content within any Web page.

Remove the CSS on many sites using this visual structure, and you will see that the content order typically runs something like this:

```
<div id="branding">Top-level heading</div>
<div id="nav_main">Main navigation</div>
<div id="content_sub">Secondary content (left)</div>
<div id="content_main">Main content (right)</div>
<div id="nav_sub">Secondary navigation</div>
<div id="site_info">Legal and copyright information</div>
```

Here the order of the content follows a table-based layout, and in essence the designer has done little more than replace table cells with semantically named divisions.

Optimize the content order with or without styles

Looking at the previous example with no style sheet attached, you will see you could make many improvements to the order. The Web Content Accessibility Guideline 1.0 specification clearly states what you should do:

> *(6.1) Organize documents so they may be read without style sheets. For example, when an HTML document is rendered without associated style sheets, it must still be possible to read the document. [Priority 1]. When content is organized logically, it will be rendered in a meaningful order when style sheets are turned off or not supported.*
>
> —WCAG 1.0 specification (www.w3.org/TR/WAI-WEBCONTENT/)

Another important issue, of course, is not only content order, but navigation order.

Navigation

The two areas of navigation are related but kept separate, one near the top of the source order and the other near the bottom. Sharing a common parent <div> and having their own identities would subtly add more semantic meaning to both navigation lists:

```
<div id="nav">
<ul id="nav_main">
<li>Main navigation</li>
</ul>

<ul id="nav_sub">
<li>Secondary navigation</li>
</ul>
</div>
```

You could then place *both* these navigation lists either near the beginning or near the end of your document source and use CSS positioning to place them visually wherever you require for your design.

Branding and content

You could write the two related content areas in the order they appear onscreen and not in the order that makes sense without styles.

You will also see that the branding area, which typically will contain a top-level heading, is separated from the content that follows. Actually, in this example, the heading does not require a containing `<div>`, because you can apply styles to the heading to create the same visual result:

```
<h1>Top-level heading</h1>
```

Swapping the order of the content `<div>` elements and placing the heading directly before them restores the relationship between the heading and content:

```
<h1>Top-level heading</h1>
<div id="content_main">Main content</div>
<div id="content_sub">Secondary content</div>
```

This revised order will better suit the needs of visitors who cannot see the visual layout (**Figure 1.24**):

```
<h1>Top-level heading</h1>
<div id="content_main">Main content (right)</div>
<div id="content_sub">Secondary content (left)</div>
<div id="nav">
<ul id="nav_main">
<li>Main navigation</li>
</ul>
<ul id="nav_sub">
<li>Secondary navigation</li>
</ul>
</div>
<div id="site_info">Legal and copyright information</div>
```

Using CSS, you have greater control over layout than was ever possible with table-based designs. You are largely free to change the visual layout of a page without altering its linear order. This greatly improves accessibility for people who access Web content using "linear browsers" such as screen readers. When CSS styles are removed or not available, what remains is well-ordered content.

With the positioning tools offered by CSS and an increased knowledge of how you can use them effectively, it is time to finally let presentational markup sleep the long sleep. You can help it rest in peace by learning to adopt a content-out approach.

1.24 Left: The most appropriate order for the content, 1 through 9.
Right: That order superimposed on the visual design.

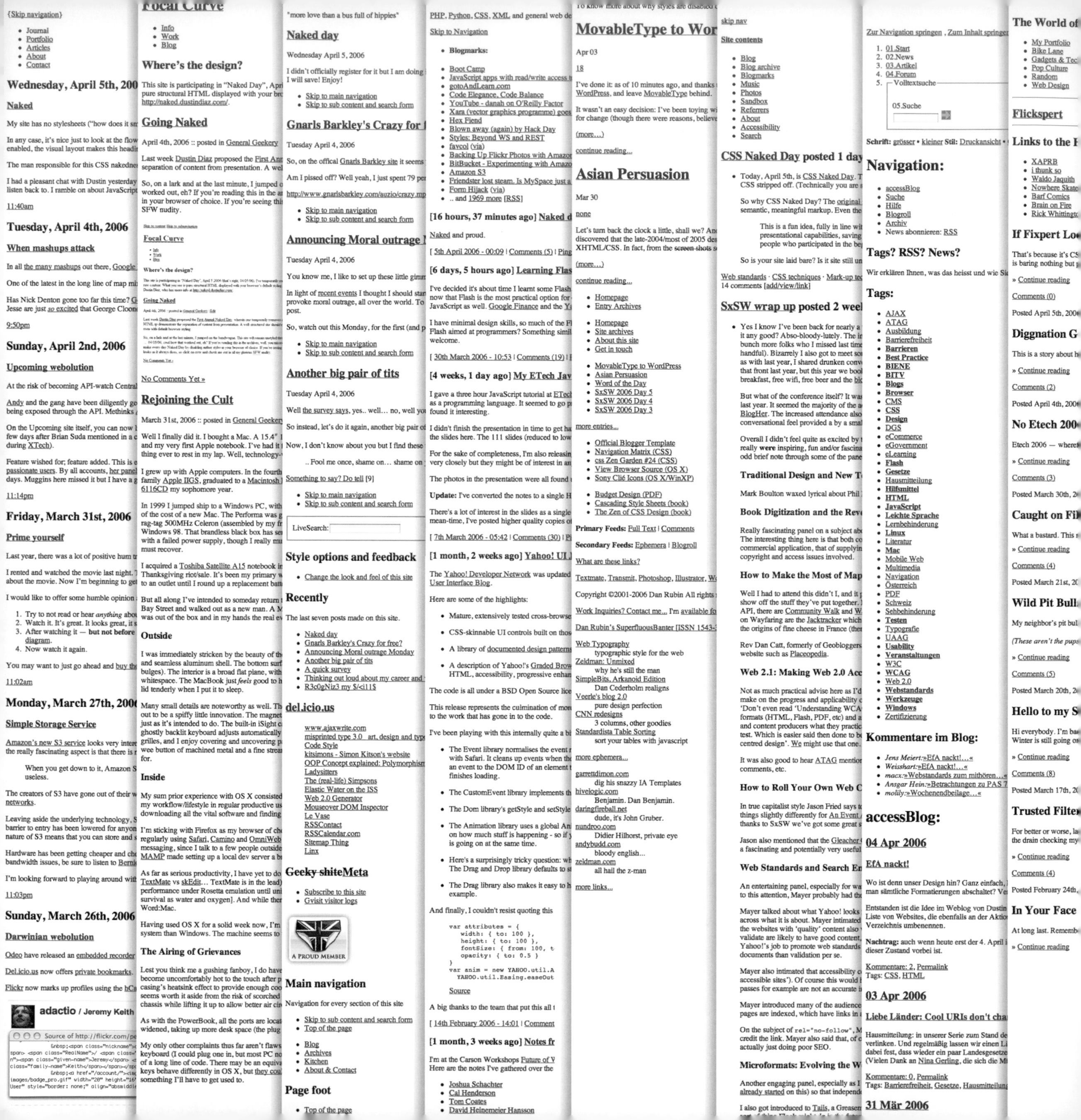

[Skip navigation]

- Journal
- Portfolio
- Articles
- About
- Contact

Focal Curve

- Info
- Work
- Blog

Where's the design?

This site is participating in "Naked Day," a day of pure structural HTML displayed with your browser's default styles. http://naked.dustindiaz.com/.

Going Naked

April 4th, 2006 :: posted in General Geekery

Last week Dustin Diaz proposed the First Annual Naked Day, a separation of content from presentation. A well...

So, on a lark and at the last minute, I jumped on and worked out, eh? If you're reading this in the all standard in your browser of choice. If you're seeing this without SFW nudity.

- Skip to main navigation
- Skip to sub content and search form

Rejoining the Cult

March 31st, 2006 :: posted in General Geekery

Well I finally did it. I bought a Mac. A 15.4" PowerBook and my very first Apple notebook. I've had it for a week now and the thing never to rest in my lap. Well, technology—

I grew up with Apple computers. In the fourth grade my family Apple IIGS, graduated to a Macintosh LC 6116CD my sophomore year.

In 1999 I jumped ship to a Windows PC, with the bulk of the cost of a new Mac. The Performa was a rag-tag 500MHz Celeron (assembled by my friend) running Windows 98. That brandless black box has served me well with a failed power supply, though I really must recover.

I acquired a Toshiba Satellite A15 notebook in a Thanksgiving riot/sale. It's been my primary machine to an outlet until I round up a replacement battery.

But all along I've intended to someday return to Apple. Bay Street and walked out as a new man. A Mac was out of the box and in my hands the real my...

Outside

I was immediately stricken by the beauty of the seamless aluminum shell. The bottom surface (with bulges). The interior is a broad flat plane, with whitespace. The MacBook just feels good to have lid tightly when I put it to sleep.

Many small details are noteworthy as well. The plug just as it's intended to do. The built-in iSight camera ghostly backlit keyboard adjusts automatically grilles, and I enjoy covering and uncovering the wee button of machined metal and a fine stream for.

Inside

My sum prior experience with OS X consisted of my workflow/lifestyle in regular productive use, downloading all the vital software and finding

I'm sticking with Firefox as my browser of choice, regularly using Safari, Camino and OmniWeb. For messaging, since I talk to a few people outside of MAMP make setting up a local dev server a breeze.

As far as serious productivity, I have yet to do the TextMate vs skEdit... TextMate is in the lead performance under Rosetta emulation until another survival as water and oxygen). And while there's a Word:Mac.

Having used OS X for a solid week now, I understand system than Windows. The machine seems to

The Airing of Grievances

Lest you think me a gushing fanboy, I do have some complaints. The heat of the casing's heatsink becomes uncomfortably hot to provide enough coverage seems worth it aside from the risk of scorched chassis while lifting it up to deliver air circulation.

As with the PowerBook, all the ports are located widened, taking up more desk space (the plug...

My only other complaints thus far aren't flaws in keyboard (I could plug one in, but most PC notebooks) of a long line of code. There may be an equivalent keys behave differently in OS X, but they could something I'll have to get used to.

"more love than a bus full of hippies"

Naked day

Wednesday April 5, 2006

I didn't officially register for it but I am doing it! I will save! Enjoy!

- Skip to main navigation
- Skip to sub content and search form

Gnarls Barkley's Crazy for free?

Tuesday April 4, 2006

So, on the official Gnarls Barkley site it seems...

Am I pissed off? Well yeah, I just spent 79 pence...

http://www.gnarlsbarkley.com/auzio/crazy.mp3

- Skip to main navigation
- Skip to sub content and search form

Announcing Moral outrage Monday

Tuesday April 4, 2006

You know me, I like to set up these little gimmicks...

In light of recent events I thought I should start to provoke moral outrage, all over the world. To round post.

So, watch this Monday, for the first (and possibly...

.. Fool me once, shame on... shame on...

Something to say? Do tell [9]

- Skip to main navigation
- Skip to sub content and search form

LiveSearch:

Style options and feedback

- Change the look and feel of this site

Recently

The last seven posts made on this site.

- Naked day
- Gnarls Barkley's Crazy for free?
- Announcing Moral outrage Monday
- Another big pair of tits
- A quick survey
- Thinking out loud about my career and
- R3c0gNiz3 my $/<i11$

del.icio.us

- www.ajaxwrite.com
- misprinted type 3.0 _ art, design and type
- Code Style
- kitsimons - Simon Kitson's website
- OOP Concept explained: Polymorphism
- Ladysitters
- The (real-life) Simpsons
- Elastic Man on the ISS
- Web 2.0 Generator
- Mouseover DOM Inspector
- Le Vase
- RSSContact
- RSSCalendar.com
- Sitemap Thing
- Linx

Geeky shiteMeta

- Subscribe to this site
- Gvisit visitor logs

A PROUD MEMBER

Main navigation

Navigation for every section of this site.

- Skip to sub content and search form
- Top of the page
- Blog
- Archives
- Kitchen
- About & Contact

Page foot

- Top of the page

PHP, Python, CSS, XML and general web dev

Skip to Navigation

- **Blogmarks:**
  - Boot Camp
  - JavaScript apps with read/write access to
  - gotoAndLearn.com
  - Code Elegance, Code Balance
  - YouTube - danah on O'Reilly Factor
  - Xara (vector graphics programme) goes
  - Hex Fiend
  - Blown away (again) by Hack Day
  - Styles: Beyond WS and REST
  - favcol (via)
  - Backing Up Flickr Photos with Amazon
  - BitBucket - Experimenting with Amazon
  - Amazon S3
  - Friendster lost stream. Is MySpace last...
  - Form Hijack (via)
  - .. and 1969 more [RSS]

[16 hours, 37 minutes ago] Naked d...

Naked and proud.

[5th April 2006 - 00:09 | Comments (5) | Ping

[6 days, 5 hours ago] Learning Flas

I've decided it's about time I learnt some Flash now that Flash is the most practical option for JavaScript as well. Google Finance and the Y...

I have minimal design skills, so much of the Fl Flash aimed at programmers? Something simi welcome.

[30th March 2006 - 10:53 | Comments (19) | H

[4 weeks, 1 day ago] My ETech Java

I gave a three hour JavaScript tutorial at ETech as a programming language. It seemed to go p found it interesting.

I didn't finish the presentation in time to get ha slides here. The 111 slides (reduced to lone...

For the sake of completeness, I'm also making th very closely but they might be of interest in an...

The photos in the presentation were all found

Update: I've converted the notes to a single H

There's a lot of interest in the slides as a single mean-time, I've posted higher quality copies on

[7th March 2006 - 05:42 | Comments (30) | Pi

[1 month, 2 weeks ago] Yahoo! UI

The Yahoo! Developer Network was updated User Interface Blog.

Here are some of the highlights:

- Mature, extensively tested cross-brows
- CSS-skinnable UI controls built on thos
- A library of documented design pattern
- A description of Yahoo!'s Graded Brow

The code is all under a BSD Open Source lice

This release represents the culmination of mor to the work that has gone in to the code.

I've been playing with this internally quite a bi

- The Event library normalises the event with Safari. It cleans up events when the an event to the DOM ID of an element t finishes loading.
- The CustomEvent library implements th
- The Dom library's getStyle and setStyle
- The Animation library uses a global An on how much stuff is happening - so if y is going on at the same time.
- Here's a surprisingly tricky question: wh The Drag and Drop library defaults to u
- The Drag library also makes it easy to h example.

And finally, I couldn't resist quoting this

```
var attributes = {
  width: { to: 100 },
  height: { to: 100 },
  fontSize: { from: 100, t
  opacity: { to: 0.5 }
}
var anim = new YAHOO.util.A
  YAHOO.util.Easing.easeOu
```

Source

A big thanks to the team that put this all t

[14th February 2006 - 14:01 | Comment

[1 month, 3 weeks ago] Notes fr

I'm at the Carson Workshops Future of V Here are the notes I've gathered over the

- Joshua Schachter
- Cal Henderson
- Tom Coates
- David Heinemeier Hansson

To know more about why styles are disabled

MovableType to Wor

Apr 03

18

I've done it: as of 10 minutes ago, and thanks WordPress, and leave MovableType be.

It wasn't an easy decision: I've been toying wi for change (though there were reasons, believe

(more...)

continue reading...

Asian Persuasion

Mar 30

Let's turn back the clock a little, shall we? And discovered that the late-2004/most of 2005 des XHTML/CSS. In fact, from the screen shots we

(more...)

continue reading...

- Homepage
- Entry Archives

- Homepage
- Site archives
- About this site
- Get in touch

- MovableType to WordPress
- Asian Persuasion
- Word of the Day
- SxSW 2006 Day 5
- SxSW 2006 Day 4
- SxSW 2006 Day 3

more entries...

- Official Blogger Template
- Navigation Matrix (CSS)
- css Zen Garden #24 (CSS)
- View Browser Source (OS X)
- Sony Clié Icons (OS X/WinXP)

- Budget Design (PDF)
- Cascading Style Sheets (book)
- The Zen of CSS Design (book)

Primary Feeds: Full Text | Comments

Secondary Feeds: Ephemera | Blogroll

What are these links?

The Yahoo! Developer Network was updated User Interface Blog.

Copyright ©2001-2006 Dan Rubin All rights

Work Inquiries? Contact me... I'm available fo

Dan Rubin's SuperfluousBanter [ISSN 1543-

Web Typography
typographic style for the web

Zeldman: Unmixed
why he's still the man

SimpleBits, Arkanoid Edition
Dan Cederholm realigns

Veerle's Blog 2.0
pure design perfection

CNN redesigns
3 columns, other goodies

Standardista Table Sorting
sort your tables with javascript

more ephemera...

garrettdimon.com
dig his snazzy IA Templates

hivelogic.com

daringfireball.net
dude, it's John Gruber.

nundroo.com
Didier Hilhorst, private eye

andybudd.com
Here's a surprisingly tricky question: wh

zeldman.com
all hail the z-man

more links...

---

skip nav

Site contents

- Blog
- Blog archive
- Blogmarks
- Music
- Photos
- Sandbox
- Referrers
- About
- Accessibility
- Search

CSS Naked Day posted 1 day

- Today, April 5th, is CSS Naked Day. T CSS stripped off. (Technically you are

So why CSS Naked Day? The original... semantic, meaningful markup. Even the

This is a fun idea, fully in line with presentational capabilities, saving people who participated in the be

So is your site laid bare? Is it still

Web standards · CSS techniques · Mark-up te
14 comments [add/view/link]

SxSW wrap up posted 2 week

- Yes I know I've been back for nearly a it any good? Abso-bloody-lutely. The bunch more folks who I missed last tim handful). Bizarrely I also got to meet as with last year, I shared drunken conv that front last year, but this year we boo breakfast, free wifi, free beer and the blo

But what of the conference itself? It was last year. It seemed the majority of the a BlogHer. The increased attendance also conversational feel provided a by a smal

Overall I didn't feel quite as excited by really were inspiring, fun and/or fascina odd brief note through some of the pane

Traditional Design and New T

Mark Boulton waxed lyrical about Phil ...

Book Digitization and the Rev

Really fascinating panel on a subject ab The interesting thing here is that both c commercial application, that of supplyin copyright and access issues involved.

How to Make the Most of Map

Well I had to attend this didn't I, and it show off the stuff they've put together. API, there are Community Walk and W on Wayfaring are the Jacktracker which the origins of fine cheese in France (the

Rev Dan Catt, formerly of Geoblogger website such as Placeopedia.

Web 2.1: Making Web 2.0 Acc

Not as much practical advise here as I'd make on the progress and applicability of 'Don't even read 'Understanding WCA formats (HTML, Flash, PDF, etc) and a and content producers what they practic test. Which is easier said then done to b centred design'. We might use that in...

It was also good to hear ATAG mention comments, etc.

How to Roll Your Own Web C

In true capitalist style Jason Fried says things slightly differently for An Event thanks to SxSW we've got some great s

Jason also mentioned that the Gleacher a fascinating and potentially very usefu

Web Standards and Search E

An entertaining panel, especially for wa to this attention, Mayer probably had th

Mayer talked about what Yahoo! looks across what it is about. Mayer intimated the websites with 'quality' content also validate are likely to have good content, Yahoo!'s job to promote web standards documents than validation per se.

Mayer also intimated that accessibility accessible sites). Of course this would pages for example are not an accurate re

Mayer introduced many of the audience pages are indexed, which have links in th

On the subject of rel="no-follow", M credit the link. Mayer also said that, of actually just doing poor SEO.

Microformats: Evolving the W

Another engaging panel, especially as I also started on this) so that independe

---

Zur Navigation springen | Zum Inhalt springen

1. 01.Start
2. 02.News
3. 03.Artikel
4. 04.Forum
   - Volltextsuche
5. 05.Suche

Schrift: grösser | kleiner Stil: Druckansicht |

Navigation:

- accessBlog
- Suche
- Hilfe
- Blogroll
- Archiv
- News abonnieren: RSS

Tags? RSS? News?

Wir erklären Ihnen, was das heisst und wie Si

Tags:

- AJAX
- ATAG
- Ausbildung
- Barrierefreiheit
- Barrieren
- Best Practice
- BIENE
- BITV
- Blogs
- Browser
- CMS
- CSS
- Design
- DGS
- eCommerce
- eGovernment
- eLearning
- Flash
- Gesetze
- Hausmittel
- Hilfsmittel
- HTML
- JavaScript
- Leichte Sprache
- Lernbehinderung
- Linux
- Literatur
- Mac
- Mobile Web
- Multimedia
- Navigation
- Österreich
- PDF
- Schweiz
- Sehbehinderung
- Testen
- Typografie
- UAAG
- Usability
- Veranstaltungen
- W3C
- WCAG
- Web 2.0
- Webstandards
- Werkzeuge
- Windows
- Zertifizierung

Kommentare im Blog:

- Jens Meiert: »EfA nackt!...«
- Weisshart: »EfA nackt!...«
- macx: »Webstandards zum mithören...«
- Ansgar Hein: »Betrachtungen zu PAS 7
- molily: »Wochenendbeilage...«

accessBlog:

04 Apr 2006

EfA nackt!

Wo ist denn unser Design hin? Ganz einfach, w man sämtliche Formatierungen abschaltet? Ver

Entstanden ist die Idee im Weblog von Dustin Liste von Websites, die ebenfalls an der Aktion Verzeichnis umbenommen.

Nachtrag: auch wenn heute erst der 4. April dieser Zustand vorbei ist.

Kommentare: 0, Permalink
Tags: CSS, HTML

03 Apr 2006

Liebe Länder: Cool URIs don't cha

Hausmitteilung: in unserer Serie zum Stand de verlinken. Und regelmäßig sehen wir einen Li dabei fest, dass wieder ein paar Landesgesetze (Vielen Dank an Nina Gerling, die sich die Mü

Kommentare: 0, Permalink
Tags: Barrierefreiheit, Gesetze, Hausmittel

31 Mär 2006

The World of

- My Portfolio
- Bike Lane
- Gadgets & Te
- Pop Culture
- Random
- Web Design

Flickspert

Links to the F

- XAPRB
- i thunk so
- Waldo Jaquith
- Nowhere Skate
- Barf Comics
- Brain on Fire
- Rick Whitting

If Fixpert Lo

That's because it's baring nothing but ...

» Continue reading

Comments (0)

Posted April 5th, 20

Diggnation G

This is a story about t

» Continue reading

Comments (2)

Posted April 4th, 20

No Etech 200

Etech 2006 – where

» Continue reading

Comments (3)

Posted March 30th, 2

Caught on Fil

What a bastard. This r

» Continue reading

Comments (4)

Posted March 21st, 2

Wild Pit Bull

My neighbor's pit bul

(These aren't the pup

» Continue reading

Comments (5)

Posted March 20th, 2

Hello to my S

Hi everybody. I'm bac Winter is still going o

» Continue reading

Comments (8)

Posted March 17th, 2

Trusted Filter

For better or worse, la the drain checking my

» Continue reading

Comments (4)

Posted February 24th,

In Your Face

At long last. Remembe

» Continue reading

Semantics Is Meaning

In technical terms, *meaning* is often also described as *semantics* and has become a hot topic among designers and developers. Even among those who have been working with markup for a while, disagreements still often occur over choosing the most appropriate markup to add the most fitting meaning. Molly E. Holzschlag sums this up nicely:

> In markup, semantics is concerned with the meaning of an element and how that element describes the content it contains.
>
> —Molly E. Holzschlag (www.informit.com/articles/article.asp?p=369225&rl=1)

CSS Naked Day

A world (wide Web) without style might seem an odd concept, but increasingly many designers have been considering how their pages would behave in such a world.

In an attempt to encourage designers to focus on the "naked" structure behind their visual designs, Dustin Diaz proposed removing the CSS style sheets from their sites for one day (**facing page**).

Diaz's aim was to highlight the use of meaningful markup and the importance of structure and content ordering. Along the way, it also confused a good many visitors, who no doubt thought their browser was broken when many sites that day appeared in only the default browser styles.

CSS Naked Day illustrated the need for designers to structure and order content logically before beginning any work on accomplishing a visual design.

It clearly showed that with no distracting visual layout, the meaningful structure of your naked content becomes clear: Visitors can more easily see headings and hierarchy, and they can more easily identify paragraphs, quotations, and lists.

Such meaningful markup and structure simplifies design. Everyone will benefit from an altogether simpler user experience, one that will be as easy to navigate on any device from a large monitor to a small-screen mobile phone.

Note

CSS Naked Day was supported by one of the cocreators of CSS, Håkon Wium Lie, plus more than 700 designers who shed their virtual clothes and showed the world nothing but their naked content. You can find out more about why so many designers stripped off their styles at http://naked.dustin diaz.com.

Translating meaning into markup:
The Markup Is Right

Writing meaningful markup can be simple when you approach it from the content, not the presentation. Rather than starting by asking "What XHTML elements do I need to accomplish this design?" ask yourself "What is this?" and "What does this mean?"

Before you think about the language of XHTML, think about the language you speak and how you would explain the content, and then translate what you have said into markup.

Imagine for a moment you are on a TV quiz show called *The Markup Is Right*. You're a little nervous, but the slick host starts with an easy question to help you feel comfortable.

QUIZ MASTER: "What is this?"

YOU: "It's a top-level heading."

This simply translates to the "most important heading," and in markup, it's an <h1>:

<h1>BritPack and destinations</h1>

Play on

Luckily, *The Markup Is Right* is not one of those difficult quiz shows with a $100,000,000 top prize; it's more of a teatime quiz where the questions start easy and then don't get a whole lot more difficult. "Let's play on," says the host.

QUIZ MASTER: "What is this?"

YOU: "It's a list of names, in no particular order, and each name is a link."

This simply translates to an "unordered list of items (the names) where each link is an anchor," and in markup it looks like this:

```
<ul>
<li><a href="http://www.rachelandrew.co.uk">Rachel Andrew</a></li>
<li><a href="http://www.markboulton.co.uk">Mark Boulton</a></li>
<li><a href="http://www.andybudd.com">Andy Budd</a></li>
<li><a href="http://www.collylogic.com">Simon Collison</a></li>
<li><a href="http://dean.edwards.name">Dean Edwards</a></li>
</ul>
```

You're feeling confident, not even sweating under the lights; the prize is already in sight.

QUIZ MASTER: "You're doing well; the final question for this round is, what is this?"

YOU: "It's a block of text that I am quoting from Patrick Griffiths's HTML Dog Web site."

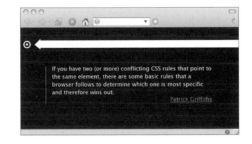

This translates into markup language as follows:

```
<blockquote>
<p>If you have two (or more) conflicting CSS rules that point to the same
element, there are some basic rules that a browser follows to determine which
one is most specific and therefore wins out.</p>
<p><cite>
<a href="http://www.htmldog.com/">Patrick Griffiths</a>
</cite></p>
</blockquote>
```

You're doing well

At this stage in the game, what the content "looks like" is not important; what matters is meaning. The elements you have chosen have not been for their appearance, and even in basic text browsers, the meaning of the content will be clear.

Picturing the content-out design

After a short break for commercials, you are back in the hot seat, and the smarmy host is aching to get you sweating in this round, the pictures round.

QUIZ MASTER: "I'm going to show you three pictures, and I want you to describe the content you want to convey from each picture and then translate that into markup. Here is your first picture."

NUMBER 1: HORSES

YOU: "It's a picture of several jockeys on horses, each wearing different colored jerseys. The picture has a title, Par for the Horse. Translate that into markup and you have this":

```
<h2>Par for the Horse</h2>
<ul>
<li>Red</li>
<li>Blue</li>
<li>Pink</li>
<li>Green</li>
<ul>
```

You add for a bonus point, "If I wanted a particular horse to link to the horse owner's Web site, I could add an anchor around the color, and because those linked words do not properly describe the contents of the pages I am linking to, I would add a title attribute to those links":

```
<li><a href="http://www.stuffandnonsense.co.uk" title="Andy Clarke's personal site">Red</a></li>
```

```html
<h2>Par for the Horse</h2>
<ul>
  <li>Red</li>
  <li>Blue</li>
  <li>Pink</li>
  <li>Green</li>
</ul>
```

NUMBER 2: A RACE

YOU: "It's a race and there is an implicit order to the runners. I would also like to list the runners' names and entrance numbers and links to their personal profiles":

```
<ol>
<li>2312 <a href="2312.html">Paul Weller</a></li>
<li>0605 <a href="0605.html">Bruce Foxton</a></li>
<li>1992 <a href="1992.html">Rick Buckler</a></li>
<li>2011 <a href="2011.html">Peter Townsend</a></li>
<li>2205 <a href="2205.html">Roger Daltrey</a></li>
<li>1966 <a href="1966.html">John Entwistle</a></li>
</ol>
```

```
<ol>
  <li>2312 <a>Paul Weller</a></li>
  <li>0605 <a>Bruce Foxton</a></li>
  <li>1992 <a>Rick Buckler</a></li>
  <li>2011 <a>Peter Townsend</a></li>
  <li>2205 <a>Roger Daltrey</a></li>
  <li>1966 <a>John Entwistle</a></li>
</ol>
```

NUMBER 3: A TAXI QUEUE

YOU: "This one is a little trickier to mark up because there is more detail in the content I want to convey: the taxi number and its driver's name, plus the license plate number and the taxi's position in the rank.

"This information is ideally suited to a table because it is tabular data. I will use table headers to give the content more structure, use a table row for each taxi, and add a caption to the table that describes its contents":

```
<table>
<tr>
<th>Taxi number</th>
<th>Driver name</th>
<th>License plate</th>
<th>Position in rank</th>
</tr>

<tr>
<td>8K33</td>
<td>Aaron Gustafson</td>
<td>666 DOM</td>

<td>1</td>
</tr>

</table>
```

I wish someone gave huge prizes for writing meaningful markup, but the biggest winners will be your visitors. Even if you go home with only a cuddly toy or a toasted sandwich maker, your documents will be smaller, more meaningful, and more accessible if you follow the content-out approach.

```
<table>
  <tr>
    <th>Taxi Number</th>
    <th>Driver Name</th>
    <th>License Plate</th>
    <th>Position In Rank</th>
  </tr>
  <tr>
    <td>8K33</td>
    <td>Aaron Gustafson</td>
    <td>666 DOM</td>
    <td>1</td>
  </tr>
</table>
```

What does the content tell you?

If you are a developer who still works in an environment where designers deliver to you completed design visuals, they can help you choose the most appropriate markup to maintain the meaning of their content in a number of ways.

Designers can add short notes directly to a design visual, perhaps on a separate layer inside a Photoshop or Fireworks file. This can be a powerful way to specify that meaning must be preserved and can also be highly effective when designers and developers work side-by-side and make a simple but effective education or communication tool (**Figure 1.25**).

Meaningful descriptions can include the following:

- "This list has no order."
- "An ordered list of top-selling items."
- "A top-level heading."
- "A quotation from a happy customer."

These descriptions contain no presentational information and help clarify the meaning of each design element without a designer ever having to leave the cozy confines of Photoshop.

Moving meaningfully along

By now you have learned that designing for a modern Web requires you to think differently about the ways you write meaningful, semantic markup. Rather than considering the visual layout as your starting point, as so often has been the case until now, you have seen the importance of starting with the "naked" content and working outward, adding appropriately identified divisions until accomplishing your design—all with a minimal amount of markup and none of the presentational hacks that have stalked the Web for so long.

So if you're ready, next you'll learn how to put these ideas into practice by working through a series of short exercises that will help you become more familiar with markup in the Transcendent CSS approach.

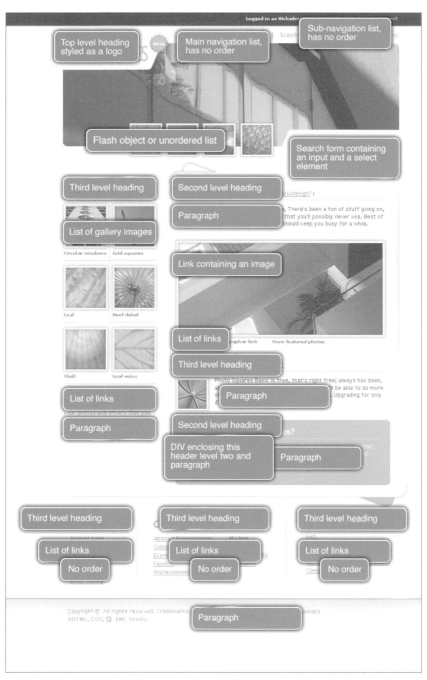

Top level heading styled as a logo

Main navigation list, has no order

Sub-navigation list, has no order

Flash object or unordered list

Search form containing an input and a select element

Third level heading

Second level heading

Paragraph

List of gallery images

Link containing an image

List of links

Third level heading

List of links

Paragraph

Second level heading

Paragraph

DIV enclosing this header level two and paragraph

Paragraph

Third level heading

Third level heading

Third level heading

List of links

List of links

List of links

No order

No order

No order

Paragraph

1.25 Clarifying the meaning of each design element

Marking Up the World

Earlier in this chapter, you learned about the importance of writing meaningful and well-ordered markup as the basis for implementing your designs. You also saw that in the past, visual presentation dictated the elements you chose and the order in which you wrote them. Using the content-out approach, you can free your markup once and for all of presentational thinking. Through some simple examples, you learned that you can, at last, separate meaning and presentation.

Now it's time to put those lessons into practice through a series of fine-art exercises. You'll start by looking at new examples and thinking about the meaning they convey, and then you'll write markup that appropriately describes that meaning. You'll start with lists, the basis of much standards-based code.

All the world's a list; every item must play its part

If you strip away the style sheets from most standards-based pages, you will find an abundance of lists; unordered, ordered, and definition lists have become the stalwarts of meaningful markup.

You will find that standards-savvy designers have put lists to many different uses, including everything from simple groups of links to tabbed-style navigation to product listings in e-commerce stores. Some designers have also stretched the semantics of lists and used them for laying out form inputs and their labels.

Lists are all around us, even in the real world. Sure, you have to-do lists and shopping lists, but take the nine examples (**opposite**); in each, a list is appropriate for one or more areas of content. The type of list you choose will depend on the content you want to convey.

Are the books in Example 1 in any order? They may have been stacked on the shelf at random after pulling them straight out of a dusty box. If that were the case, then an unordered list would be the most appropriate. However, it's possible that their owner placed them in the order they were published or, this case, the volume number. If this were true, then the order would dictate that an ordered list would be most appropriate:

```
<ol>
<li>Deals in Diamonds</li>
<li>But Ill He Lived</li>
<li>Devilweed</li>
<li>The Taste of Proof</li>
</ol>
```

Example 1

Now look at Example 5. It would be unlikely that these motorcycles have been parked in order of color or even in order of the year they were made. More likely, their riders parked in the next available space. To list them by model, color, or even the owner name, you would use an unordered list because they were parked in no specific order:

```
<ul>
<li>Green</li>
<li>Gray</li>
<li>Blue</li>
<li>Purple</li>
</ul>
```

Example 5

Example 8

If history is your thing, Example 8 shows three medieval helmets. Perhaps you need to convey their ages and list the helmets in chronological order. However, many times you will need to convey more detailed information about a list of items. In the case of each helmet, you might want to list not only its name but also a short description of its design and how the design affected the wearer's performance in a battle or joust.

Although definition lists were invented strictly to mark up definition terms and their descriptions, many designers have stretched the semantics and used them in instances like this to join "name" and "value" pairs. In this example, you would mark up the name of the helmet using a definition term, <dt>, and mark up the description using a definition data element, <dd>. This combination of terms and definitions has extended the usefulness of the definition list far beyond that for which it was originally intended:

```
<dl>
<dt>Bassinet Helmet</dt>
<dd>To protect the neck against sword strokes a chainmail "net" is added to
the back portion of the helmet.
</dd>

<dt>Medieval Helmet</dt>
<dd>It had a comb like the Morion but gave better protection by the hinged
cheek pieces. In battle an additional front protection could be added.</dd>
</dl>
```

Lists as far as the eye can see

By looking at the remaining examples and considering the content you want to convey with them, you'll find that you'll use lists in every instance. It's your job to hunt them down.

Unfortunately, with only forty XHTML elements at your disposal and only three types of lists, sometimes you will need to combine lists with other elements to give them more precise meaning.

```html
<dl>
  <dt>Bassinet Helmet</dt>
  <dd>To protect the neck against sword stokes a chainmail "net" is added to the back portion of the helmet.</dd>
  <dt>Medieval Helmet</dt>
  <dd>It had a comb like the Morion but gave better protection by the hinged cheek pieces. In battle an additional front protection could be added.</dd>
</dl>
```

Note

What's an XHTML compound, you ask? To learn more about XHTML and XHTML compounds, you can download the full presentation of "The Elements of Meaningful XHTML" at http://tantek.com/presentations/2005/09/elements-of-xhtml/.

"If I have two beans and then add two more beans, what do I have?"

Often you can use lists in combination with other structural elements to create new XHTML *compounds*. XHTML compounds provide meaning that is more specific than is possible with just a single element.

I'll use the example of a conversation between two of my favorite comedy characters, Captain Blackadder and Private Baldrick from *Blackadder Goes Forth*. What elements should you use to mark up this conversation, given that no `<conversation>` element exists in XHTML?

Headings and paragraphs are not precise enough to say *conversation*, and although many designers might be tempted to use a definition list, a conversation is not strictly *terms* or *definitions*. What is needed is a combination of meaningful elements that together form a compound to describe a conversation. Building precise XHTML compounds are simple when you design from the content out.

A plan so cunning you could brush your teeth with it

What are conversations, and what happens in them? No matter what is said or who says what, in conversations people say words, and they do so over a period of time.

In XHTML you already have the `<blockquote>` element to describe what a person says:

```
<blockquote>
<p>The British Empire at present covers a quarter of the globe, while the
German Empire consists of a small sausage factory in Tanganyika. I hardly
think that we can be entirely absolved of blame on the imperialistic front.
</p>
</blockquote>
```

You also have the `<cite>` element for the name of the person who is being quoted:

```
<cite>Captain Blackadder</cite>
```

What is missing now is an element that can group who is speaking, and what they're saying, in the order that took place during the conversation.

From the speakers and quotations at the center, you can work outward, wrapping that content inside another element that was designed to add order; cunningly, it was named an *ordered* list:

```
<ol>
<li>
<cite>Blackadder</cite>
<blockquote>
<p>If I have two beans and then I add two more beans, what do I have?</p>
</blockquote>
</li>

<li>
<cite>Baldrick</cite>
<blockquote>
<p>Some beans</p>
</blockquote>
</li>

<li>
<cite>Blackadder</cite>
<blockquote>
<p>Yes and no. Let's try again shall we? I have two beans, then I add two more
beans. What does that make?</p>
</blockquote>
</li>

<li>
<cite>Baldrick</cite>
<blockquote>
<p>A very small casserole.</p>
</blockquote>
</li>

<li>
<cite>Blackadder</cite>
<blockquote>
<p>Yes. To you Baldrick, the Renaissance was just something that happened to
other people, wasn't it?</p>
</blockquote>
</li>
</ol>
```

Combining elements that have rich, semantic meaning to form compounds is an ideal way to extend the meaning of your content.

Note

The <address> element is possibly one of the most badly named elements in XHTML. It was not designed for use with physical addresses but with contact information for a particular page, such as the e-mail address for the author of the content.

Send me an hCard from San Francisco

Take a look at this photograph of San Francisco, one of my favorite cities in the world. Like San Francisco itself, a lot is going on here; for instance, you can see a lot of streets with a lot of buildings that contain a lot of businesses.

How do you think you would mark up a city like this? "With more markup than there is room for in this book" would be one answer, but not the one I want. A more correct answer would be "It depends." Specifically, it depends on the information you are aiming to convey.

Like all towns and cities great and small, San Francisco has streets, and those streets have numbered buildings. This implies that if you were aiming to list the buildings in any one street, then an ordered list would be the most appropriate element:

```
<ol>
<li>665 3rd Street, San Francisco, 94107, California</li>
</ol>
```

What if you are interested in marking up the address of a particular building? Your first thought might be to grab hold of the nearest <address> element. Sadly, you would be wrong.

Despite the unfortunate name of the <address> element, no element in XHTML was designed for use with a physical address or location. And no elements exist that can adequately describe a street, postal code, or state.

Earlier you were introduced to the concept of microformats to add more precise meaning by using special class attributes on some elements. Here too you can work from the content out and use microformats, in particular the *hCard* microformat, to create meaning in your page.

You can enclose each line of your address in a <span> element and give each line a precise attribute to reflect the contents of that line:

```
<span class="street-address">665 3rd Street</span>
<span class="locality">San Francisco</span>
<span class="postal-code">94107</span>
<span class="region">California</span>
```

In place of an *<address>* element, you should provide a context for these address parts by enclosing them all in another <span> element:

```
<span class="adr">
<span class="street-address">665 3rd Street</span>
<span class="locality">San Francisco</span>
<span class="postal-code">94107</span>
<span class="region">California</span>
</span>
```

Finally, you should add a `class` attribute of `vcard` to the list item to ensure both real people and software applications can read the complete compound, one of the key benefits of using microformats.

Learning to keep your eyes wide open

Looking around you and noting the implicit meaning of what you see can become an interesting, if a little geeky, way to pass the time on journeys to and from your studio. Wherever you go, you can extract meaning from the following:

• Advertising hoardings and billboards

• Signage

• Shop window displays

In fact, you can extract meaning from almost anything in the world. If you, like me, don't get out as often as you should, look for semantics in the pages of newspapers or magazines or on packaging. You'll be surprised at how much nutritional, semantic information appears on your box of morning cereal.

You should start seeing markup appearing before your eyes, everywhere you look. But if you start hearing voices, I suggest you contact your doctor immediately.

Working from the "contents"

In fact, if you are similar at all to me, when you start thinking about the semantic meaning of the objects around you, you will notice yourself wondering how to mark up almost everything you touch.

Flicking through the pages of magazines and newspapers, you will begin to wonder not only what markup would be most appropriate to the content, but also how you might accomplish a design element with CSS.

Given the example of a Contents page from a gardening magazine (**Figure 1.26**), let's work through how you might arrive at the meaningful markup to represent it.

1.26 **Taking on a magazine layout**

With an initial glance, you might first think about dividing this page into two columns, using two divisions: one for the written content on the left and one on the right to hold the images. But presentational thinking often results in presentational markup, and working outward from the content will help you achieve minimal, meaningful markup.

Scribble notes

You can use different techniques to help you visualize markup in cuttings you make from newspapers or magazines; one of my favorite methods is to write notes either on the cutting or on tracing paper taped over the cutting in my scrapbook (**Figure 1.27**). You can scribble notes about the meaning of the content and your thoughts about the most appropriate elements.

1.27 Making notes

Visualize the magazine markup

Looking at this example, a number of elements spring immediately to mind:

- A top-level heading, `<h1>`, for the word *Contents* because it is the most important heading on the page

- Second-level headings, `<h2>`, for the words *Gardens & Houses* and *Features*

GARDENS & HOUSES
13 Seasonal display Make an elegant Easter arrangement with the first-flowering spring shrubs
15 Emporium Inspiring ideas for the home and

- All contained in a division: a lower-level heading, `<h3>`; a list of page numbers and titles that are featured on the cover, `<ul>`; and a thumbnail picture of the cover of the magazine, `<img>`

35 The good life Inspiration and practical advice for would-be smallholders. By Molly E. Holzschlag
65 Keep **Your greenhouse green** Tips from the experts on how to stay green in your greenhouse
86 20/20 Vision: Ways to become village of the

But what about the two lists of articles and the images on the right? These require a little more abstract thinking. But you might be surprised at just how simple the solutions to problems like this can be when you start at the essence of the content.

Each contains the "title" of an internal page and a short description of what the reader might find on that page if she turns to it. Headings—in this case, third-level headings, `<h3>`—can form the titles of the pages, and simple paragraphs, `<p>`, make up the descriptions:

<h3>Seasonal Display**</h3>**

<p>Make an elegant Easter arrangement with the first-flowering spring shrubs**</p>**

1.28 Ordering the list

Order, please

Because the pages are listed in the order they appear in the magazine, an ordered list, <ol>, will give extra meaning to the lists (**Figure 1.28**):

```
<ol>
<li>
<h3>The Good Life</h3>
<p>Inspiration and practical advice for would-be smallholders. By Molly E.
Holzschlag.</p>
</li>

<li>
<h3>20/20 Vision: Ways to become village of the year</h3>
<p>Ensure your village stands out. By Patrick H. Lauke</p>
[etc.]
</ol>
```

Add in links

You will also need to add links to other pages inside the headings for each article; after all, you can't have a page without at least one link, can you?

```
<li>
<h3><a href="81.html">20/20 Vision: Ways to become village of the year</a></h3>
<p>Ensure your village stands out. By <a href="lauke.html">Patrick H. Lauke</a>
</p>
</li>
```

That is essentially the entire structural markup you will need to convey the meaning of this page's content.

At this point you might be wondering, but what about the images? Where are the <img> elements? Where will they appear in the flow of the document? Remember when I said the images would require a little more abstract thinking? Looking again at the images, you will see that their *function* is to *highlight* particular articles by illustrating them with an image and giving the reader the page number of that article. In essence, their function is no different from any of the other article links you have so meaningfully placed inside your ordered lists (**Figure 1.29**).

Place emphasis

Your next task is to identify these important articles individually and give them all additional semantic *emphasis* in your markup.

You can start by giving the list item for these special articles an individual identity, logically the page number on which the articles appear. Because XHTML does not allow an `id` attribute to begin with a numeral, you can prefix your `id` attribute with a letter, in this case *p* (for *page*):

```
<li id="p89">
<h3><a href="89.html">Fresh spring styles</a></h3>
<p>Discover how to create three very different decorating schemes. By
<a href="smith.html">Dori Smith</a> and <a href="mclellan.html">Drew McLellan
</a></p>
</li>
```

All four of these articles should be emphasized in some way as being featured articles; luckily, the emphasis element, <em>, is waiting and willing to help you.

You will wrap the emphasis around the name of each article and its link to the article page:

```
<li id="p89">
<h3><em><a href="89.html">Fresh spring styles</a></em></h3>
<p>Discover how to create three very different decorating schemes. By
<a href="smith.html">Dori Smith</a> and <a href="mclellan.html">Drew McLellan
</a></p>
</li>
```

You will use these `id` attributes and emphasis to style these featured articles differently than you style all the others.

Complete the markup

Your completed markup has created a meaningful, well-ordered flow of "contents" ready to be styled with CSS. Take a look at the completed markup, and compare it to the markup guide to see the relationships between your elements and how the completed page will look when styled with CSS (**Figure 1.30 and Figure 1.31, next page**).

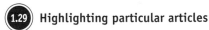

1.29 **Highlighting particular articles**

Contents

August 2006   ISSUE NO. 232

GARDENS AND HOUSES

Seasonal display Make an elegant Easter arrangement with the first-flowering spring shrubs

Emporium Inspiring ideas for the home and garden. Compiled by Ben Henick

Easter cheer Celebrate with pretty table decorations and simple seasonal gifts. By D.L. Byron, Chris Casciano and Chris Kaminski

In the garden A monthly guide to growing organically. By Derek Featherstone

Fresh spring styles Discover how to create three very different decorating schemes. By Dori Smith and Drew McLellan

Wild at heart Wildwife and native species flourish in the informal garden of a charming farmhouse. By Ian Lloyd

The bare essentials Plain colours and weathered acessories add style and space to a Sussex cottage. By Matt May and Meryl K. Evans

FEATURES

The good life Inspiration and practical advice for would-be smallholders. By Molly E. Holzschlag

Keep your greenhouse green Tips from the experts on how to stay green in your greenhouse

20/20 Vision: Ways to become village of the year Ensure your village stands out. By Patrick H. Lauke

Lifting the lid on packaging Discover how you can help reduce the 10 million tonnes of waste discarded in Britain each year. By Porter Glendinning

Seasonal impresssions The tiny garden of Dori Smith's cottage in the Tamar Valley yields all the flowers she needs to create her decorative tiles. By Rachel Andrew and Steve Champeon

89

65

132

22

COUNTRY SCENE
HOUSES GARDENS FOOD CRAFTS

COVER STORIES

Spring property special page 47 Britain's most desirable homes page 49 The best market towns page 50 20 ways to improve village life page 86 Packaging campaign page 103 Decorating ideas for the season page 113 Eat weeds & stay fit! page 132

 1.30 Creating a well-ordered flow of contents

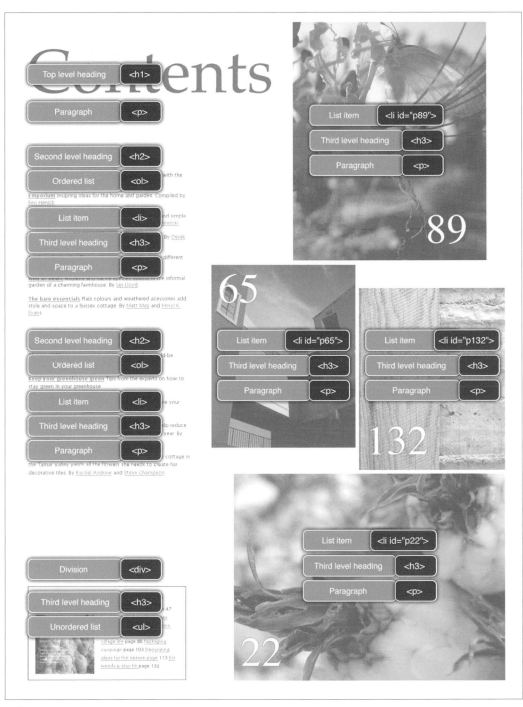

1.31 Marking up the content

Time to Process
What You Have Learned

Having learned about how to look for meaning in unusual places, how to give your markup more precise meaning by combining elements into "compounds" and using microformats, and how to separate the natural order of your content from your visual goals, it's time to start processing all this new information.

In Part 2, "Process," you will take a fresh look at the design and development process. You will learn some exciting new ways to start your designs, learn how to use wireframes more effectively, and go step-by-step through the process of turning a design into a prototype using meaningful markup and CSS.

2 Process

Find the perfect workflow.

Focus on interactive prototypes.

Follow best practices for creating prototypes.

Searching for a Perfect Workflow

During 2005 I worked with a company that was driven by technology and process rather than creativity. Planning and procedures were considered more important than creative experimentation. In this company, dry-wipe boards full of mantras and flow diagrams lined the walls, making me almost long for those dreadful "soar like an eagle" motivational posters so loved by business managers who read *1001 Ways to Energize Employees* on their days off!

Every day, designers and developers alike were subject to the ritual humiliation of reporting on what they had achieved the previous day and what they hoped to accomplish the next. (Sometimes, out of sheer belligerence, I would say, "I thought about tabs.") It was a miserable experience that left us all handcuffed due to a rigid process that gave little room for creativity.

Most Web design workflows continue to follow traditional patterns for design and development. Despite the best intentions, adopting these outdated patterns can limit both your creativity and your efficiency. They can also negatively impact how you work and how you communicate with others during the process.

Looking for a better way

Visiting with a variety of other designers in organizations and companies large and small, I see many similarities with my own experiences, particularly in the way designers often work separately from the technical developers and others working on the same project.

We need to find a better way, one that values the creative process, enhances the overall quality of the final product, and improves the working relationships between all involved.

The key to developing a new process is to give everyone a central point around which to focus. This focal point should not be presentation, as it has been in the past, but the meaningful content that we convey to our visitors. And although some of the techniques that designers and developers have used in the past still have many merits, these techniques are often disconnected from each other. To work more effectively, we need a way to better connect them.

The Web is a dynamic and interactive medium. The best way to join these disconnected tasks is to focus the efforts of everyone involved—information architects and others working primarily with content, visual designers, and technical developers—on the same things that make up the essence of the Web. Using content, meaningful XHTML markup, and CSS to develop interactive prototypes makes the connection and helps designers, developers, and other specialists do their jobs better and more efficiently.

It's easy to understand why many devices of the early planning stages—content site maps, flow diagrams, and wireframes—use static images, but the Web is an interactive medium. Whereas wireframes and static designs can only hint at the interactivity of a finished Web site, interactive prototypes can do so much more. To make the most of the medium, we should work *using* the medium.

Why should we do this?

We should create a new workflow for the following reasons:

- To improve our knowledge and understanding of all parts of the design and development process
- To help us better communicate the organization and relationships in content
- To convey this meaning and these relationships through our visual designs and layouts
- To improve our efficiency and enable technical developers to implement a design and add functionality much earlier in the process

In this part, you will find new ways to make all this happen. You will learn best practices for making wireframes and interactive prototypes and will finish by making an interactive prototype using all the techniques you learn about in this part.

Following a content-based process

Content is often said to be king, a king who demands the attention of everyone in the design and development life cycle, including information architects, user experience and accessibility strategists, visual designers and technical developers, and copywriters and editors. Content in the form of text, links, photos, audio, and video is the foundation of any site.

In Part 1, "Discovery," you were introduced to the content-out approach to markup. Taking this approach a stage further, you will see how this approach creates an opportunity for you to build a completely new type of workflow. In this new process, content is the primary focus, influencing every stage of planning, designing, and developing. The content-based process includes many familiar steps (**Figure 2.1, left to right**):

1. Gather the content.
2. Work with wireframes to organize and present that content.
3. Create static designs to demonstrate creative concepts and layout ideas.
4. Write meaningful markup that structures the content.
5. Work with CSS to implement the design.

2.1 Following the steps of a content-based process

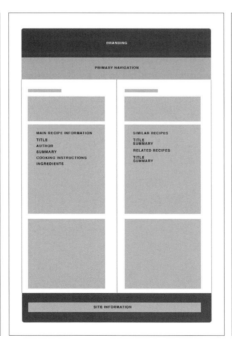

All these steps lead to the creation of an interactive prototype, which you can use to better communicate with everybody on your team and with your clients. The interactive prototype helps designers make design iterations and refinements and test them with visitors and with clients. The interactive prototype also provides a solid platform for technical developers to create fully interactive experiences with scripting and programming.

If by now your heart is pounding in anticipation, start by looking at gathering content from your clients and other sources.

```
<!DOCTYPE html PUBLIC "-//W3C//DTD XHTML 1.0 Strict//EN" "http:/
xhtml1/DTD/xhtml1-strict.dtd">
<html xmlns="http://www.w3.org/1999/xhtml" xml:lang="en" lang="e
<head>
<meta http-equiv="Content-Type" content="text/html; charset=utf-
<title>Transcending CSS - Cookr!</title>

<link rel="stylesheet" type="text/css" href="layout.css" />
<link rel="stylesheet" type="text/css" href="colors.css" />
<link rel="stylesheet" type="text/css" href="typography.css" />
</head>

<body id="cookr-co-uk" class="recipe">

<div id="branding">
<h1><a href="/">Cookr!</a></h1>
<blockquote>
<p>A great place to store and share your favorite recipes</p>
<p><cite>Kimberley Blessing</cite></p>
</blockquote>
</div>

<div id="nav_main">

<p>Bonjour Monsiour <a href="#">Collison</a></p>

<h2>Site features</h2>
<ul id="nav_features">
<li id="nav_signup"><a href="#">sign up!</a></li>
<li id="nav_dishup"><a href="#">dish up!</a></li>
<li id="nav_washup"><a href="#">wash up!</a></li>
</ul>

<h2>Tools</h2>
<ul id="nav_tools">
<li id="nav_account"><a href="#">Your account</a></li>
<li id="nav_help"><a href="#">Help</a></li>
<li id="nav_logout"><a href="#">Log out</a></li>
<li id="nav_rss"><a href="#">Nutritious RSS</a></li>
</ul>
</div>

<div id="content" class="clear_children">
<div id="content_main" class="pc cc_tallest">

<h2>Raisin bread</h2>
<p>Tea breads, half-way between bread and a cake are popular for
```

```
/* Normalizes margin, padding */
body, div, dl, dt, dd, ul, ol, li, h1, h2, h3, h4, h5, h6, pre,
input, p, blockquote, th, td
{ margin : 0; padding : 0; }

/* Normalizes font-size for headers */
h1,h2,h3,h4,h5,h6 { font-size : 100%; }

/* Removes list-style from lists */
ol,ul { list-style : none; }

/* Normalizes font-style and font-weight to normal */
address, caption, cite, code, dfn, em, strong, th, var
{ font-style : normal; font-weight : normal; }

/* Removes list-style from lists */
table { border-collapse : collapse; border-spacing : 0; }

/* Removes border from fieldset and img */
fieldset,img { border : 0; }

/* Left-aligns text in caption and th */
caption,th { text-align : left; }

/* Removes quotation marks from q */
q:before, q:after { content :''; }


/* layout.css */

html { text-align : center; }

body {
position : relative;
width : 770px;
margin : 0 auto;
text-align : left; }

div#content {
position : relative;
width : 100%; }

div#content_main {
left : 0;
width : 50%;
padding : 1em 0; }
```

As long as we have the outline and breakdown

of how content is organized and prioritized on

a page, we do not need to have the final content

in place until the site is completely built.

—KELLY GOTO, Goto Media
www.wise-women.org/features/kelly_goto/

Gathering Your Content

Goto's assertion (**facing page**) that "we do not need to have the final content" is effective when you are working at a higher level and are dealing with the overall shape and structure of your pages. However, this process breaks down when working with the specifics of markup. This perspective begs the question, how do you convey the meaning of content through markup when you have no precise content to work with?

Note: It has been a common working practice in both print and Web design for designers to lay out their pages using Greeking text (the familiar *Lorem Ipsum*). Other designers prefer to use short paragraphs of text from works in the public domain, such as *Moby Dick*, or covered under the Creative Commons license. Mock text doesn't provide the meaning you want in order to begin immediately marking up your documents semantically.

Ensuring that content is delivered on time and in the right format is not only a concern for visual designers and technical developers. Information architects and others who organize content also depend on it, as visual designers and even search engine optimization specialists.

You have many ways to ensure you receive content so your job can run more smoothly:

- Work with your clients to create inventories of existing content.
- Provide your clients with a *new content brief*, which gives an overview of the new content that will likely be required and who will be required to work on the different areas.
- Include milestone dates in your contracts, and use Basecamp or even a simple spreadsheet to keep track of content delivery.

Note: You can learn more about content briefs from D. Keith Robinson's article "Content Brief" at www.7nights.com/asterisk/archives05/2005/05/content-brief. You can learn about the collaborative project management tool Basecamp at www.basecamphq.com.

Working with Wireframes

Traditional wireframes are black-and-white diagrams that illustrate blocks of content, navigation, or functionality. They have been a familiar sight to Web designers and developers and are broadly understood by both clients and Web professionals (**Figure 2.2**).

2.2 **Detailing a wireframe**

Used as a tool to communicate content and structure without the distractions of color and imagery, wireframes remain an important part of the design process.

They can help designers do the following:

- Storyboard a visitor's path through a site.
- Work quickly through a series of layout iterations (**Figure 2.3**) before the costly job of creative design and technical development begins.

Although wireframes are not quite shake-and-bake, almost anyone can easily create wireframes with OmniGraffle from the Omni Group or even PowerPoint from Microsoft, with little or no knowledge of Web technologies. Just like pouring boiling water onto an instant Pot Noodle, using common software to create simple wireframes is easy. It is perhaps because of this ease that many people have come to regard making wireframes as an inexpensive way of proofing concepts.

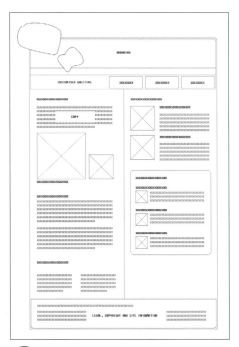
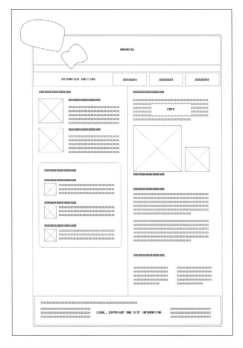
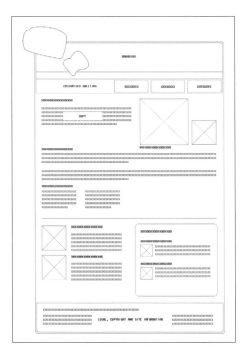

2.3 **Working through a series of layout iterations**

Where traditional wireframes fail

Frederick Barnard has been credited with saying "a picture is worth a thousand words" in the advertising journal *Printer's Ink*. Sadly, what worked for Barnard in 1921 is not altogether relevant eighty-five years later. However much care you take in creating them and however detailed or well annotated you make them, traditional wireframe images can only hint at what will become rich content and navigation on the Web.

Images work just fine for static designs to show creative concepts, color, and typography, but using them as prototypes for interactive Web pages is flawed from the start. Using images makes it difficult to mimic even the simplest forms of interaction such as :hover, :focus, or :target states (**Figure 2.4**).

A further drawback of wireframes is that they are often created long before a visual designer begins the job of creating page-layout concepts. Sometimes they include not only information about content and relationships, but also page-layout instructions such as the location of branding and content areas, sidebars, navigation, and footers.

Many visual designers, when presented with wireframes that contain so much detail, feel they have little room to express their creativity. Decisions over design and layout have already been made *before* the job of visual design has even started. Cases like these are common and problematic because the designer's valuable input has been overlooked.

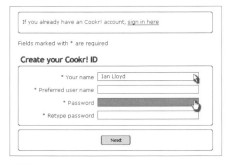

2.4 Using images makes it hard to show interaction

Improving the approach using granular wireframes

To help avoid being overly prescriptive and dictating the complete layout of a page, some have advocated using more granular wireframes. These break down important features into smaller pieces, such as the following for a Web application or an e-commerce site: account creation, customer sign-in, customization options, e-commerce checkout, navigation, and search interfaces.

This type of wireframe helps designers stay creative, because they do not specify the layout of an entire page. However, they are still far from ideal:

- They lack the capability to describe the semantic meaning of elements or the relationships between them to visual designers.
- Despite their precision, they often fail to describe in sufficient detail all the information that technical developers need to understand complex functionality or interactivity.

Although traditional wireframes can provide a broad indication of a finished product, they are often mistakenly used as benchmarks for how a layout will ultimately look. Worst of all, they reinforce the idea that Web pages should be pixel-perfect reproductions of frozen images. Often, they lock a design into one fixed display type and rarely take into account the need to design for users of alternative browsers, such as screen readers or mobile devices.

Are wireframes a good value for the money?

It is a popular misconception that making wireframes is an inexpensive part of design and development; in the context of a modern workflow, they represent much less value for the money.

Prototyping of any kind is often thought to involve working on materials that will ultimately be discarded before creating a final product. If you start your process with images as a wireframe, you can quickly turn this notion into a self-fulfilling prophecy. When I look at the hundreds of wireframes I have made, all now gathering digital dust in my archives, I can picture the thousands of hours that went into creating them. Because I approached these wireframes as part of a throwaway process, that is exactly what they became.

In addition, they may seem quick and easy to make, but in reality wireframes rarely consider every aspect of the complex nature of interactive Web pages. Issues such as pagination, error or status messages, and visitor feedback are rarely tackled at the wireframing stage, and by not including them, the missing work is simply moved to a stage later in the process (**Figure 2.5**).

2.5 **Dealing with error messages**

Finally, wireframes rarely convey all the complete information, and a range of supporting material such as site maps, page descriptions, or functional specifications almost always accompanies them. On large-scale projects, writing, reading, and keeping track of this documentation can add to the complexity and costs involved.

Traditional wireframes and interaction

If the simple interaction of a flexible, liquid layout is hard to convey using images, try to imagine how difficult the complex functionality now common on sites using interactive media such as Macromedia Flash and technologies such as Ajax and DOM (Document Object Model) scripting might be. Jeffrey Zeldman may have said it best:

> *Wireframing Ajax is a bitch.*
>
> —Jeffrey Zeldman (www.alistapart.com/articles/web3point0)

When you are designing e-commerce sites similar to Amazon, you can more easily convey the process of adding an item to a shopping cart and proceeding through the checkout process using images (**Figure 2.6**). Even some of Amazon's slickest user features such as 1-Click ordering present no real challenges to an experienced designer.

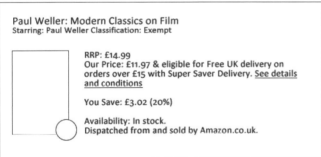

Paul Weller: Modern Classics on Film
Starring: Paul Weller Classification: Exempt

RRP: £14.99
Our Price: £11.97 & eligible for Free UK delivery on orders over £15 with Super Saver Delivery. <u>See details and conditions</u>

You Save: £3.02 (20%)

Availability: In stock.
Dispatched from and sold by Amazon.co.uk.

READY TO BUY
Price: £8.97
Availability: Usually dispatched with 24 hours

(Add to Shopping Basket)
or
(Buy now with 1 Click)
Dispatch to:

[Andy Clarke ▼]
☐ Add giftwrap/message

Your 1-Click order has been placed

Thank you

The following item will be dispatched to Andy Clarke via First Class

Paul Weller: Modern Classics on Film (DVD)

(Review or edit your 1-Click orders)

• Change address, quantities or payment method
• Change item quantities
• Apply or change gift options
• Apply a gift certificate or promotional code to your order

Continue 1-Click shopping. If you 1-Click other items within the next 90 minutes, we'll minimise your delivery costs by combining items into as few deliveries as possible.

(Continue Shopping)
on the Amazon.co.uk home page.

2.6 **Wireframing exercise with a one-click order process**

Note: For more thoughts on prototyping Ajax, read Kevin Hale's article "A Designer's Guide to Prototyping Ajax" at http://particletree.com/features/a-designers-guide-to-prototyping-ajax/.

But in Ajax-driven applications, where users can invoke complex behaviors with simple text input or a mouse click, images are rarely capable of describing sufficient detail on a single screen.

An interesting case in point is Flickr, Yahoo's popular photo storage and sharing application. Flickr is a complex mix of markup, CSS, Flash, and Ajax that gives its visitors an immersive user experience. Some of Flickr's tools, such as adding a tag, editing a title, or changing a description, might cause fewer headaches in wireframing with images.

Flickr's more complex user features for adding a note to a photo or organizing photos into sets through its drag-and-drop interface would prove extremely difficult to represent in a traditional wireframe with even a long series of images.

Proofing functionality of this complexity would be a tough job for even the most patient designer and would involve creating images of every stage of user interaction, clearly a job few designers would relish.

Many variables get overlooked when creating

wireframes or other paper documents.

Factors such as state, security, error messages,

level of effort, page flow, DOM scripting

and other dynamic elements can be ignored

or misrepresented.

—GARRETT DIMON
www.digital-web.com/articles/
just_build_it_html_prototyping_and_agile_development

Lorem ipsum dolor sit amet, consectetur adipisicing elit, sed do eiusmod tempor incididunt ut labore et dolore magna aliqua. Ut enim ad minim veniam, quis nostrud exercitation ullamco laboris nisi ut aliquip ex ea commodo consequat. Lorem ipsum dolor sit amet, consectetur adipisicing elit, sed do eiusmod tempor incididunt ut labore et dolore magna aliqua. Ut enim ad minim veniam, quis nostrud exercitation ullamco laboris nisi ut aliquip ex ea commodo consequat.

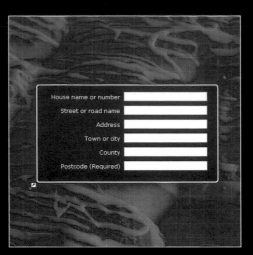

House name or number
Street or road name
Address
Town or city
County
Postcode (Required)

Lorem ipsum dolor

Lorem ipsum dolor sit amet, consectetur adipisicing elit, sed do eiusmod tempor incididunt ut labore et dolore magna aliqua.Lorem ipsum dolor sit amet, consectetur adipisicing elit, sed do eiusmod tempor incididunt ut labore et dolore magna aliqua. Lorem ipsum dolor sit amet .

Lorem ipsum dolor sit
Lorem ipsum dolor sit
Lorem ipsum dolor sit
Lorem ipsum dolor sit
Lorem ipsum dolor sit
Lorem ipsum dolor sit

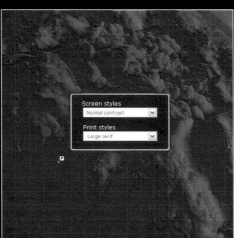

Screen styles
Normal contrast

Print styles
Large serif

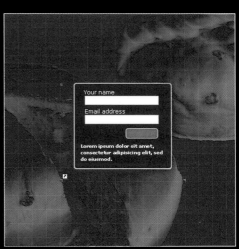

Your name

Email address

Lorem ipsum dolor sit amet, consectetur adipisicing elit, sed do eiusmod.

Search this site

Advanced search | Search tips

Lorem ipsum dolor sit

Lorem ipsum dolor sit amet, consectetur adipisicing elit, sed do eiusmod tempor incididunt ut labore et dolore magna aliqua

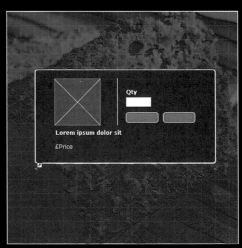

Qty

Lorem ipsum dolor sit

£Price

Using symbols to add greater detail

Sometimes you will need to provide more detail in a visual way. Developing a library of reusable graphic components, or *symbols*, that provide this extra level of detail and can be dragged and dropped on grey boxes can be highly effective.

For much of my own design and layout work, my preferred layout application is Macromedia Fireworks, not least for its capability to store graphic symbols that I use from project to project in its library. I have made a simple symbol for each of the common user interface elements I use on a regular basis (**Figure 2.7**):

- Grid design variations
- Greeking text
- Common e-commerce interface elements
- Search areas
- Form fieldsets and other form elements

   Tip: This technique is also possible in other graphic and layout tools.

You should keep these symbols deliberately minimal and free from any creative flourishes. By dragging and dropping these symbols on grey boxes, you can add more detail to the parts of your wireframes that require it.

2.7 Several elements created in Fireworks as "symbols"

Tips for working with grey boxes

Grey boxes can help make collaboration between information architects, visual designers, and technical developers better.

When organizing information for Web sites, you can implement the following tips to better relate your work to the work of visual designers and developers while at the same time preserve the meaning of the content relationships you have defined:

- Define the source order of the content.
- Think about how that content will look without style; will it be easy to read, and will the order make sense?
- Visually highlight any relationships: This will ultimately help identify necessary divisions and show areas of similar but not related information.
- Use established naming conventions

cookr! BETA

Bonjour Monsiour Collison!

sign up!   **dish up!**   **wash up!**

Raisin bread (Eric Fung)

Tea breads, half-way between bread and a cake are popular for tea, as they keep well and can be made in advance. Soda bread is a good substitute for yeast bread in an emergency, and can be made shortly before it is required.

Instructions

I worked on 9 strands at a time, letting them relax before rolling and stretching it a bit further. In all, it took us about an hour to finish. We braided the stands then coiled them around a stainless steel bowl that we covered in tinfoil.

Bread Basket Chef baked them in a hot oven until the dough set, then removed the metal bowls and inverted the basket to dry out the inside. When she removed them from the oven, the outside was browned but the inside was still a bit soft, so we finished drying them at home. I'm not all that excited about this product: while it's edible and interesting to admire, I much prefer something I can eat.

Ingredients

5ml bicarbonate of soda	100g butter
2.5ml cream of tartar	2.5ml ground ginger
275g plain flour	5ml ground mace
100g butter	2.5ml ground all spice

Similar recipes

Challah

For the challah, we mixed up a very tacky dough that clung to the bowl, the hook and the table. Mindful of Chef's instructions to use as little flour as possible.

Baguettes

We used both hands, one on top of the other, to press out most of the gas and pulled the dough into a rectangle. Then, with the short-end facing us, we folded it in three.

You might also like

Lemon Blueberry Muffins

The recipe in the link is half the original recipe which yields about 18 large muffins. I always cut down on the butter in this recipe

Pistachio and Dried Fruit Cake

The author says her mother makes this cake during Lent so it is a coincidence that I made it for the Easter weekend.

Brownie Berry Tower

For the final class of this course, we made a tall cake, with brownie layers sandwiching two kinds of cream and strawberries.

cookr BETA

BETA UNTIL THE CABBAGE HAS BOILED

2.8 Creating a static design

Creating Static Designs

Static designs are important in conveying ideas about look and feel, page layouts, and interface designs to clients and other stakeholders (**Figure 2.8**). Although static designs should indicate how the finished product will look, they are also mistakenly used as benchmarks, leaving little room for later flexibility or even behaviors such as liquid page layouts.

Many designers have asked when static design visuals, or *comps* as they're often referred to, fit best in a contemporary Web design workflow. Should they come at the beginning? Should they come before making wireframes or grey boxes, or should they come later? The answer will depend on your own working environment.

To answer this question, you should ask yourself, what purpose are these static designs going to accomplish? If they are designed to illustrate only general shape and style, you can work on them throughout the process and refine them right up until the end because the specific details of the layout may not depend on them. However, if static designs are intended to show the specifics of layout details, they will likely be completed and signed off on far earlier in the process.

Moving faster through the design workflow

In the past, finalizing and signing off on static designs has always preceded other stages in the design and development process. Writing markup and CSS waited while static designs were completed, and it was even less likely that expensive activities such as scripting or programming would start until later.

One of the most important advantages of the content-based workflow is that these other areas of work do not have to wait until static designs are complete. Grey boxes and other supporting materials can give not only visual designers but also technical developers and others all the information they need, giving them a head start to begin their work from the same basis of content as designers.

Even when markup has been written and perhaps more complex functionality added to a prototype, visual designers can continue to experiment with design ideas or even different layouts, safe in the knowledge that CSS will allow them to implement their designs without breaking the work of other people in their team (**Figure 2.9**).

2.9 Giving variety to layout

Markup guides as training aids

Some information architects and designers who are new to the concepts of semantics and writing meaningful rather than presentational markup find it difficult to relate a visual layout to XHTML.

Markup guides help them visually associate markup to design. Working regularly with these guides can help demystify markup and the XHTML elements that are commonly used.

Adding markup guides to static designs

Markup guides are designed to show the simple outline of the markup that is most appropriate to convey the meaning of any element during the design process. They do this directly on the static design and can be used to do the following:

- Show the hierarchy or structure of the content.
- Help advise technical developers of the most appropriate markup to use.

Imagine for a moment that a visual designer shows two blocks of text. The first is plainly styled; the second is styled bolder and in larger type. One problem that technical developers often face is how to interpret the visual design as markup when the precise meaning of an element is not obvious through the visual design. For example, in **Figure 2.10**, can you tell that the second block of text is a quotation rather than a normal paragraph?

Whether you choose to work on paper by printing your grey boxes and writing your markup and any accompanying notes onto that or to work electronically by adding the guides directly to your grey box files, using markup guides will help everyone involved in the process (**Figure 2.11**).

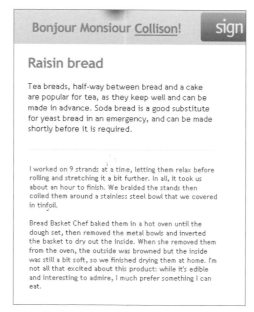

 Highlighting the difficulties when precise meaning is not obvious

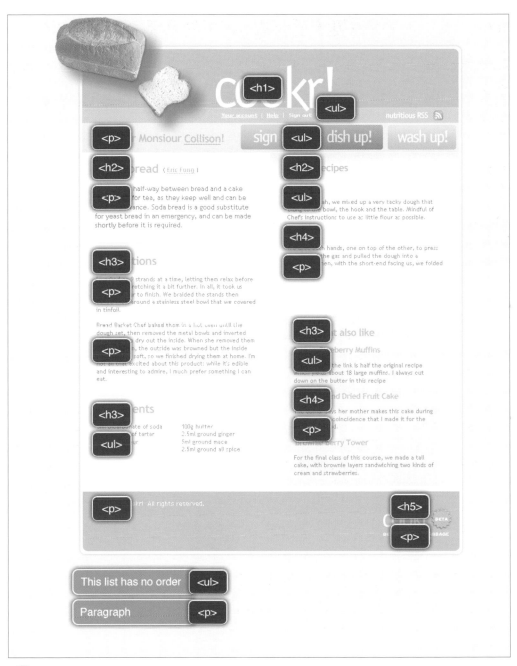

2.11 Laying markup over a static design

Using Interactive Prototypes

It's easy to understand why many devices of the early planning stages—content site maps, flow diagrams, and wireframes—use static images, but the Web is an interactive medium. Whereas wireframes and static designs can only hint at the interactivity of a finished Web site, interactive prototypes can do so much more. To make the most of the medium, we should work *using* the medium.

By creating interactive prototypes using valid, meaningful markup and CSS, designers can use the prototypes to demonstrate their designs, and developers can easily add more functionality with Ajax and related technologies to create a fully working prototype.

You might at first think that making prototypes using hand-coded XHTML and CSS would take more time than creating images, particularly if you have experience with your wireframing application or have a library of reusable symbols you use by dragging and dropping.

However, using XHTML and CSS does allow you to work faster:

- You can use one or multiple CSS files to lay out your prototypes.
- You can use CSS styles for layout, color, and typography across any number of pages.
- You can make rapid changes without changing your markup.
- You can preview multiple design variations using the same content.

These interactive prototypes also enable visual designers to make faster and more frequent design iterations, try new ideas, and rearrange layouts, all without altering the structure or order of the content.

Interactive prototypes make it real

When you demonstrate your designs in a Web browser, you allow your clients to interact with them in a more meaningful way. Even though your prototype may not be fully functional, your clients will be able to interact with it more than with a static image, reducing the possibility for misunderstandings.

If you are following modern Web standards

practices, these pages are probably built with

XHTML for structure and CSS for markup.

XHTML is an excellent structure that can

serve as the basis for a wireframe that can later

be transitioned into a prototype and eventually

designed via CSS.

—NICK FINCK
www.blueflavor.com/ed/information_architecture/
recyclable_information_archite.php

Clients become engaged when they can interact with HTML wireframes. Clients not only enjoy the process more, but they also get a better contextual understanding of the features than with paper prototypes.

—Jeff Gothelf, Boxes and Arrows (www.boxesandarrows.com/ view/practical_applications_visio_or_html_for_wireframes)

Interactive prototypes are powerful tools for presenting your designs to your clients. When clients provide feedback, you can implement suggestions immediately; if the changes don't work, your clients will see the results right away, and you can easily roll back to a previous iteration. Working in this way rapidly speeds up the process of gaining client approval for your designs, even when working with clients spread across different continents and time zones.

Creating reusable code

When you develop using meaningful markup and CSS, you can reuse much of your work. This will save you significant amounts of development time because your work is far less likely to need duplicating. When you follow the same strict coding practices as you would when making your final product, your work during prototyping will not be thrown away.

If you approach your work with the goal of keeping and reusing it, then most everything you do will survive to the end. By adopting this method, you will almost always increase your speed and reduce costs for your studio, organization, managers, and clients.

Model behavior for wireframes and prototypes

With new ways of improving communication between all of those working on organizing content, it is time to learn best practices and learn how to use a Web browser and a range of extensions for organizing your style sheets efficiently.

WYSIWYG: What you see, or short-sighted?

The WYSIWYG design environment in applications such as Macromedia Dreamweaver, with its built-in templates and drag-and-drop library items, have already played a large part in the transition to using HTML for prototyping. These tools have made it far easier for people to make HTML prototypes without a wide knowledge of markup, CSS, or best practices.

With WYSIWYG editors being designed to create the markup for you, you might at first think that hand-coding XHTML and CSS would take more time and be less efficient than using a WYSIWYG editor, particularly if you have experience with your wireframing application or have a library of reusable assets that you use by dragging and dropping. But that isn't necessarily the case.

The following are some advantages of using XHTML and CSS prototypes over those created with WYSIWYG editors:

WYSIWYG	Standards-based markup and CSS
Requires you to buy a WYSIWYG application such as Dreamweaver or Adobe GoLive.	Requires only a basic Web editor or plain-text editor such as Notepad for Windows or TextEdit for Mac OS X.
Requires you to be experienced in an application that will rarely be useful in developing the final pages.	Requires you to have only a basic knowledge of markup and CSS.
Your markup is likely to be presentational and more likely to be difficult to maintain and reuse.	Your markup will be structured, well ordered, and meaningful. You will reuse much of your markup and CSS.
Changes to your visual layout will often require you to change markup and source order across many pages.	Editing linked or imported CSS files can update any number of pages from only one file.

In the same way an author makes an outline before writing a book, [the grey box method] serves as my visual outline before creating a design. Breaking this into steps makes you consider your design choices and foundation before you are swept away by the details of your visual decisions.

—JASON SANTA MARIA
www.jasonsantamaria.com/archive/2004/05/24/grey_box_method.php

Following Best Practices for Interactive Prototyping

It is important to understand that even though I present the steps in a linear order, the process is not. The content-based process is not a set of hard-and-fast guidelines but a series of steps to improve your workflow, whether you are a lone designer with multiple roles or you work as part of a larger team.

Choosing a development browser

When developing, testing, and demonstrating your interactive prototypes, you should avoid the quirks and issues of older browsers. Having a stable browser platform to act as your development environment and sticking with it throughout the workflow process is essential.

It is important to let others know about your choice so they understand that if they look at your work in any different browser, the results may not look the same.

Your choice of browser will depend on several factors. If you are designing for an internal company environment where the majority of people reading your pages use Microsoft Internet Explorer 5 on Windows 2000, Explorer 5 might, sadly, be the most logical choice because even after several years this browser still ships as part of that operating system. It might also be appropriate to choose Safari if your visitors largely use that browser. Using a browser that has strong support for CSS and a range of development tools available to work with it will make the job of developing and testing that much easier.

Using browser extensions

Although Internet Explorer 7 has its own tools and a developer toolbar, Mozilla Firefox is the development browser most standards-aware designers will choose because of the sheer quantity and quality of its developer extensions. The Mozilla Web site currently contains more than 190 developer extensions for Firefox, with more being added almost daily.

You will be using browser extensions throughout the exercises in this book. Two of my favorite extensions for Firefox are Chris Pederick's Web Developer extension and Firebug.

Note: You can find the developer extensions for Firefox at http://addons.mozilla.org/.

Use the Web Developer extension

The most essential developer extension is Chris Pederick's Web Developer extension for Firefox and other Mozilla browsers. Pederick's browser toolbar extension includes so many useful features that an entire book could be written (and perhaps will be) on how to use it (**Figure 2.12**).

Note: Download the free Web Developer extension at http://chrispederick.com/work/webdeveloper/.

Explore the DOM with Firebug

Firebug is a useful Firefox extension that makes it easy to explore the DOM. Firebug then logs JavaScript, CSS, and other errors to a console. You can also use your keyboard to move through the DOM, and any node you select will be highlighted in the page (**Figure 2.13**).

Note: You can find Firebug at http://addons.mozilla.org/firefox/1843/.

2.12 The Show Element Information feature in the Web Developer extension

2.13 Using Firebug to explore the DOM

Live editing your CSS with the Web Developer extension

Some of the powerful tools within the Web Developer extension are the controls for the specific CSS files and styles that are loaded into the browser. These tools make it simple for you to change the look of your prototype page without directly editing your CSS files in an external editor, and this process is particularly effective when you want immediate feedback.

One of the most useful features of the Web Developer extension is the Edit CSS panel, which allows you to change styles and then preview the results without ever leaving your browser.

Imagine for a moment that your client or manager has had feedback from user tests. The tests tell you that the default type size you originally chose is too small to meet their needs. This is not an unusual comment, so don't take it to heart; many designers love text so small that it can leave older visitors with their noses pressed against the screen.

Select Edit CSS from the toolbar menu, and a panel will appear with all the styling information from your inline styles and external style sheets, all organized neatly into tabs.

To change your base font size, select the correct tab (here typography.css), and increase the percentage text size that you defined on the `<body>` element:

```
body {
font : 82%/1.5 "Trebuchet MS", "Lucida Grande","Lucida
Sans Unicode", Verdana, sans-serif; }
```

The results will appear immediately in the browser.

When any changes have been approved, use the Edit CSS panel to save the new font size to your external style sheet.

Working directly in your development browser can save you considerable time. You can try, test, and (if successful) save even large-scale changes to layout, all without ever reaching for your favorite Web editor.

Keeping your <div> elements to a minimum

Adding more `<div>` elements than necessary will make the likelihood of errors far greater. To avoid this problem during the markup phase, you should keep your markup as minimal as possible.

Start with only structural elements such as headers, paragraphs, lists, and quotations, and work from the content out, before adding any divisions.

Then, keep your `<div>` elements to a minimum, adding them progressively as needed but not more than you need. This approach will help you keep your working documents and the final prototype as free from presentational or unnecessary markup as possible.

Ensuring your markup stays valid

Poorly written markup will always eat into your valuable time by forcing you to first find errors and then correct them. Testing your markup regularly to ensure that no validation errors have slipped in is not only wise, but it can be essential to working efficiently. Writing valid markup will pay dividends; it will reduce any margin for error and give you a firm foundation on which to build your designs.

Choosing positioning over floats

Using floats has become almost a de facto standard method for creating column layouts using CSS. Floats were originally not intended for page layout, but they do their best of a tough job. However, they have a fragility that can often lead to frustration during this phase because sometimes all it takes for float-dependent layouts to fall apart is the addition of italicized text or an image that is a single pixel wider than the floated column that contains it.

The solution lies in CSS positioning. Understanding the basics of absolute, relative, and fixed positioning can sometimes be more difficult than understanding the relative simplicity of floats. However, mastering positioning with its enormous potential for layout flexibility and its more robust behavior will be one of the most rewarding challenges you can take on when learning CSS.

Whereas float-dependant layouts can easily fall apart at the slightest nudge, positioned layouts can support supersized images or gigantic text without failing, making them ideal

 2.14 Sticking out of the side of a parent element

to use during this phase. Although you may later choose to rework the CSS to use floats and some positioning, the generally accepted current recommendation is to use positioning in this phase and make changes later.

The problem with floats

Contemporary Web browsers follow the W3C (World Wide Web Consortium) specification in which a 200-pixel-wide element, such as a division, should always be 200 pixels wide. Wider elements placed inside it would simply stick out of the side; the result might look ugly, but the layout will remain intact (**Figure 2.14**).

The developers of early versions of Internet Explorer had other ideas. They developed their browser to expand a container to fit the width of its contents. So, the same 200-pixel-wide column containing a 220-pixel-wide image would expand to 220 pixels. This can cause a floated column to drop underneath its neighbor column, breaking your layout (**Figure 2.15**).

Although you can solve problems with floats when you have more time, time is often in short supply when you are making your prototypes.

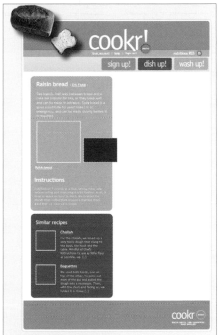

2.15 A floated element dropping down

Dividing your CSS into multiple files

Whereas people might disagree over whether a single, linked, or imported CSS file is more manageable in a final product than many separate ones, you can best solve that argument by studying the context of the situation. One fact is certain, however; while building the interactive prototype, using multiple files has distinct advantages.

For example, you could break a prototype into the following separate files:

- Layout styles including display properties, floats and positioning, widths and heights, and padding and margins (layout.css)
- Color styles including background properties, colors, and images, as well as text colors (color.css)
- Typographical information including font families and sizes, line heights, letter spacing, and text decorations (type.css)

For simplicity and to reduce the number of style sheets that are linked to and from your markup, you might choose to link to one file and import your additional style sheets into that using the @import at-rule.

To work correctly, your imported style sheets must appear at the top of the style sheet above any other rules:

```
@import url(color.css);
@import url(type.css);
[ remaining layout.css rules ]
```

So far, you have learned that using meaningful markup and CSS to make interactive prototypes will help you achieve lightweight, semantic code; accessible content; and flexible design. This kind of prototype also helps you communicate more efficiently with your colleagues and clients.

HTML prototyping and full-on agile development of Web applications are increasingly viable options that help minimize communication gaps and assumptions and deliver more accurate results sooner. If you haven't considered it, now may be the time.

—GARRETT DIMON
www.digital-web.com/articles/
just_build_it_html_prototyping_and_agile_development/

Practicing the Process

It's time for you put into practice the workflow and techniques you have learned. In this section, you will move through the stages of the content-based workflow with the goal of creating an interactive prototype from one of three static design visuals using meaningful markup and CSS.

Looking at the ingredients

Let's imagine for a moment that you have the pleasure of working on a new design for a start-up company. This company has shiny new offices and enough venture capital to run a small country with change to spare. This new company, Cookr!, is building an exciting Web application that will enable its visitors to upload and share recipes on the Web.

The first stage in the process is for you to gather all the content and organize it, taking care to be sensitive to search engine, usability, and accessibility concerns.

Opening the grey boxes

Here the grey box method is ideal for describing the content that will appear on any given page and the relationships inherent between areas of that content. Grey boxes are easy to create, and they give visual designers just the right amount of information without limiting any of the ideas they might have for how the page layout should look.

For this simple page, grey boxes are representing two primary areas (**Figure 2.17**):

- Content of interest
- Navigation and tools

Content and navigation have been further divided into the following:

- Content includes an individual recipe's main content, including its description, ingredients, and cooking instructions.
- Navigation includes links to account features and tools that help visitors use the site.

To provide more detailed information, these grey boxes could be part of a larger set of documentation that might include a page description document or other notes about content and functionality.

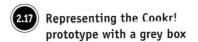

2.17 **Representing the Cookr! prototype with a grey box**

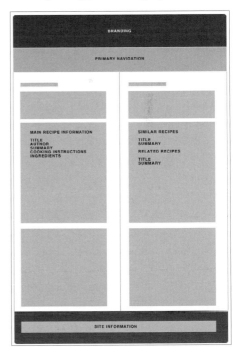

Looking at the static design visuals

Creating static designs will likely always be part of the creative design process. For this project, assume you have created three static designs. The client has initially chosen one that best reflects their branding and the emotions they want the site to evoke (**Figure 2.18**).

Writing content-out markup

Whatever role you play in the process, work can begin now on creating a meaningful XHTML document. You will build this document from the content that was described and organized into grey boxes. You can work on this markup even while the intricacies of the visual design are still being finalized. This gives everybody involved in the project a head start.

Although it might be tempting to use the visual layout as the basis for the structure of your markup, this could lead to you overusing elements, particularly `<div>` elements. This will also result in establishing your content order primarily to accomplish the visual layout rather than it making sense when no style sheets are available. To avoid presentational markup and ordering problems, begin by first looking at the content and then working out from the meaning.

2.18 **Giving three static designs for the Cookr! project**

Visualizing the structure

If you refer to the grey boxes and static design visuals, you will see that the page you are prototyping has several important areas of content:

- A main recipe that contains information about how to make it, plus its ingredients
- Similar and alternative recipes

The static design contains expected site features including branding, navigation, and site information that are unrelated to the main content. I often refer to these features as *site furniture*.

Main content

We already know that the name of the site, Cookr!, is important for identifying the site. It's so important, in fact, that it is appropriate to use the top-level heading <h1> to describe it in markup.

Now turn your attention to the main recipe information, which includes its name followed by a short description (**Figure 2.19**).

Raisin bread (Eric Fung)

Tea breads, half-way between bread and a cake are popular for tea, as they keep well and can be made in advance. Soda bread is a good substitute for yeast bread in an emergency, and can be made shortly before it is required.

Raisin bread

2.19 Getting a close-up look at the main recipe information

Note

Some developers prefer to use a top-level heading, on the home page only, for the name of the site. On other pages, they use an <h1> element for the page's unique title and not for the name of the site.

Note

You can find all the files you need for this example and the others in the book at www.transcendingcss.com/support/.

Looking at this content, two elements should spring to mind:

- A heading for the recipe name, in this case a second-level heading, <h2>
- A paragraph, <p>, for the recipe description

Here are the elements:

`<h2>`Raisin bread`</h2>`

`<p>`Tea breads, halfway between bread and a cake, are popular for tea, as they keep well and can be made in advance. Soda bread is a good substitute for yeast bread in an emergency and can be made shortly before it is required.`</p>`

You should see a similar pattern to the structure of the cooking instructions, but with one subtle difference. If you refer to the grey boxes, you will see that these instructions and ingredients are part of the main recipe content marked up with an <h2> element. To maintain a well-structured outline, you should choose lower-level headings for all the content that falls under that heading (**Figure 2.20**).

`<h3>`Instructions`</h3>`

`<p>`I worked on 9 strands at a time, letting them relax before rolling and stretching them a bit further. In all, it took us about an hour to finish. We braided the strands and then coiled them around a stainless steel bowl that we covered in tinfoil.`</p>`

`<p>`Bread Basket Chef baked them in a hot oven until the dough set, then removed the metal bowls, and inverted the basket to dry out the inside. When she removed them from the oven, the outside was browned but the inside was still a bit soft, so we finished drying them at home. I'm not all that excited about this product: while it's edible and interesting to admire, I much prefer something I can eat.`</p>`

Finally, the main recipe content contains a list of ingredients, in no particular order. Here you should use an unordered list, rather than any other type, to provide the structure (**Figure 2.21**).

`<h3>`Ingredients`</h3>`

Instructions

I worked on 9 strands at a time, letting them relax before rolling and stretching it a bit further. In all, it took us about an hour to finish. We braided the stands then coiled them around a stainless steel bowl that we covered in tinfoil.

Bread Basket Chef baked them in a hot oven until the dough set, then removed the metal bowls and inverted the basket to dry out the inside. When she removed them from the oven, the outside was browned but the inside was still a bit soft, so we finished drying them at home. I'm not all that excited about this product: while it's edible and interesting to admire, I much prefer something I can eat.

2.20 **Close-up of the instructions**

Ingredients

5ml bicarbonate of soda	100g butter
2.5ml cream of tartar	2.5ml ground ginger
275g plain flour	5ml ground mace
	2.5ml ground all spice

2.21 **Close-up of the ingredients**

```
<ul>
<li>5<sup title="Milliliters">ml</sup> bicarbonate of soda</li>
<li>2.5<sup>ml</sup> cream of tartar</li>
<li>275<sup title="Grams">g</sup> plain flour</li>
<li>100<sup>g</sup> butter</li>
<li>2.5<sup>ml</sup> ground ginger</li>
<li>5<sup>ml</sup> ground mace</li>
<li>2.5<sup>ml</sup> ground allspice</li>
</ul>
```

You might have noticed that at no stage have I been asking any questions about how this content is going to look, concentrating instead on the content's meaning and the elements most appropriate to describe it.

Secondary content

Now turn your attention to the similar recipes area. They appear on the right of the static design, but you should not be concerned about that at this stage because it does not matter where this content will be positioned visually.

The similar recipes links give visitors an opportunity to look at related recipes should the main recipe not quite be what they need. Here you can see two alternative recipes listed, although many more could be listed (**Figure 2.22**). The heading is simple enough to deal with; in this case I have chosen to use a third-level heading, <h3>.

```
<h3>Similar recipes</h3>
```

Similar recipes

Challah
For the challah, we mixed up a very tacky dough that clung to the bowl, the hook and the table. Mindful of Chefs instructions to use as little flour as possible, we [..]

Baguettes
We used both hands, one on top of the other, to press out most of the gas and pulled the dough into a rectangle. Then, with the short-end facing us, we folded it in three [..]

2.22 **Close-up of similar recipe links**

What about the alternative recipes information that follows this heading?

Challah

For the challah, we mixed up a very tacky dough that clung to the bowl, the hook, and the table. Mindful of Chef's instructions to use as little flour as possible.

Baguettes

We used both hands, one on top of the other, to press out most of the gas and pulled the dough into a rectangle. Then, with the short end facing us, we folded it in three.

You would be correct if you thought this content suggests that headings and paragraphs would be appropriate, but you would also be overlooking that these recipes are part of a series, and as such they form a list. But what type of list?

The titles and accompanying text are not strictly definition terms and descriptions, so using a definition list would be stretching the semantic use of the <dl> element. Because the list has no order, it is appropriate to use an unordered list with list items that contain each heading and a paragraph. This forms a meaningful XHTML compound:

```
<ul>
<li>
<h4><a href="#">Challah</a></h4>
<p>For the challah, we mixed up a very tacky dough that clung to the bowl, the
hook, and the table. Mindful of Chef's instructions to use as little flour as
possible.</p>
</li>

<li>
<h4><a href="#">Baguettes</a></h4>
<p>We used both hands, one on top of the other, to press out most of the gas
and pulled the dough into a rectangle. Then, with the short end facing us, we
folded it in three.</p>
</li>
</ul>
```

Note: XHTML *compounds* are combinations of two or more elements in XHTML that each have their own meaning. When combined, the elements create a more precise meaning together than they do separately. The concept of XHTML compounds emerged from the microformats community rather than the W3C. You can learn more about XHTML compounds in "The Elements of Meaningful XHTML" by Tantek Çelik at www.tantek. com/presentations/2005/09/elements-of-xhtml/.

Finally, you can take an identical approach for the links to related recipes (**Figure 2.23**):

```
<h3>You might also like</h3>

<ul>
<li>
<h4><a href="#">Lemon Blueberry Muffins</a></h4>
<p>The recipe in the link is half the original recipe that yields about 18
large muffins. I always cut down on the butter in this recipe.</p>
</li>

<li>
<h4><a href="#">Pistachio and Dried Fruit Cake</a></h4>
<p>The author says her mother makes this cake during Lent, so it is a
coincidence that I made it for the Easter weekend.</p>
</li>

<li>
<h4><a href="#">Brownie Berry Tower</a></h4>
<p>For the final class of this course, we made a tall cake, with brownie
layers sandwiching two kinds of cream and strawberries.</p>
</li>
</ul>
```

With both the main and additional areas of content complete, it's a good time to preview your document in your development browser to see the structure of your content. It's also a great time to validate your markup to ensure that no errors have crept in along the way.

Adding your first divisions

By now it should be clear that these two content areas are separate but are also related. You can group each into a division, and to add further meaning, you can give each one an identity that relates to the meaning of the content it contains:

 Close-up of related recipes

```
<div id="content_main">
Main content
</div>

<div id="content_sub">
Secondary content
</div>
```

Because the two areas are related, you can enclose them both inside a content division to further cement their relationship:

```
<div id="content">
<div id="content_main">
Main content
</div>

<div id="content_sub">
Secondary content
</div>
</div>
```

Each of these three meaningfully labeled divisions will soon become an opportunity for you to add your visual style.

Adding the site furniture

With your content areas complete, it is time to add the branding area, navigation, and site information that form the site's furniture. This furniture will appear on every page of your site. Once again, start working from the content out, tackling each area in turn.

Branding

Your document contains two pieces of branding information: the site's name that is graphically presented as a logo in the static design and a tag line that the visual design has intended not to be visible. Think of this hidden tag line as a piece of embedded information that will be useful to visitors using browsers that do not support style sheets and also to search engines (**Figure 2.24**):

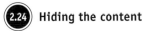

2.24 **Hiding the content**

```
Cookr!
A great place to store and share your favorite recipes
Kimberly Blessing
```

You have already decided on an <h1> element for the site name, but what about the tag line? In its basic form, this tag line is a quotation from a happy customer, and the <blockquote> element is a perfect choice. You can also take this opportunity to cite the source of the quotation by including the <cite> element:

```
<blockquote>
<p>A great place to store and share your favorite recipes</p>
<p><cite>Kimberly Blessing</cite></p>
</blockquote>
```

You can now relate both the site name and the tag line in a division to give them an extra level of meaning and get the added advantage of a hook for styling those elements:

```
<div id="branding">
<h1>Cookr</h1>
<blockquote>
<p>A great place to store and share your favorite recipes</p>
<p><cite>Kimberly Blessing</cite></p>
</blockquote>
</div>
```

Adding navigation

It is now time for you to address the elements you will need for the navigation area. Although this navigation might at first look complex with its different visual styles, by working from the content out you will realize that it is no more complex than other areas of your document (**Figure 2.25**).

2.25 **Close-up of the navigation**

Looking at this navigation in the static design and grey boxes, you will see several distinct types of links:

- A personalized welcome message containing a link from the visitor's name
- Account, help, and sign-out links (tools)
- Image links for the "sign up," "dish up," and "wash up" features
- A link to the site's RSS feed

I suggest you start by establishing the order of importance of these links.

1. Welcome message (for a returning visitor)
2. Features
3. Tools
4. RSS feed

You can now choose the appropriate markup for these lists, working in that order:

```
<p>Bonjour Monsiour <a href="#">Collison</a></p>

<ul id="nav_features">
<li><a href="#">sign up!</a></li>
<li><a href="#">dish up!</a></li>
<li><a href="#">wash up!</a></li>
</ul>

<ul id="nav_tools">
<li><a href="#">Your account</a></li>
<li><a href="#">Help</a></li>
<li><a href="#">Log out</a></li>
<li><a href="#">Nutritious RSS</a></li>
</ul>
```

You can now extend the meaning of these navigation list items by giving each a unique identity that reflects the function of the list that each contains:

```
<p>Bonjour Monsiour <a href="#">Collison</a></p>

<ul id="nav_features">
<li id="nav_signup"><a href="#">sign up!</a></li>
<li id="nav_dishup"><a href="#">dish up!</a></li>
<li id="nav_washup"><a href="#">wash up!</a></li>
</ul>
```

```
<ul id="nav_tools">
<li id="nav_account"><a href="#">Your account</a></li>
<li id="nav_help"><a href="#">Help</a></li>
<li id="nav_logout"><a href="#">Log out</a></li>
<li id="nav_rss"><a href="#">Nutritious RSS</a></li>
</ul>
```

I also suggest you add headings to both of these lists:

```
<h2>Site features</h2>
```

```
<h2>Tools</h2>
```

These headings will not be visible in the browser but will help visitors who will not be able
see the visual design. You can think about these hidden headings as embedded helpers to
further clarify the lists that follow them.

Cement the relationship between headings and lists by grouping these elements inside
their own uniquely identified division:

```
<div id="nav_main">
<p>Bonjour Monsiour <a href="#">Collison</a></p>

<h2>Site features</h2>
<ul id="nav_features">
<li id="nav_signup"><a href="#">sign up!</a></li>
<li id="nav_dishup"><a href="#">dish up!</a></li>
<li id="nav_washup"><a href="#">wash up!</a></li>
</ul>
```

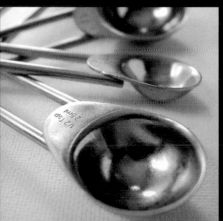

```
<h2>Tools</h2>
<ul id="nav_tools">
<li id="nav_account"><a href="#">Your account</a></li>
<li id="nav_help"><a href="#">Help</a></li>
<li id="nav_logout"><a href="#">Log out</a></li>
<li id="nav_rss"><a href="#">Nutritious RSS</a></li>
</ul>
</div>
```

Site information footer

Finally, you can turn to the footer that will contain the site information. Typically this might include a copyright statement, legal information, and perhaps a link to the start of the page (**Figure 2.26**).

Although the visual designer has chosen not to show these elements, you will see by looking at the grey boxes that the content should be present in the document. Deciding on the elements for this content should be straightforward to you by now: a heading containing an anchor to the top of the page and two paragraphs all grouped together within a site-information division:

```
<div id="site_info">

<h5><a href="#cookr-co-uk" title="Back to top">Cookr!</a></h5>
<p>Beta until the cabbage has boiled</p>
<p>Copyright Cookr! All Rights Reserved</p>

</div>
```

Once again, this is a good opportunity to preview your document in your development browser and to validate your markup to ensure it doesn't contain any errors.

2.26 Showing detail of site-information footer including a link to the top of the page

Arranging content into a meaningful order

Having decided on the most appropriate, meaningful elements to describe your content, it is time to place them in a logical order. Before you dive back into your markup, I suggest you start by listing the content in the most logical order (**Figure 2.27**):

1. Branding (site name and tag line)

2. Navigation

3. Main content

4. Supplementary content

5. Site information

2.27 **Ordering the content in a logical manner**

This list will become your document's content order. For easy scanning through the order, I have added numbered comments that relate to this order.

I have now also added the <html>, <head>, and <body> elements and my chosen DOCTYPE to form a complete XHTML document:

```
<!DOCTYPE html PUBLIC "-//W3C//DTD XHTML 1.0 Strict//EN" "http://www.w3.org/TR/
xhtml1/DTD/xhtml1-strict.dtd">
<html xmlns="http://www.w3.org/1999/xhtml" xml:lang="en" lang="en">

<head>
<title>Cookr! | Raisin bread</title>
<meta http-equiv="content-type" content="text/html; charset=utf-8" /> </head>

<body id="cookr-co-uk" class="recipe">

<!-- 1. Branding -->
<div id="branding">
<h1>Cookr!</h1>
<blockquote>
<p>A great place to store and share your favorite recipes</p>
<p><cite>Kimberly Blessing</cite></p>
</blockquote>
</div>

<!-- 2. Navigation -->
<div id="nav_main">

<p>Bonjour Monsiour <a href="#">Collison</a></p>

<h2>Site features</h2>
<ul id="nav_features">
<li id="nav_signup"><a href="#">sign up!</a></li>
<li id="nav_dishup"><a href="#">dish up!</a></li>
<li id="nav_washup"><a href="#">wash up!</a></li>
</ul>

<h2>Tools</h2>
<ul id="nav_tools">
<li id="nav_account"><a href="#">Your account</a></li>
```

```
<li id="nav_help"><a href="#">Help</a></li>
<li id="nav_logout"><a href="#">Log out</a></li>
<li id="nav_rss"><a href="#">Nutritious RSS</a></li>
</ul>
</div>

<div id="content ">
<!-- 3. Main content -->
<div id="content_main">

<h2>Raisin bread</h2>
<p>Tea breads, halfway between bread and a cake are popular for tea, as they
keep well and can be made in advance. Soda bread is a good substitute for
yeast bread in an emergency and can be made shortly before it is required.</p>

<h3>Instructions</h3>
<p>I worked on 9 strands at a time, letting them relax before rolling and
stretching them a bit further. In all, it took us about an hour to finish. We
braided the strands and then coiled them around a stainless steel bowl that we
covered in tinfoil.</p>

<p>Bread Basket Chef baked them in a hot oven until the dough set, then
removed the metal bowls, and inverted the basket to dry out the inside. When
she removed them from the oven, the outside was browned but the inside was
still a bit soft, so we finished drying them at home. I'm not all that excited
about this product: while it's edible and interesting to admire, I much prefer
something I can eat.</p>

<h3>Ingredients</h3>
<ul>
<li>5<abbr title="Mililitres">ml</abbr> bicarbonate of soda</li>
<li>2.5<abbr>ml</abbr> cream of tartar</li>
<li>275<abbr title="Grammes">g</abbr> plain flour</li>
<li>100<abbr>g</abbr> butter</li>
<li>2.5<abbr>ml</abbr> ground ginger</li>
<li>5<abbr>ml</abbr> ground mace</li>
<li>2.5<abbr>ml</abbr> ground all spice</li>
</ul>
</div>
```

```
<!-- 4. Supplementary content -->
<div id="content_sub">

<h3>Similar recipes</h3>

<ul>
<li>
<h4><a href="#">Challah</a></h4>
<p>For the challah, we mixed up a very tacky dough that clung to the bowl, the
hook, and the table. Mindful of Chef's instructions to use as little flour as
possible.</p>
</li>
<li>
<h4><a href="#">Baguettes</a></h4>
<p>We used both hands, one on top of the other, to press out most of the gas
and pulled the dough into a rectangle. Then, with the short end facing us, we
folded it in three.</p>
</li>
</ul>

<h3>You might also like</h3>

<ul>
<li>
<h4><a href="#">You might also like</a></h4>
<p>The recipe in the link is half the original recipe that yields about 18
large muffins. I always cut down on the butter in this recipe.</p>
</li>
<li>
```

```
<h4><a href="#">Pistachio and Dried Fruit Cake</a></h4>
<p>The author says her mother makes this cake during Lent, so it is a
coincidence that I made it for the Easter weekend.</p>
</li>

<li>
<h4><a href="#">Brownie Berry Tower</a></h4>
<p>For the final class of this course, we made a tall cake, with brownie
layers sandwiching two kinds of cream and strawberries.</p>
</li>
</ul>
</div>
</div>

<!-- 5. Site information -->
<div id="site_info">
<h5><a href="#cookr-co-uk" title="Back to top">Cookr!</a></h5>
<p>Beta until the cabbage has boiled</p>
<p>Copyright Cookr! All Rights Reserved</p>
</div>

</body>
</html>
```

With all your markup elements in place, it is a great idea to once again preview your document in your browser and take the opportunity to validate your markup before you move on
to implementing the design with CSS.

Implementing the static design with CSS

With your markup written and validated, it is time to develop the CSS to implement the static design.

For flexibility, I suggest you divide your CSS across three separate style sheets, in the way I demonstrated earlier:

- Layout styles including display properties, floats and positioning, widths and heights, and margins and padding. Name this style sheet layout.css.
- Color styles including background properties, colors, and images, as well as text colors. Name this style sheet color.css.
- Typographical information including font families and sizes, line heights, letter spacing, and text decorations. Name this style sheet typography.css.

To reduce the number of style sheets that are linked from your XHTML document, it is common practice to link to only one style sheet, as follows:

```
<link rel="stylesheet" type="text/css" href="layout.css" />
```

Then import the remaining style sheets into that by using the @import at-rule:

```
@import url(color.css);
@import url(typography.css);
```

Building your layout

The first style sheet you will work with will contain all aspects of the visual layout that has been defined in the static design; in this instance, it's a two-column layout with branding at the top, navigation, and a site-information area at the bottom.

I suggest you start by overriding all the browser styles, which will appear if you do not provide a style. Furthermore, different browsers have different style defaults. By overriding, or *normalizing*, the way elements are styled by the browser, you'll gain far more control—both within the CSS and across the browsers that will interpret it:

```
/* Normalizes margin, padding */
body, div, dl, dt, dd, ul, ol, li, h1, h2, h3, h4, h5, h6, pre, form, fieldset,
input, p, blockquote, th, td
{ margin : 0; padding : 0; }
```

```
/* Normalizes font-size for headers */
h1,h2,h3,h4,h5,h6
{ font-size : 100%; }

/* Removes list-style from lists */
ol,ul
{ list-style : none; }

/* Normalizes font-style and font-weight to normal */
address, caption, cite, code, dfn, em, strong, th, var
{ font-style : normal; font-weight : normal; }

/* Removes borders and spacing from tables */
table
{ border-collapse : collapse; border-spacing : 0; }

/* Removes border from fieldset and img */
fieldset,img
{ border : 0; }

/* Left-aligns text in caption and th */
caption,th
{ text-align : left; }

/* Removes quotation marks from q */
q:before, q:after
{ content :''; }
```

Working from the body

The static design in this example is a common, centered, fixed-pixel-width layout. In this type of design, you can use an outer container or wrapper division to constrain the design to the center of the browser window. You can eliminate the need for this division by using the <html> and <body> elements to fix and center your design:

```
html {
text-align :  center; }
```

Note

Read more about normalizing browser styles at http://tantek.com/log/2004/09.html#d06t2354 and at http://meyerweb.com/eric/thoughts/2004/09/15/emreallyem-undoing-htmlcss/.

```
body {
width : 770px;
margin : 0 auto;
text-align : left; }
```

Here, a fixed width and autoright and autoleft margins placed in the <body> element will center the design within <html>.

Creating a positioning context

The expected behavior of any absolutely positioned element is to be positioned according to any offsets in relation to the following:

• Its closest positioned ancestor

• In the absence of a positioned ancestor, the root element <html>

Because your design will use <body>, rather than a container <div>, to center the design, you can apply relative positioning to the <body> element to establish it as a positioning context for other positioned elements within the design:

```
body {
position : relative;
width : 770px;
margin : 0 auto;
text-align : left; }
```

To implement the static design using positioning (as I recommended earlier in the discussion about CSS in the workflow), you will create two equal columns.

In your markup, both of the columns, `content_main` and `content_sub`, are situated inside an outer division, `content`. To create a positioning context for these two columns, you will add `position : relative;` to the division labeled `content`:

```
div#content {
position : relative;
width : 100%; }
```

Creating your two columns

Now you are ready to make two equal columns and use absolute positioning to place the columns to the left and right. To accomplish the static design, you will give each column an equal width, with the main content positioned to the left edge of its container and the additional content positioned 50 percent from the container's left edge:

```
div#content_main {
left : 0;
width : 50%;
padding : 1em 0; }
```

```
div#content_sub {
left : 50%;
width : 50%;
padding : 1em 0; }
```

Using this method will create two robust columns that can support supersized images or even gigantic text without breaking the integrity of your design.

Switching the columns

What will you do if your client asks at this point, "Do you think the main content would look better on the right, rather than on the left?"

CSS positioning allows you to switch the position of the two columns without changing the source order of your document, even if one of your colleagues is still developing the markup (**Figure 2.28**):

```
div#content_main {
position : absolute;
left : 50%;
width : 50%; }
```

```
div#content_sub {
position : absolute;
left : 0;
width : 50%; }
```

It is equally as simple to change the proportions of your layout by adjusting both the widths of the two columns and their horizontal positions. For example, to alter the layout to 70/30 percent proportions, you can alter the column rules to the following:

```
div#content_main {
position : absolute;
left : 70%;
width : 30%; }

div#content_sub {
position : absolute;
left : 0;
width : 70%; }
```

2.28 Switching the position of the two columns

Arranging the furniture

With much of the more complex layout positioning now complete, you should add a combined rule that will give all of your remaining layout divisions a width:

```
div#branding, div#nav_main, div#site_info {
width : 100%; }
```

Ah, but a gotcha is hiding here. If you preview your layout in a browser, you will notice immediately that the site-information section, which you intended to be at the foot of the page, has risen up and overlaps the content of your columns. This is not a bug, either in your CSS or in your browser; it is the result of using absolute positioning to create your columns, which means you can easily fix this using the Inman position clearing method.

RELATIVELY SPEAKING

Relative positioning often confuses people who are new to CSS positioning, largely because the term *relative* makes people wonder "relative to what?"

Relatively positioned elements are positioned relative to the normal flow. *Normal flow* is the natural, expected flow of the content within the browser window. Imagine looking at a plain document, marked up with content, headers, and paragraphs only. Then resize the browser window using the lower-right corner. Watch the text while making your browser window smaller and you'll notice the text flows down and to the left. Any element in the normal flow flows with the document logic (**Figure 2.29**).

A relatively positioned box is offset in relation to its natural position within the normal flow. When an element is relatively positioned from its original location in the normal flow, it leaves behind it the space it would normally have occupied. Other elements cannot flow into this "ghosted" space because the element is still considered by the browser to actually be in the normal flow, not out of it (**Figure 2.30**).

2.29 Box in normal flow

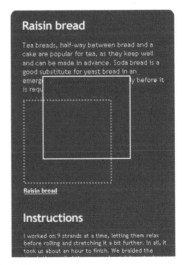

2.30 Relatively positioned box leaving a space behind

Understanding absolute positioning

An *absolutely positioned* element is positioned first to its closest positioned ancestor. If there is no positioned ancestor, the element is positioned to the root element <html> (**Figure 2.31**).

Absolutely positioned elements are considered to be out of the normal flow of the document. Therefore, text and other elements can flow up into any space the element was taking up prior to being offset (**Figure 2.32**).

 2.31 An element absolutely positioned to root

 2.32 Normal flow intact, with other elements flowing up to fill the space

Using Inman position clearing to fix your footer

During the prototyping phase, you can use a combination of JavaScript and CSS to force this site information to drop below the absolutely positioned columns. Inman position clearing uses JavaScript to position the site-information <div> element underneath the absolutely positioned columns once the browser has calculated their heights.

For this solution to work, you must place a link to the script immediately prior to the closing </body> tag in your XHTML:

```
<script type="text/javascript" src="si-clear-children.
js"></script>
</body>
```

To enable this script to work its magic, you need to add several extra class attributes to your content divisions in your XHTML:

```
<div id="content" class="c clear_children">
<div id="content_main" class="pc cc tallest">
Main content
</div>
```

```
<div id="content_sub" class="sc">
Additional content
</div>
</div>
```

```
/* =si_clear_children */
.pc,.sc { position : absolute; top: 0; left: 0; }
.clear_children,.cc_tallest { position: relative; }
/*\*/* html .clear_children { display: inline;}/**/
.cc_tallest:after { content: ''; } /* PREVENTS A REDRAW
BUG IN SAFARI */
```

Your site-information footer will now take its rightful place underneath the two columns.

> **Note:** You can find out more about Inman position clearing at www.shauninman.com/plete/2006/05/ clearance-position-inline-absolute.

Moving on, or handing over?

In a team environment, this is another opportunity for you to hand over your work to another team member or a different department, for example, to add functionality or perhaps CMS (Content Management System) integration. This basic layout (**Figure 2.33**) provides your technical developers with a robust platform on which to develop while you continue working to accomplish the full static design.

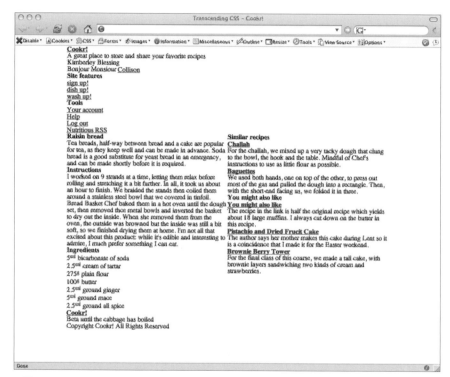

2.33 Viewing the prototype with only layout styles applied

Basic color styles

Now it's time for you to add the background colors and images for your page backgrounds and content areas:

```
html {
background-color : #f1efe2; }
```

```
div#content {
background-color : #fff; }

div#site_info {
background : transparent url(site_info.png) no-repeat 0 0; }
```

Building brand

If you refer to the static design, you'll see the branding area features a rounded-corner, green background image, and a logo and image that break out of the top and left of the design. Here's the markup that was chosen for this area:

```
<div id="branding">
<h1>Cookr!</h1>
<blockquote>
<p>A great place to store and share your favorite recipes</p>
<p><cite>Kimberly Blessing</cite></p>
</blockquote>
</div>
```

You'll add some room above the branding area to make space for positioning your logo and image by adding top padding to your <body> element:

```
body {
padding-top : 50px; }
```

Style the branding by giving it a height that matches its background image:

```
div#branding {
height : 120px;
background : transparent url(branding.png) no-repeat 0 0;  }
```

Adding the logo

To create the effect of the logo and image breaking out of the branding area, you will use negative offset values on the absolutely positioned <h1> element. This will move them outside the <body> element:

```
h1 {
position : absolute;
top : -10px;
left : -80px;
}
```

To accomplish the static design, you will need the branding images to overlap the naviga-tion below it. To ensure that these images always remain in the foreground and above any other positioned elements, give your heading a high z-index:

```
div#branding {
position : relative;
z-index : 10; }
```

> **Note:** You can read all about z-index and image replacement in my article "Z's not dead baby, Z's not dead" at http://24ways.org/advent/zs-not-dead-baby-zs-not-dead/.

For this design, you will need to replace the <h1> element with an alpha-transparent PNG image. So many image replacement techniques now exist that it can be hard to keep up-to-date. I suggest you use the simple and reliable Phark method:

```
h1 {
position : absolute;
top : -60px;
left : -80px;
width : 588px;
height : 253px;
background : transparent url(h1.png) no-repeat;
text-indent : -9999px; }
```

This method hides the header text by using negative text indentation to the point where it disappears off the left edge of the browser viewport. You can use a similar technique for moving the tag line out of view. This text will still be available to visitors who cannot see the visual design:

```
div#branding blockquote {
position : absolute;
top : -9999px;
}
```

(2.34) Completed branding

The branding area is now complete with the header styled, the site logo in place, and the tag line moved out of view (**Figure 2.34**).

Styling the navigation

With your branding complete, it is time to turn your attention to the slightly more complex navigation area. If you refer to the markup you created for the navigation division, you will see you included a paragraph and two unordered lists. You gave each of the lists, and the items they contain, unique identities:

```
<div id="nav_main">

<p>Bonjour Monsiour <a href="#">Collison</a></p>
<h2>Site features</h2>
<ul id="nav_features">
<li id="nav_signup"><a href="#">sign up!</a></li>
<li id="nav_dishup"><a href="#">dish up!</a></li>
<li id="nav_washup"><a href="#">wash up!</a></li>
</ul>

<h2>Tools</h2>
<ul id="nav_tools">
<li id="nav_account"><a href="#">Your account</a></li>
<li id="nav_help"><a href="#">Help</a></li>
<li id="nav_logout"><a href="#">Log out</a></li>
<li id="nav_rss"><a href="#">Nutritious RSS</a></li>
</ul>
</div>
```

You can now put each of those attributes to good use by selecting these elements using their id attributes.

But before you turn your attention to the elements, you'll start by preparing their parent, the division you labeled nav_main. Add a background image and a height that matches that image:

```
div#nav_main {
position: relative;
height : 50px;
background : #edc025 url(nav_main.png) no-repeat 0 0; }
```

Because so many of its children will be positioned, you should establish the parent as the positioning context and set a low z-index because you'll want some of these positioned elements to sit behind others on the page:

```
div#nav_main {
z-index : 1;
height : 90px;
background : #edc025 url(nav_main.png) no-repeat 0 0; }
```

Features navigation

You will start by using absolute positioning to place the features navigation list on the right of the navigation area:

```
ul#nav_features {
position : absolute;
top : 35px;
left : 325px;
margin : 0;
width : 440px;
height : 50px; }
```

Ready to add the images that form the features navigation buttons? Opt for a simple solution that places all three buttons as a background image to the features list. Then, lay each of the anchors over the background image by using absolute positioning and giving each anchor an explicit height and width:

```
ul#nav_features {
position : absolute;
top : 35px;
left : 325px;
margin : 0;
width : 440px;
height : 50px;
background : transparent url(nav_features.png) no-repeat; }

ul#nav_features li {
display : inline;  }

li#nav_signup {
left : 0; }

li#nav_dishup {
left : 150px; }
```

```
li#nav_washup {
left : 300px; }

li#nav_signup a, li#nav_dishup a, li#nav_washup a {
display : block;
height : 50px;
width : 140px;
text-indent : -9999px; }
```

Tools navigation

You will form the tools navigation list from simple text links. Once again you will use
absolute positioning to place this list where the design demands:

```
ul#nav_tools {
position : absolute;
top : 3px;
left : 280px;
margin : 0;
width : 460px; }
```

You should style each list item to display inline rather than as a block that will occupy
a space on a line below:

```
ul#nav_tools li {
display : inline; }
```

To create an even space between each of the anchors, add a margin and padding to each
of the anchors, and then reset these styles on specific links by selecting them with their
list item's id name:

```
ul#nav_tools li a {
margin-right : 10px;
padding-right : 10px; }

li#nav_logout a. li#nav_rss a {
margin-right : 0;
padding-right : 0; }
```

You can position the link to the site's RSS feed using both positioning and image replacement:

```
li#nav_rss {
position : absolute;
right : 0;
width : 120px;
height : 25px; }
```

```
li#nav_rss a {
display : block;
width : 120px;
height : 25px;
text-indent : -9999px; }
```

Getting up close and personal

Style and position the paragraph containing the site's personalized welcome message to returning visitors:

```
div#nav_main p {
position : absolute;
top : 45px;
left : 35px;
margin : 0; }
```

Hide the embedded alternate headers by moving them off the top of the screen:

```
div#nav_main h2 {
position : absolute;
top : -9999px; }
```

You've styled each of the different navigation elements using a combination of text and images (**Figure 2.35**).

2.35 **Completed navigation**

Styling the footer

All that remains is to complete the styling of the site information. This area contains a level-five heading, <h5>, and two paragraphs:

```
<div id="site_info">
<h5><a href="#cookr-co-uk" title="Back to top">Cookr!</a></h5>
<p>Beta until the cabbage has boiled</p>
<p>Copyright Cookr! All Rights Reserved</p>
</div>
```

Once again you will use absolute positioning to style the heading and "hide" one of the paragraphs from view. Your first tasks are to establish the division as a positioning context for its absolutely positioned child elements and give it a height that matches its background image:

```
div#site_info {
position : relative;
width : 100%,
height : 120px;
background : transparent url(site_info.png) no-repeat 0 0; }
```

Using image replacement

Replacing the text of this heading should be a familiar process to you by now. Once again I suggest using the Phark method for its simplicity:

```
div#site_info h5 {
position : absolute;
right : 10px;
bottom : 10px;
width : 150px;
height : 70px;
background : transparent url(h5.png) no-repeat; }
```

```
div#site_info h5 a {
display : block;
width : 150px;
height : 70px;
text-indent : -9999px; }
```

The semantic framing of the pages in

(X)HTML makes it all the way to production

in 95% of the projects. The time savings with

XHTML wireframes has been about a quarter

to a third of the development time saved.

—THOMAS VANDER WAL
www.vanderwal.net/random/category.php?cat=84

Positioning the paragraphs

Your final task in styling the footer is to position the paragraph containing the copyright notice. Although your document has two paragraphs of text, the static design dictates that only the second of the two is visible.

Here you can use the power of adjacent sibling selectors to target the second paragraph without affecting the first, all without adding further `class` or `id` attributes to achieve this presentational result.

Apply styles to both of the paragraphs in the site-information area, once again using absolute positioning to place both paragraphs in the same place:

```
div#site_info p {
position : absolute;
left : 10px;
top : 10px;
margin : 0; }

div#site_info h5 + p {
text-indent : -9999px; }
```

If you preview the result in your browser, you will see that both paragraphs now occupy the same space, hardly an attractive result. Your next move will be to hide only the first paragraph, moving it off the left of the browser viewport, by using an adjacent sibling selector and a large amount of negative text indent (**Figure 2.36**).

Completed footer styles

Understanding elements of typographical style

With your main design styling complete, it's time to turn your attention to typography. I suggest you write all your typographical styles in a separate typography.css style sheet:

```
body {
font : 72%/1.5 "Trebuchet MS", "Lucida Grande","Lucida Sans Unicode", Verdana,
sans-serif; }

h2, h3, h4, p, ul, blockquote {
margin : 0 20px .75em; }

h2, h3 {
margin-bottom : .15em;
font : 200% "Trebuchet MS", "Lucida Grande","Lucida Sans Unicode", Verdana,
sans-serif;
font-weight : bold;
letter-spacing : -1px; }

li > h4 { margin-left : 0; }

p {
font-size : 100%; }

h2 + p {
font-size : 110%; }

li > p { margin-left : 0; }

a:link, a:visited {
text-decoration : none; }
```

You can follow these with your text colors that you have derived from your static design:

```
body {
color : #333; }

h2, h3 {
color : #88a308; }

div#nav_main p {
font-size : 160%;
color : #88a308; }
```

```
div#site_info p {
color : #fff; }

a:link, a:visited {
color : #f90; }

ul#nav_tools a {
color : #fff; }
```

Add the typographic styles, and you've completed the interactive prototype (**Figure 2.37**).

Putting It All Together

You now have a working interactive prototype, a far cry from the traditional result of a static image. This prototype, built with meaningful markup and CSS, enables interaction designers and developers to take development further by adding enhanced functionality using Ajax or related technologies.

I hope you have seen that this method not only makes the most of lightweight, meaningful markup and CSS, which are two of the major advantages when working with Web standards, but that this method is about far more than the mechanics of markup and style sheets.

If you are a lone designer who creates static designs, markup, and CSS, this method is an ideal design framework to give you more flexibility. Proofing your ideas using markup and CSS, in addition to working in Photoshop, enables you to see the realities of your designs far earlier in the process. It allows you to try new ideas and to rapidly see what works and what doesn't. You can find out earlier how your designs will work when adapted for the Web and see how your layouts will behave when implemented as a flexible, rather than as a frozen, layout.

If you work as part of a larger team where designers work separately from technical developers, these prototypes have many advantages for both designers and developers. For designers, they give all the creative advantages and also provide an ideal way to collaborate with technical developers. They show the real meaning of the content and demonstrate the meaningful markup that should be used and maintained throughout the entire process.

For technical developers, these standards-based prototypes offer the firm foundation for development that no other method of static design, wireframe, or prototype can offer: valid, meaningful markup on which to continue developing with microformats, DOM scripting, and any other type of technical programming and development. These prototypes are the ideal starting point for developing feature-rich content by using Ajax or similar combinations of technologies, all without breaking the carefully crafted work of a visual designer.

In large organizations where many people with many different skills work together to make the final product, quality of workmanship and time spent in design and development are both critical factors. By working in parallel, iterative tracks from the same sound foundation of meaningful XHTML, visual designers and technical developers of all kinds can work on a project in sync, with fewer margins for error and less time spent undoing other people's hard work.

3

Inspiration

Explore the divine proportion.

Design with grids in mind.

Discover that inspiration is everywhere.

Introducing Grid-Based Design

When you sit back in your comfy chair, close your eyes, and think about grids, what are the first ideas that spring to mind? I suppose that if your chosen career path has led you to wear a pointy hat and direct traffic, your mind might jump first to those yellow "don't-enter-unless-your-exit-is-clear" grids at busy road junctions. But I'm assuming you chose instead to design for the Web and your ideas about grids are somewhat different. Still, there are parallels in the way some designers and some traffic police think about grids—that they are about rules or regulations, rather than about flexibility.

Technically speaking, *grids* are a combination of vertical columns, horizontal fields, and white space gutters. Translating that grid terminology into CSS, you can think in terms of divisions, margins, and padding (**Figure 3.1**).

Designers often think working with grids can be a restrictive rather than a creative process. They think basing a design on a series of columns and fields will limit their ability to make designs that break out of the literal box; in reality, the opposite in true.

My aim is to show you that designing with grids will lead to more, rather than fewer, creative opportunities; your designs will go in new directions, and using grids will provide you with a solid foundation for experimenting with new ideas.

I'll begin with the theory behind designing grids in the context of Web design. You will then see how grids have been used across different media, and you will finish by using grids that have been influenced by other media to bring a fresh look to some of the common layouts and interface elements you design every day.

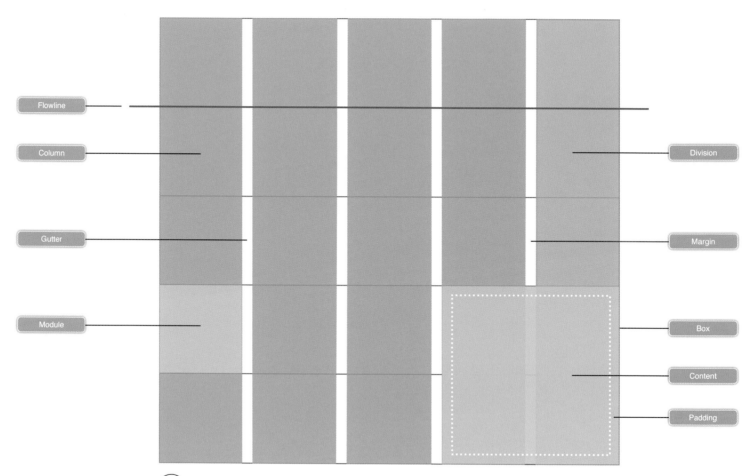

Flowline

Column

Gutter

Module

Division

Margin

Box

Content

Padding

3.1 Comparing grid design and CSS terminology

The designer and the grid

I remember art-school lectures about proportion and balance. But as a fine-arts student, I preferred to spend my time in the printmaking room rather than in the lecture hall.

As with many designers working on the Web today, I was schooled in neither the theory nor the importance of using grids. It was only after I began working on the Web professionally that I became aware of their importance in helping make well-balanced designs. When I started reading about grids, I found that much of the information about them seemed to have little relevance to modern-day Web design.

Some of these discussions focus on mathematics and talk of the famous Fibonacci sequence. As someone who finds it difficult to remember the PIN numbers of two of my credit cards at any one time, mathematics was never a favorite subject.

When I began to consciously consider the grids I use in my everyday design work, I realized their tremendous flexibility, and I began to look for unusual grids I could bring into my designs.

When you start to look for examples of grid design in action, you won't have to look far. Open your morning newspaper or pick up a copy of a favorite magazine, and you'll see grids everywhere. When you take a drive through your neighborhood, grids appear in the design of buildings and in modern cities, even in the layout of the roads on which you are driving. The horizontal and vertical lines inherent in grids are almost everywhere in the world that we humans have designed for ourselves.

Grid design is a skill that is important for every designer to learn. Learning to work with their composition and proportions is one of the foundations for great design.

It is a mistake to think designing with grids is about making designs conforming to a rigid structure; in fact, the opposite is true. Grids help designers create arrangements and patterns that "feel right" and that people find comfortable to use.

Grids serve as a guide to designers to follow when they are placing objects on a page. They provide structure and add rhythm to a design. Using them helps designers create compositions that are easier for a reader to scan. Grids also present information in a way that is more neatly organized and therefore easier to follow.

Note

In *The Book of Calculating* in 1202, Fibonacci's number progression involved adding two numbers to arrive at the next in the sequence:

1, **2** (1+1), **3** (2+1), **5** (3+2), **8** (5+3), and so on

That's always handy to remember when you're out shopping.

Thinking outside the grid

In her article for *A List Apart* magazine, author Molly E. Holzschlag explores the common ground between the uses of grids in the design of urban spaces with their use in Web design. You can find the article at www.alistapart.com/articles/outsidethegrid/.

At some level, every designer is trying to bring order to the world; it's the secret reason we all practice this craft for a living. And there's no better tool for achieving order in design than the grid.

—KHOI VINH, DESIGNER
www.subtraction.com

3.2 Designing with grids helps usability and accessibility

Look at the example of the two page layouts here (**Figure 3.2**). On the left, the lack of structure makes the page seem cluttered and chaotic. On the right, the reader can more easily understand the visual structure of the content. Applying this to the Web helps both usability and accessibility without requiring the designer to write a single line of code.

Sometimes a grid is subconscious to the layout and merely influences the visitor to follow particular patterns; at other times, its presence can be overt and define the design. The choice of whether to place the grid center stage or allow it to fade into the background will fall to the designer and the goals of a particular design.

The divine proportion and the rule of thirds

Many of the theories of grid design have a basis in the proportions that occur in the natural world and even in our own bodies. Take a look at your arms and note the distance between the tips of your fingers and your wrist. Compare it to the distance between your fingertips and your elbow.

Unless your genes include more gorilla DNA than you'd like your friends to know about, I'm guessing the distance between your fingertips and wrist is a third of the distance to your elbow. It's this divine proportion that has found its way into the thinking of a great many artists and designers throughout history.

A List Taken Apart

As computer monitors get larger and their resolutions get higher, many Web designers are tempted to make designs that fit just inside the now common 1024 × 800 pixel resolution.

When the online Web design magazine A List Apart launched a new design in 2005, much of the discussion around its design centered on the decision to use a fixed-width, 1024-pixel layout (**Figure 3.3**).

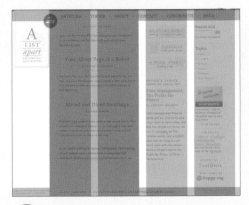

3.3 Dissecting A List Apart's structural grid

After the design was launched, I was lucky to interview A List Apart's designer Jason Santa Maria, and question him about the decision to drop support for window widths smaller than 1024 pixels. Santa Maria explained:

> ALA (A List Apart) has always tried to be one of those sites at the front of the pack. We don't support 800 × 600 anymore, nor do we 640 × 480. Do you? People flipped when sites stopped supporting 640 × 480, now no one says a word. Things change. Trust me, you are going to see more sites stretching out their legs and putting their feet up.

—Jason Santa Maria
(www.stuffandnonsense.co.uk/archives/a_list_taken_apart.html)

Although the desire to design for the highest resolutions is understandable, it is important to remember that resolution does not always equal the width of a visitor's Web browser. Visitors running Windows often keep their windows maximized to the full screen area, but many will be running their browsers with sidebars that contain bookmarks, browsing history, and more. These sidebars can quickly reduce horizontal screen space (**Figure 3.4**).

Note: Jakob Nielsen offers his advice on designing for flexibility at www.useit.com/alertbox/screen_resolution.html.

Mac users rarely extend their browsers to the full monitor width, so even when you consider the widescreen format of many Apple monitors, you can never trust that the browser window will be as wide as the screen area. Designer John Oxton explains:

> I will continue to allow the 800 × 600 platform full access to my sites because until a month ago I had a screen that could only cope with a maximum of 1024 × 768 and with my browser side bar open, sites that allow access for 800 × 600 worked nicely.

—John Oxton (http://joshuaink.com/blog/383/800-by-600)

3.4 Reducing horizontal screen space

No doubt, the question of whether designers should attempt to develop their designs as fixed-width, liquid, or elastic layouts will continue to be debated for a long time to come.

Tommy Olsson has examined the advantages and disadvantages of each type of layout at www.autisticcuckoo. net/archive.php?id=2004/07/21/ fixed-liquid-elastic.

Technically speaking, the *divine proportion* is a visual representation of the number Phi (pronounced "fi"), or the number 1.618033988749895. Don't worry, for all practical purposes you won't need to dust off your scientific calculator; when I mention the divine proportion, you'll just need the first three numbers (rounded up to 1.62), and sometimes even fewer.

So, what does advanced mathematics have to do with design, and why am I talking about using a method for composition that has been around for centuries when working in a medium as young and dynamic as the Web?

Using the divine proportion as a guide when composing your layouts can help improve the balance of your designs, whether you are designing for a fixed-size piece of paper or a flexible browser window. The divine proportion has been used throughout the history of architecture, art, and design and is as important today as it was centuries ago.

The divine proportion for the Web

Whereas the canvas width in print design is determined by the width of the media—a newspaper, a magazine page, a conventional sheet of paper, or even a poster—the canvas size on the Web is not fixed. It is determined by the browser window width minus any open sidebars.

Arguments will no doubt continue to rage on between those who prefer to make fixed-width designs for what they think is the average minimum window width (nominally 800 pixels) and those who believe designs should be flexible to make the most of a visitor's screen space, no matter what the window size.

Now you can put the theory into action by using the divine proportion to create harmonious layouts for both fixed-pixel width and flexible designs.

Fixed-pixel width design

For the first example, you will be creating a common fixed-pixel design that sits just inside an 800-pixel width browser window. For now you can forget about the actual window width or whether a visitor has any sidebars open. It has become common practice to shave off 30 pixels to allow for scroll bars, arriving at the width of 770 pixels so favored by many fixed-pixel aficionados.

Fire up your calculator, and divide 770 by 1.62. Unless you need new batteries, you should arrive at 475 pixels, a useful width for main content that also provides a comfortable line length for reading text onscreen. Now take those 475 pixels away from your total width. This will give you a sidebar width of 295 pixels, which is ample room for supplementary content and even a good-sized search input (**Figure 3.5**).

Many designers start their designs by deciding on an arbitrary width, often a width they stick to regardless of the content they are presenting. You can also work with the divine proportion in the other direction. Imagine that the site you are designing features a large branding image, perhaps one that has been carried over from an offline advertising campaign. Using the divine proportion, you can calculate the correct overall width from the dimensions of the image.

For this example, the image is 400 pixels wide. Multiply this by 1.62 to give you an overall design width of 648 pixels, slightly narrower than common layouts but one you can use to interesting effect (**Figure 3.6**).

You can then divide these columns using the same proportions to create an interesting microgrid to create a balanced structure for even the smallest design elements on your page (**Figure 3.7**).

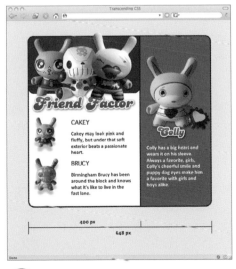

3.5 Establishing correct column width

3.6 Calculating layout width from an image

3.7 Creating microgrids

Rule Britannia

If pixel perfection is your thing, several tools and methods can help you ensure that your elements are lining up with the proportions of your grid.

You can apply CSS background images to almost any XHTML element, including block-level divisions, paragraphs, lists, or inline elements. For precision, add a background image of a ruler to an element (**Figure 3.8**).

Note: You can download a handy premade ruler image courtesy of Greg Storey at www.airbagindustries.com/archives/airbag/ruler.php.

Chris Pederick's Web Developer extension for Firefox contains both a handy ruler that you can drag over any element in your browser window and line guides that ensure your elements line up in the way you intended.

For a way to add measuring tools in any browser that supports JavaScript, you can create bookmarklets that use PNG image alpha-transparency to add a grid-pad image either to the <body> of the page or to a division overlaid onto your design (**Figure 3.9**).

Note: Andy Budd's Layout Grid Bookmarklets are available for you to bookmark at www.andybudd.com/archives/2006/07/layout_grid_bookmarklet/.

Although these techniques and tools are not strictly part of grid-based design, they can prove extremely useful when placing your design elements in your layout grids.

SUBTRACTION GRID IMPOSITION

One easy way of ensuring that your designs stay on the grid when implementing them with markup and CSS is to use the CSS background-image property to keep your grid visible as you work.

Although visual tools including Macromedia Dreamweaver have long had features to place tracing images, Khoi Vinh has brought this technique back to the surface.

Note: You can find out more about Khoi Vinh's grid imposition method at www.subtraction.com/archives/2004/1231_grid_computi.php.

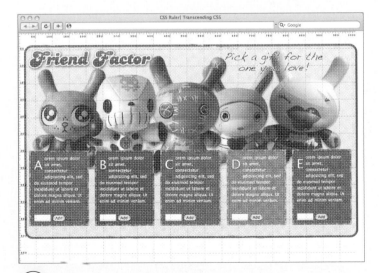

3.8 Adding a ruler image

3.9 Overlaying a grid-pad image

Elastic design

Whereas on the Web the number and width of columns that are used in a design are often chosen arbitrarily, this has not been the case with the design of newspapers. In newspaper design, the column count and proportions have always been based on the width of the *measure*, the number of characters of text in a horizontal line. Because traditional broadsheet newspapers use a larger format, they can have more columns yet keep the width of the measure to a level that keeps reading comfortable.

Line length and readability are perhaps more important onscreen than they are on paper. Designs based on em units will shrink and grow as the visitor changes the font size in their browser, keeping line lengths to a more optimum width for easy reading.

This "elastic," em-based design technique can prove extremely effective. It has been put to varied uses including designs planted in the CSS Zen Garden as well as the homepage of Mozilla.

For his Elastic Lawn (www.csszengarden.com/?CSSfile=/063/063.css) design for the CSS Zen Garden (**Figure 3.10**), designer Patrick Griffiths chose a width of 48 em for his layout. To use Phi to find the divine proportions for this design, divide 48 em by 1.62, and you get the following:

Overall content	Main content	Sidebar
48 em	29 em	19 em

3.10 Patrick Griffiths's em-based design, Elastic Lawn, at three different text sizes.

 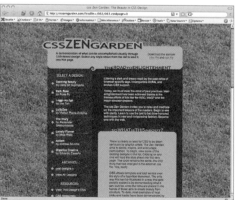 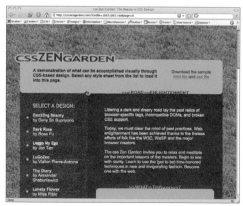

To give you the proportions for your design details, you can subdivide this grid again to create a set of fully elastic microgrids.

The homepage of Mozilla (**Figure 3.11**) shows great elastic design in action. Using ems allows the content area to shrink and grow when the visitor changes the size of the text. To ensure that text lines do not stretch beyond a comfortable width, the Mozilla designers have limited the maximum width of their content to 70 em:

```
body {
min-width: 610px;
margin: 20px; }

#container {
max-width: 70em;
margin: 0 auto;
}
```

3.11 www.mozilla.org

Part 3: Inspiration   **195**

About em units

An *em* is a "relational" unit of measurement, which, when used on the Web, will change when a visitor either increases or decreases the default text size in her Web browser. Technically speaking, one em is equal to the distance that is equal to the type size. For example, 1 em of 12-point type is 12 points. You can find out more about em units and the measure, plus find an interesting follow-up discussion, at www.markboulton.co.uk/journal/comments/five_simple_steps_to_better_typography/.

A note about gutters

In Web design, gutters are not the spaces alongside the pavement that are filled with potato crisp packets and cigarette ends; instead, *gutters* are the gaps separating columns, and they prevent text or images in separate columns from butting into each other.

I prefer to add left and right margins or padding to a column's child elements to create the effect of gutters, rather than applying margins or padding to the columns themselves. This avoids the need to use a box model hack when designing for Internet Explorer 5 and 5.5 for Windows (or Internet Explorer operating in "quirks" mode).

Using Mozilla's width as your starting point, divide its 70 em by 1.62 to establish the divine proportions for the elastic content area and sidebar. You get the following:

Overall content	Main content	Sidebar
70 em	43 em	27 em

Interestingly, Mozilla's designers have chosen to use percentages rather than ems for the widths of their columns. This allows their flexible design to shrink and grow when both the text and the window is resized:

```
#side {
float: left;
width: 23%; }

#mainContent {
float: right;
width: 75%; }
```

Whether you choose to implement fully elastic layouts or a combination of elastic and fluid layouts, these techniques work equally as well as fixed-pixel designs when working with grids.

Fully flexible layouts

Grid system design has historically been based on fixed sizes. Designers working on the Web have had to adapt many traditional techniques to accommodate the variety of platforms, windows, and browsing environments on the Web.

It is this visitor control over the browsing environment that makes the Web so different from other forms of screen and print media. Any changes to text size, screen resolution, or the size of the browser window can impact a design enormously. The challenge is for Web designers to create a flexible design that will adapt to these changing conditions. It is here that a well-designed grid can often help you.

Giving up control over the width of a design can be a tough challenge for even seasoned Web designers who may be more comfortable creating fixed-pixel designs. Designing a grid using flexible percentages can create the most powerful layouts for your designs. A fluid grid will expand and collapse along with a visitor's window, and they make no assumptions about window size or resolution. This type of layout will also better accommodate visitors with open sidebars of browsing history or bookmarks.

Here once again, the divine proportion can prove to be a powerful tool for designing a flexible, asymmetrical grid. Starting with a 100 percent browser width, divide by 1.62 to give you the harmonious widths of both the main content area and the sidebar.

Overall content	Main content	Sidebar
100%	62%	38%

A few words about line length

Reading text on a computer screen is more difficult and tiring than reading on paper. Ensuring that your content can be read comfortably is essential if you want your readers to enjoy reading your content.

The *Web Style Guide: Basic Design Principles for Creating Web Sites*, by Patrick J. Lynch and Sarah Horton, says this: "Research shows that reading slows and retention rates fall as line length begins to exceed the ideal width, because the reader then needs to use the muscles of the eye and neck to track from the end of one line to the beginning of the next line. If the eye must traverse great distances on the page, the reader is easily lost and must hunt for the beginning of the next line."

Restricting the length of any lines of text by using `max-width` is just one of the ways you can make your content more appealing.

Joe Clark has written an interesting article about line lengths when reading from a screen at http://blog.fawny.org/2005/09/21/measures/.

Now, to ensure that the line length of your text content does not become uncomfortable, you can choose to limit the overall width of your design. Following the example set by Mozilla, you might choose to limit your design to 70 em here by setting `max-width` on the `<body>` element:

```
body {
width : 100%;
max-width: 70em;
```

So far, all the grids you have explored have been based on the divine proportion or golden section. These are known as *asymmetrical* grids because of the proportions, or ratios, of their columns. Another highly useful grid design is already in use across many different mediums but is found less often on the Web. This is known as a *symmetrical* grid.

Rational grid design

Designers choose to work with grids for many reasons. Grids also help maintain consistency, particularly over a large number of pages. In a printed book, the number of pages is limited by practical considerations such as size and weight. The number of pages it can contain does not limit a Web site. Establishing this consistency of layout will help visitors navigate both individual pages and entire sites. This is one of the key goals of designing good Web usability (**Figure 3.12**).

Grids also help the designer organize branding, content, and navigation into spaces. With the enormous variety of objects now vying for a visitor's attention, it is the precision and flexibility that comes from designing a solid symmetrical grid, based on a rational ratio, that can help a designer bring order to that potential chaos.

Symmetrical grids are divided into a number of equal width columns, such as six, eight, or sometimes even more columns, in what is known as a *rational* ratio. This symmetrical layout helps create balance across the design but at the same time gives the designer a greater number of layout options by enabling him to create "supercolumns" by allowing content to span across two or more columns.

The ratios of the columns in a rational grid do not always end in a symmetrical or even a balanced design. You can create many interesting and unusual asymmetric designs by starting with a symmetrical grid to give you a solid structure and the correct proportions for your elements.

One of my favorite layout techniques starts by first defining a grid and then creating rectangles and other shapes whose proportions are defined by the grid. Moving these elements inside the grid and even allowing them to overlap, often suggests interesting new ideas for layout.

3.12 **Establishing consistency in layout at http://web.burza.hr/**

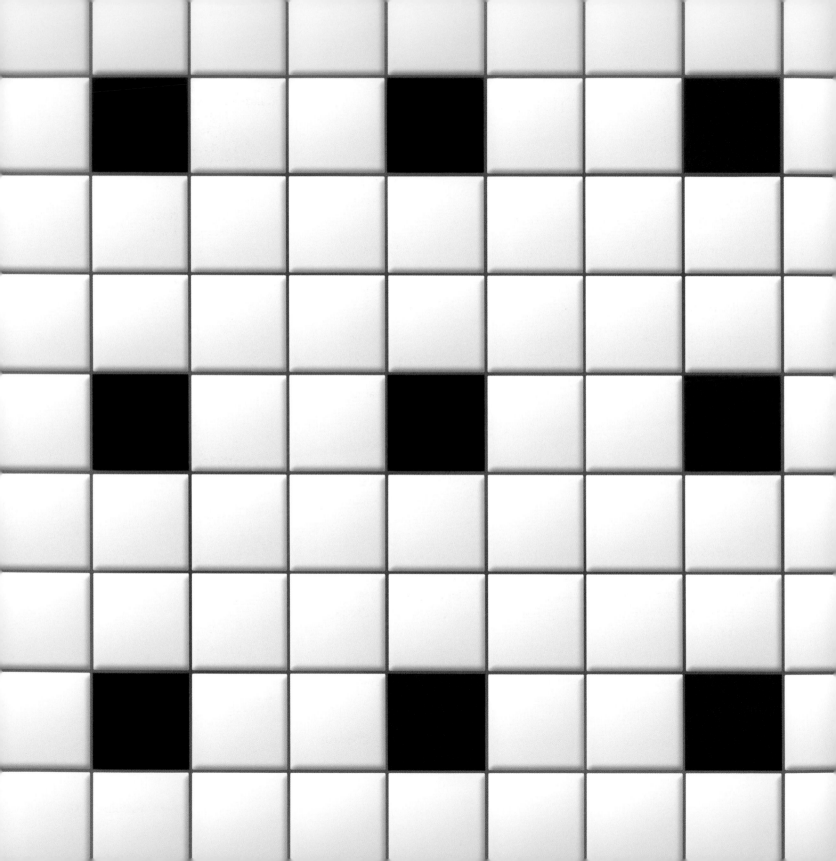

Grids in Contemporary Web Design

For me, one of the most enjoyable parts of the creative process is the freedom to experiment. It can be fun and rewarding to push paint around a canvas or make cuttings from magazines and move them around a collage to see what happens.

Often the most exciting results can come from the most unexpected of combinations. If something doesn't work, it doesn't matter; scrunch up those pieces of paper, throw them into a corner, and start again. The worst thing that can happen is that your mother, partner, or office cleaner will complain about your blatant disregard for tidiness.

Many times my decisions over layout and proportions happen organically and are not backed by any logic—and almost never by mathematics. I'm sure as a designer that I'm not unusual in occasionally designing layouts in a happy-go-lucky, feel-good fashion. Only much later in my design career did I see the enormous creative opportunities that designing with grids can offer.

Grid design has become a popular topic of conversation among Web designers, and many are turning to grids to help them make stunning and distinct designs. I want to share with you some of my personal favorite sites that have made strong use of grid-based design techniques.

Subtraction

One of the most talked about grid-based designs is the striking, black-and-white Subtraction. In addition to using stark imagery and minimalist typography, designer Khoi Vinh has used a powerful eight-column grid to underpin every aspect of his design (**Figure 3.13**).

In many grid-based designs, the grid takes a backseat. In Subtraction, the grid positively climbs into the front seat and grabs hold of the steering wheel (**Figure 3.14**). Every aspect

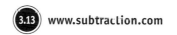

3.13 www.subtraction.com

of the design is bound to the grid with almost obsessive precision. The grid dictates the size and position of each of the elements in the branding area, including the logo and the search input. Navigation links also align perfectly to the grid structure, and it is because of this attention to detail that the links are not overshadowed by the large image below them, an image that spans all eight columns (**Figure 3.15**).

Subtraction's eight columns also combine to form four supercolumns to add focus to the articles in the main content. The reader's eye flows immediately to the main content.

Vinh added flow to what could have easily become a rigid layout by allowing his titles to span an additional column to the left. This highlights the publication time and the number of reader remarks (**Figure 3.16**).

Many designers and their clients leave no pixel untouched. Subtraction leaves much of the left column empty, and it uses white space to allow its content room to breathe. With so much content being presented on a single page, Subtraction's design could easily have become overwhelming to the reader. Vinh has prevented this information overload by cleverly using vertical height.

Subtraction continues to use its eight-column grid in even more surprising ways as you scroll down the page. The layout changes when the focus moves from internal to external content, and these two areas are cleverly divided by another large column-spanning image (**Figure 3.17**).

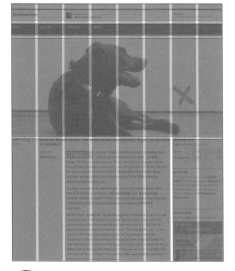

3.14 Dissecting the Subtraction grid

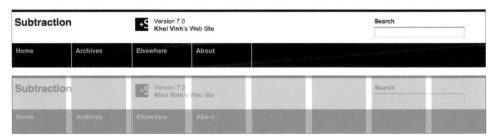

3.15 Navigating Subtraction

Vinh uses shorter fields to present his links to external sites, and every one of the eight columns features his content: dates, star ratings, link information, and navigation tools.

Note: You'll be amazed at the intricate design details that Khoi Vinh has created at www.subtraction.com.

Subtraction succeeds because of its designer's understanding of grid-based design and how this knowledge has allowed him to present his content in a structured and ordered way.

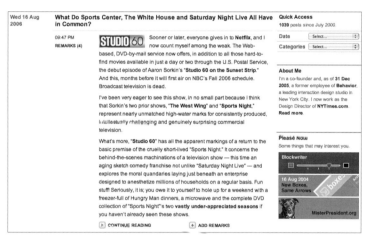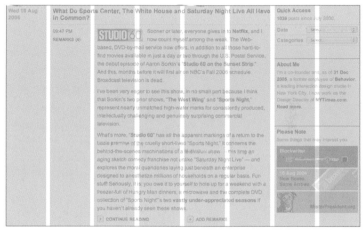

3.16 Remarking on Subtraction

3.17 Dividing and subtracting

Airbag Industries

Compared to the overt complexity of Subtraction, the design of Airbag Industries seems almost understated (**Figure 3.18**). At first glance, it might be difficult to notice the impact that its design grid makes (**Figure 3.19**).

For Airbag Industries, designer and airship enthusiast Greg Storey based his design on a subtle, four-column, symmetrical grid. Two of the columns have been combined to hold the main content for the articles. The central column, adorned with a Hawaiian beauty and palm trees, breaks a common three-column convention by drawing your attention to the central portion of the page because of its background color and imagery.

When I first saw Airbag Industries, I was initially irritated because the tops of the three columns were not aligned vertically, with the left column starting 60 pixels above the other two columns. Later I noticed that the positioning of this left column visually connects the airship image with the content below (**Figure 3.20**).

One of the design details I particularly love about Airbag Industries is that on the homepage, Storey has used the proportions of his grid to determine the size of the airship image.

3.18 www.airbagindustries.com

3.19 Investigating the Airbag grid

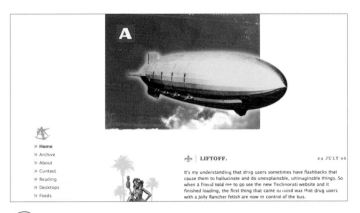

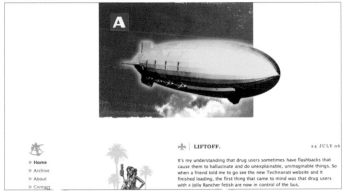

3.20 Left: The irregular alignment of the tops of the columns leads your eye into the content.
Right: The effect is lost in my modified version where the columns are straightened.

Look closely, and you will see that not only does the width of the image match the width of two of his columns but also that the airship itself, floating gracefully out of its bounding rectangle, is the width of those two columns (**Figure 3.21**).

The attention to the grid continues to the bottom of the page where the bear image also matches perfectly the width of the center column (**Figure 3.22**). On a page containing this much content I would have liked to see that this image also linked to the top of the page, but even without a link, the image bleeding off the bottom of the window is a neat way to let the visitor know they have reached the end of the content. I'm not so sure I agree with Storey's choice of alternative text for this bear image, but that can be a conversation for another day:

```
<img src="fin.jpg" alt="Grrrr" />
```

For me, what makes this site interesting is how it uses the design grid consistently across all its pages and how it uses the grid in different ways.

Note: Take a ride on Greg Storey's airship at www.airbagindustries.com.

I find the design decisions Storey has made and his clever use of a simple, symmetrical four-column grid intriguing. It demonstrates clearly that designing to a grid can suggest subtle ideas that may not have otherwise presented themselves.

3.21 Matching the width of two columns

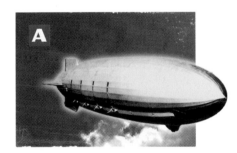

3.22 Reaching the bottom of the page

Jeff Croft

Of all the sites that rebooted for CSS Reboot, one in particular, Jeff Croft's, stood out (**Figure 3.23**)—not because of lively, colorful imagery, rounded corners, or gradient backgrounds, but because of its solid use of a design grid (**Figure 3.24**).

Note: CSS Reboot is a community Web design event where Web designers and developers from all over the world launch their CSS-based redesigns simultaneously. You can find out more and participate in a future event at www.cssreboot.com.

Many of the designs that appeared first on CSS Reboot this year divided areas of content into horizontal bands or fields. Croft's use of light text against a darker background, combined with his bands, give his design a strong horizontal focus.

Croft again uses a four-column, symmetrical grid. The main content in horizontal panels, both above and below the fold, spans two columns. This arrangement goes from the top to the bottom of the homepage. Although the horizontal stripes reduce the visual impact of vertical columns, your eyes still follow their invisible lines.

3.23 www2.jeffcroft.com

3.24 Rebooting with the solid grid

Croft's grid loses some of its structure in what is perhaps one of the most technically impressive parts of the site. The technical achievement of the site's live search draws together search results not only from his articles but also from comments, links, and even photos on Flickr. In the live search area, the results are divided into five unequal columns. These columns use a different ratio to any others used throughout the site, and the layout would be much stronger if it used the same four-column grid and moved the explanation text to underneath the results (**Figure 3.25**).

Digging deeper into Croft's CSS, I was interested to see that whereas I prefer to use margins or padding on child elements to simulate gutters, Croft chooses to use margins on his columns.

You can see this by using the Outline Custom Elements feature of the Web Developer extension to outline the divisions (**Figure 3.26**).

Note: Dig deeper and learn more about how Jeff Croft implemented his design at http://www2.jeffcroft.com.

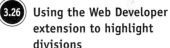

3.26 Using the Web Developer extension to highlight divisions

3.25 Above: Original search area layout. Below: Modified layout making use of the grid.

Veerle's Blog

Whereas Airbag Industries has a light and airy feel, Veerle Pieters' Blog uses dark gray background colors to bring her content into focus (**Figure 3.27**). This is helped by the use of a strong four-column, symmetrical grid that paradoxically results in an asymmetric rather than symmetric design (**Figure 3.28**).

3.27 Symmetric grid with an asymmetric design at http://veerle.duoh.com

3.29 Emphasizing columns with color

3.28 Designing to the grid

While the bright branding illustration spans three of the four columns, two columns join to form a supercolumn to hold the most recently published article.

On first seeing this site, I was confused why Pieters chose a lighter gray background for her previously links to older articles, because my eye was immediately drawn to that column, rather than to the content of the main article. Visiting this site on a regular basis has made this concern fade because the lighter color provides a useful way to emphasize the column structure of all the content on the page (**Figure 3.29**).

One of the design features I particularly enjoy about Veerle's blog is the way she has used a subtle shadow to emphasize the border between the third and fourth columns. Instead of overtly dividing the layout at this point, Pieters cleverly uses images to join these columns in a subtle but effective way. This adds movement to the design by drawing your eyes across all the columns (**Figure 3.30**).

Throughout its design, Veerle's blog is playful with the four-column grid, switching effortlessly between content that spans two or sometimes even three columns. This design succeeds not only by basing the layout on a grid but by also not being defined or constrained by it.

Note: Explore the subtle ways that Veerle Pieters plays with grid design at http://veerle. duoh.com/.

3.30 Drawing your eyes across columns

Lorem Ipsum

Lorem ipsum
dolor sit amet

Lorem ipsum dolor sit amet, consectetur adipisicing elit, sed do

*Lorem ipsum dolor sit amet,
consectetur adipisicing elit, sed do
eiusmod tempor incididunt ut labore
et dolore magna aliqua.*

Lorem ipsum dolor sit amet, consectetur adipisicing elit, sed do eiusmod tempor incididunt ut labore et dolore magna aliqua. Ut enim ad minim veniam, quis nostrud exercitation ullamco laboris nisi ut aliquip consequat. Lorem ipsum dolor sit amet, consectetur adipisicing elit, sed do eiusmod tempor incididunt ut labore et dolore magna aliqua. Ut enim ad minim veniam, quis nostrud exercitation ullamco laboris nisi ut aliquip consequat. Lorem ipsum dolor sit amet, consectetur adipisicing elit, sed do eiusmod tempor incididunt ut labore et dolore magna aliqua.

Lorem ipsum dolor sit amet, consectetur adipisicing elit, sed do eiusmod tempor incididunt ut labore et dolore magna aliqua. Ut enim ad minim veniam, quis nostrud exercitation ullamco laboris nisi ut aliquip consequat. Lorem ipsum dolor sit amet, consectetur adipisicing elit, sed do eiusmod tempor incididunt ut labore et dolore magna aliqua.

Lorem ipsum dolor sit amet

Lorem ipsum dolor sit amet, consectetur adipisicing elit, sed do eiusmod tempor incididunt ut labore et dolore magna.

Lorem ipsum dolor sit amet, consectetur adipisicing elit, sed do eiusmod tempor incididunt ut labore et dolore magna.

Lorem ipsum dolor sit amet, consectetur adipisicing elit, sed do eiusmod tempor incididunt ut labore et dolore magna.

Lorem ipsum dolor sit amet consectetur

Lorem ipsum dolor sit amet, consectetur adipisicing elit, sed do eiusmod tempor incididunt ut labore et dolore magna aliqua. Ut enim ad minim veniam, quis nostrud exercitation ullamco laboris nisi ut aliquip consequat.

Lorem ipsum dolor sit amet, consectetur adipisicing elit, sed do eiusmod tempor incididunt ut labore et dolore magna aliqua. Ut enim ad minim veniam, quis nostrud exercitation ullamco laboris nisi ut aliquip consequat.

Lorem ipsum dolor sit amet consectetur

Lorem ipsum dolor sit amet, consectetur adipisicing elit, sed do eiusmod tempor incididunt ut labore et dolore magna aliqua.

Lorem ipsum dolor sit amet, consectetur adipisicing elit, sed do eiusmod tempor incididunt ut labore et dolore magna aliqua.

Lorem ipsum dolor sit amet, consectetur adipisicing elit, sed do eiusmod tempor incididunt ut labore et dolore magna.

Lorem Ipsum

Lorem ipsum dolor sit amet

Lorem ipsum
dolor sit amet

Lorem ipsum dolor sit amet

Lorem ipsum dolor sit amet, consectetur adipisicing elit, sed do eiusmod tempor incididunt ut labore et dolore

Lorem ipsum dolor sit amet, consectetur adipisicing elit, sed do eiusmod tempor incididunt ut labore et dolore magna aliqua. Ut enim ad minim veniam, quis nostrud exercitation ullamco laboris nisi ut aliquip consequat.

Lorem ipsum dolor sit amet, consectetur adipisicing elit, sed do eiusmod tempor incididunt ut labore et dolore magna aliqua. Ut enim ad minim veniam, quis nostrud exercitation ullamco laboris nisi ut aliquip consequat.

Lorem ipsum dolor sit amet, consectetur

Lorem ipsum dolor sit amet, consectetur adipisicing elit, sed do eiusmod tempor incididunt ut labore et dolore magna aliqua.

Lorem ipsum dolor sit amet, consectetur adipisicing elit, sed do eiusmod tempor incididunt ut labore et dolore magna aliqua.

Lorem ipsum dolor sit amet, adipisicing elit,

Lorem ipsum dolor sit amet consectetur

*Lorem ipsum dolor sit amet,
consectetur adipisicing elit, sed do
eiusmod tempor incididunt ut labore
et dolore magna aliqua.*

Lorem ipsum dolor sit amet, consectetur adipisicing elit, sed do eiusmod tempor incididunt ut labore et dolore magna aliqua. Ut enim ad minim veniam, quis nostrud exercitation ullamco laboris nisi ut aliquip consequat. Lorem ipsum dolor sit amet, consectetur adipisicing elit, sed do eiusmod tempor incididunt ut labore et dolore magna aliqua. Ut enim ad minim veniam, quis nostrud exercitation ullamco laboris nisi ut aliquip consequat. Lorem ipsum dolor sit amet, consectetur adipisicing elit, sed do eiusmod tempor incididunt ut labore et dolore magna aliqua. Ut enim ad minim veniam, quis nostrud exercitation ullamco laboris nisi ut aliquip consequat.

Lorem ipsum dolor sit amet consectetur

*Lorem ipsum dolor sit amet,
consectetur adipisicing elit, sed do*

Lorem ipsum dolor sit amet, consectetur adipisicing elit, sed do eiusmod tempor incididunt ut labore et dolore magna aliqua. Ut enim ad minim veniam, quis nostrud exercitation ullamco laboris nisi ut aliquip consequat. Lorem ipsum dolor sit amet, consectetur adipisicing elit, sed do eiusmod tempor incididunt ut labore et dolore magna aliqua. Ut enim ad minim veniam, quis nostrud exercitation nisi ut aliquip consequat

Lorem
ipsum
dolor sit
amet,
adipisicing
eiusmod
tempor Lo
rem ipsum
dolor sit
amet,
adipisicing
elit, sed do
eiusmod
tempor.

Using contemporary six-column design

There has been a progressive decline in the popularity of the traditional eight-column newspaper grid and a widespread adoption of a simpler, six-column design. This switch has not limited the number of design variations that can be based on this layout, however, as a look at many of the inspiring newspaper designs from around the world today will demonstrate.

From across the United States, Europe, the Middle East, and beyond, millions of people consume their daily news from pages that have been designed using six columns. Many of the core design devices from traditional eight-column grids remain, and often these devices have been given new life.

Column spanning remains a key design technique and some newspapers, including *Die Welt* from Germany, use headlines that span multiple columns and are also center justified.

In many cases, the six-column design is supplemented by a seventh, slightly wider column on either the far left or the far right. This column often contains information about news items that will be found on the inside pages, not unlike the sidebar found on almost every content-rich Web page. On the next pages are four alternative content layouts based upon the grid used by France's *Le Figaro*.

LOREM IPSUM
Lorem ipsum dolor sit amet, consectetur adipisicing elit, sed.

Lorem ipsum dolor sit amet, consectetur

Lorem ipsum dolor sit amet, consectetur adipisicing elit, sed do eiusmod tempor incididunt ut labore

Lorem ipsum dolor sit amet, consectetur adipisicing elit.

Lorem ipsum dolor sit amet, consectetur adipisicing elit.

Lorem ipsum dolor sit amet, consectetur adipisicing elit.

Lorem ipsum dolor sit amet, consectetur adipisicing elit.

Lorem ipsum dolor sit amet, consectetur adipisicing elit.

Lorem ipsum dolor sit amet, consectetur adipisicing elit.

Lorem ipsum dolor sit amet, consectetur adipisicing elit, sed do eiusmod tempor

Lorem ipsum dolor sit amet, consectetur adipisicing elit, sed do eiusmod tempor incidunt ut labore et dolore magna. Lorem ipsum dolor sit amet, consectetur adipisicing elit, sed do eiusmod tempor incididunt ut labore et dolore magna

Lorem ipsum dolor sit

Lorem ipsum dolor sit amet, consectetur adipisicing elit, sed do eiusmod tempor incididunt ut labore et dolore magna aliqua. Ut enim ad minim veniam, quis nostrud exercitation ullamco laboris nisi ut aliquip consequat.

Lorem ipsum dolor sit

Lorem ipsum dolor sit amet, consectetur adipisicing elit, sed do eiusmod tempor incididunt ut labore et dolore magna aliqua. Ut enim ad minim veniam, quis nostrud exercitation ullamco laboris nisi ut aliquip consequat.

Lorem ipsum dolor sit amet, consectetur adipisicing elit, sed do eiusmod tempor incididunt ut labore et dolore magna aliqua.

Lorem ipsum dolor sit amet, consectetur adipisicing elit, sed do eiusmod tempor incididunt ut labore et dolore magna aliqua.

Lorem ipsum dolor sit amet, consectetur adipisicing elit, sed do eiusmod tempor incididunt ut labore et dolore magna aliqua.

Lorem ipsum dolor sit amet, consectetur adipisicing elit, sed do eiusmod tempor incididunt ut labore et dolore magna aliqua.

Lorem ipsum dolor sit amet, consectetur adipisicing elit, sed do eiusmod tempor incididunt ut labore et dolore magna aliqua.

LOREM IPSUM DOLOR

Lorem ipsum dolor sit

Lorem ipsum dolor sit amet, consectetur adipisicing elit, sed do eiusmod tempor incididunt ut labore et dolore magna aliqua. Ut enim ad minim ex ea commodo consequat.

Lorem ipsum dolor sit amet, consectetur adipisicing elit, sed do eiusmod tempor incididunt ut labore et dolore magna aliqua.

Lorem ipsum dolor sit amet, consectetur adipisicing elit, sed do eiusmod tempor incididunt ut labore et dolore magna aliqua. Ut enim ad minim veniam, quis nostrud exercitation ullamco laboris nisi ut aliquip ex ea commodo consequat.

The six-column grid based on France's _Le Figaro_

LOREM IPSUM
Lorem ipsum dolor sit amet, consectetur adipisicing elit, sed.

Lorem ipsum dolor sit amet, consectetur

Lorem ipsum dolor sit amet, consectetur adipisicing elit, sed do eiusmod tempor incididunt ut labore

Lorem ipsum dolor sit amet, consectetur adipisicing elit, sed do eiusmod tempor incididunt ut labore et dolore magna aliqua. Ut enim ad minim veniam, quis nostrud exercitation ullamco laboris nisi ut aliquip ex ea commodo consequat. Lorem ipsum dolor sit amet, consectetur adipisicing elit, sed do eiusmod tempor incididunt ut labore et dolore magna aliqua. Ut enim ad minim veniam, quis nostrud exercitation ullamco laboris nisi ut aliquip ex ea commodo consequat.

Lorem ipsum dolor sit amet, consectetur adipisicing elit, sed do eiusmod tempor incididunt ut labore et dolore magna aliqua. Ut enim ad minim veniam, quis nostrud exercitation ullamco laboris nisi ut aliquip ex ea commodo consequat. Lorem ipsum dolor sit amet, consectetur adipisicing elit, sed do eiusmod tempor incididunt ut labore et dolore magna aliqua. Ut enim ad minim veniam, quis nostrud exercitation ullamco laboris nisi ut aliquip ex ea commodo consequat.

Lorem ipsum dolor sit amet, consectetur adipisicing elit, sed do eiusmod tempor incididunt ut labore et dolore magna aliqua. Ut enim ad minim veniam, quis nostrud exercitation ullamco laboris nisi ut aliquip ex ea commodo consequat. Lorem ipsum dolor sit amet, consectetur adipisicing elit, sed do eiusmod tempor incididunt ut labore et dolore magna aliqua. Ut enim ad minim veniam, quis nostrud exercitation ullamco laboris nisi ut aliquip ex ea commodo consequat.

LOREM IPSUM DOLOR

Lorem ipsum dolor sit amet, consectetur

Lorem ipsum dolor sit amet, consectetur adipisicing elit, sed do eiusmod tempor incididunt ut labore et dolore magna aliqua. Lorem ipsum dolor sit amet, consectetur adipisicing elit, sed do eiusmod tempor incididunt ut labore et dolore magna aliqua.

Lorem ipsum dolor sit

Lorem ipsum dolor sit amet, consectetur adipisicing elit, sed do eiusmod tempor incididunt ut labore et dolore magna aliqua. Ut enim ad minim veniam, quis nostrud consequat.

Lorem ipsum dolor sit

Lorem ipsum dolor sit amet, consectetur adipisicing elit, sed do eiusmod tempor incididunt ut labore et dolore magna aliqua. Ut enim ad minim veniam, quis nostrud consequat.

Lorem ipsum dolor sit amet, consectetur adipisicing elit

Lorem ipsum dolor sit amet, consectetur adipisicing elit, sed do eiusmod tempor incididunt ut labore et dolore magna aliqua.

Lorem ipsum dolor sit amet, consectetur adipisicing elit, sed do eiusmod tempor incididunt ut labore et dolore magna aliqua.

Lorem ipsum dolor sit amet, consectetur adipisicing elit, sed do eiusmod tempor incididunt ut labore et dolore magna aliqua.

Lorem ipsum dolor sit amet, consectetur adipisicing elit, sed do eiusmod tempor incididunt ut labore et dolore magna aliqua.

LOREM IPSUM

Lorem ipsum dolor sit amet, consectetur adipisicing elit, sed.

Lorem ipsum dolor sit amet, consectetur adipisicing elit, sed do eiusmod tempor

Lorem ipsum dolor sit amet, consectetur adipisicing elit, sed do eiusmod tempor incididunt ut labore et dolore magna aliqua. Ut enim ad minim veniam, quis nostrud exercitation consequat.

Lorem ipsum dolor sit amet, consectetur adipisicing elit, sed do eiusmod tempor incididunt ut labore et dolore magna aliqua. Ut enim ad minim veniam, quis nostrud exercitation ullamco laboris nisi ut aliquip ex ea commodo consequat.

Lorem ipsum dolor sit amet, consectetur adipisicing elit, sed do eiusmod tempor incididunt ut labore et dolore magna aliqua. Ut enim ad minim veniam, quis nostrud exercitation ullamco laboris nisi ut aliquip ex ea commodo consequat.

Lorem ipsum dolor sit amet, consectetur adipisicing elit, sed do eiusmod tempor incididunt ut labore et dolore magna aliqua. Ut enim ad minim veniam, quis nostrud exercitation ullamco laboris nisi ut aliquip ex ea commodo consequat.

Lorem ipsum dolor sit amet, consectetur adipisicing elit, sed do eiusmod tempor incididunt ut labore et dolore magna aliqua. Ut enim ad minim veniam, quis nostrud exercitation ullamco laboris nisi ut aliquip ex ea commodo consequat.

Lorem ipsum dolor sit

Lorem ipsum dolor sit amet, consectetur adipisicing elit, sed do eiusmod tempor incididunt ut labore et dolore magna aliqua. Ut enim ad minim veniam, quis nostrud exercitation ullamco laboris nisi ut aliquip consequat.

Lorem ipsum dolor sit

Lorem ipsum dolor sit amet, consectetur adipisicing elit, sed do eiusmod tempor incididunt ut labore et dolore magna aliqua. Ut enim ad minim veniam, quis nostrud exercitation ullamco laboris nisi ut aliquip consequat.

Lorem ipsum dolor sit

Lorem ipsum dolor sit amet, consectetur adipisicing elit, sed do eiusmod tempor incididunt ut labore et dolore magna aliqua. Ut enim ad minim veniam, quis nostrud exercitation consequat.

LOREM IPSUM DOLOR

Lorem ipsum dolor sit amet, consectetur adipisicing elit

Lorem ipsum dolor sit amet, consectetur adipisicing elit, sed do eiusmod tempor incididunt ut labore et dolore magna aliqua.

Lorem ipsum dolor sit amet, consectetur adipisicing elit, sed do eiusmod tempor incididunt ut labore et dolore magna aliqua.

Lorem ipsum dolor sit amet, consectetur adipisicing elit, sed do eiusmod tempor incididunt ut labore et dolore magna aliqua.

Lorem ipsum dolor sit amet, consectetur adipisicing elit, sed do eiusmod tempor incididunt ut labore et dolore magna aliqua.

Lorem ipsum dolor sit amet, consectetur adipisicing elit, sed do eiusmod tempor incididunt ut labore et dolore magna aliqua.

Lorem ipsum dolor sit amet, consectetur adipisicing elit, sed do eiusmod tempor incididunt ut labore et dolore magna aliqua.

LOREM IPSUM

Lorem ipsum dolor sit amet, consectetur adipisicing elit, sed.

Lorem ipsum dolor sit amet, consectetur elit, sed do eiusmod tempor

Lorem ipsum dolor sit amet, consectetur adipisicing elit, sed do eiusmod tempor incididunt ut labore et dolore magna aliqua. Lorem ipsum dolor sit amet incididunt ut labore et dolore magna aliqua.

Lorem ipsum dolor sit amet, consectetur adipisicing elit, sed do eiusmod tempor incididunt ut labore et dolore magna aliqua. Lorem ipsum dolor sit amet incididunt ut labore et dolore magna aliqua.

Lorem ipsum dolor sit amet, consectetur adipisicing elit, sed do eiusmod tempor incididunt ut labore et dolore magna aliqua. Lorem ipsum dolor sit amet incididunt ut labore et dolore magna aliqua.

Lorem ipsum dolor sit amet, consectetur adipisicing elit, sed do eiusmod tempor incididunt ut labore et dolore magna aliqua. Lorem ipsum dolor sit amet incididunt ut labore et dolore magna aliqua.

Lorem ipsum dolor sit amet, consectetur adipisicing elit, sed do eiusmod tempor incididunt ut labore et dolore magna aliqua. Lorem ipsum dolor sit amet incididunt ut labore et dolore magna aliqua.

Lorem ipsum dolor sit amet, consectetur adipisicing elit, sed do eiusmod tempor incididunt ut labore et dolore magna aliqua. Lorem ipsum dolor sit amet incididunt ut labore et dolore magna aliqua.

Lorem ipsum dolor sit amet, consectetur

LOREM IPSUM DOLOR

Lorem ipsum dolor sit amet

Lorem ipsum dolor sit amet, consectetur

Lorem ipsum dolor sit amet, consectetur adipisicing elit, sed do eiusmod tempor incididunt ut labore et dolore magna aliqua. Ut enim ad minim veniam, quis nostrud exercitation ullamco laboris nisi ut aliquip ex ea commodo consequat.

Lorem ipsum dolor sit amet, consectetur adipisicing elit, sed do eiusmod tempor incididunt ut labore et dolore magna aliqua. Ut enim ad minim veniam, quis nostrud exercitation ullamco laboris nisi ut aliquip ex ea commodo consequat. Lorem ipsum dolor sit amet, consectetur adipisicing elit, sed do eiusmod ut labore et dolore magna aliqua.

Lorem ipsum dolor sit amet, consectetur adipisicing elit, sed do eiusmod tempor incididunt ut labore et dolore magna aliqua. Ut enim ad minim veniam, quis nostrud exercitation ullamco laboris nisi ut aliquip ex ea commodo consequat. Lorem ipsum dolor sit amet, consectetur adipisicing elit, sed do eiusmod ut labore et dolore magna aliqua.

Lorem ipsum dolor sit

Lorem ipsum dolor sit amet, consectetur adipisicing elit, sed do eiusmod tempor incididunt ut labore et dolore magna aliqua. Ut enim ad minim veniam, quis nostrud exercitation ullamco laboris nisi ut aliquip consequat.

Lorem ipsum dolor sit

Lorem ipsum dolor sit amet, consectetur adipisicing elit, sed do eiusmod tempor incididunt ut labore et dolore magna aliqua. Ut enim ad minim veniam, quis nostrud exercitation ullamco laboris nisi ut aliquip consequat. Lorem ipsum dolor sit amet, consectetur adipisicing elit, sed do eiusmod tempor incididunt ut labore et dolore magna aliqua.

Lorem ipsum dolor sit

Lorem ipsum dolor sit amet, consectetur adipisicing elit, sed do eiusmod tempor incididunt ut labore et dolore magna aliqua.

Lorem ipsum dolor sit

Lorem ipsum dolor sit amet, consectetur adipisicing elit, sed do eiusmod tempor incididunt ut labore et dolore magna aliqua.

Lorem ipsum dolor sit

Lorem ipsum dolor sit amet, consectetur adipisicing elit, sed do eiusmod tempor incididunt ut labore et dolore magna aliqua.

Using alternative newspaper layouts

Neither the eight-column grid nor the common six-column grid will suit every type of publication, language, or culture. In many examples, an even number of columns has given way to an uneven number such as five or seven columns. In many parts of the world and in many publications, the number of columns does not change many of the underlying principles of either newspaper or grid design.

Whether the front page is largely visual as in the example of Ukraine's *Segodnya* or text-based as in Belgium's *De Morgen*, many of the same principles of visual hierarchy, column spanning, and variation in headline type sizes and faces apply.

Of course, not every newspaper uses a grid in ways that might be familiar to Western readers. The chaotic layout of Japan's *Asahi Shimbun* might seem strange to Western eyes and is largely dictated by the Japanese language and its vertical text flow. It would be dangerous for Web designers in Western cultures to assume that all Web design should follow the same, predominantly Western model. The Web is a medium with a global reach.

> **Note:** Newseum at www.newseum.org is a site devoted to reproducing newspaper front pages from around the world every day. Typically it contains more than 500 pages from almost 50 countries.

Internationalization will become only more important in the future, as more people outside of the so-called developed nations get online. Looking at how news content is presented in other languages, character sets, and orientations will give you some idea of the challenges ahead when designing Web sites that have a truly global reach. On the next pages are four alternative content layouts based upon the grid used by Japan's *Asahi Shimbun*.

The long way round

After a journey around the world of newspapers, it's time to bring grids a little closer to home, to the homepage of a popular news site to be precise. This is no time to put your feet up, because in the next section, you will see how using a grid derived from a newspaper can work with Newsvine.

The grid layout based on Japan's *Asahi Shimbun*

Lorem ipsum dolor sit amet, consectetur

Lorem ipsum dolor sit amet, consectetur adipisicing elit, sed do eiusmod tempor incididunt ut labore et dolore magna aliqua. Ut enim ad minim veniam, quis nostrud exercitation ullamco laboris nisi ut aliquip consequat. Lorem ipsum dolor sit amet, consectetur adipisicing elit.

Lorem ipsum sit amet, consectetur adipisicing elit, sed do eiusmod tempor incididunt ut labore et dolore magna aliqua. Ut enim ad minim veniam, quis nostrud exercitation ullamco laboris nisi ut aliquip consequat. Lorem ipsum dolor sit amet, consectetur adipisicing elit, sed enim ad minim veniam, quis nostrud exercitation ullamco laboris nisi ut.

Lorem ipsum dolor sit amet

Lorem ipsum dolor sit amet, consectetur adipisicing elit, sed do eiusmod tempor incididunt ut labore et dolore magna aliqua. Ut enim ad minim veniam, quis nostrud exercitation ullamco laboris nisi ut aliquip consequat. Lorem ipsum dolor sit amet, consectetur adipisicing elit, sed do eiusmod tempor incididunt ut labore et dolore magna aliqua. Ut enim ad minim veniam, quis nostrud exercitation ullamco laboris nisi ut aliquip consequat. Lorem ipsum dolor sit amet, consectetur.

Lorem ipsum dolor sit amet, consectetur adipisicing elit, sed do eiusmod tempor incididunt ut labore et dolore magna aliqua. Ut enim ad minim veniam, quis nostrud exercitation ullamco laboris nisi ut aliquip consequat. Lorem ipsum dolor sit amet, consectetur adipisicing elit, sed do eiusmod temp.

Lorem ipsum dolor sit amet, consectetur adipisicing elit, sed do eiusmod tempor incididunt ut labore et dolore magna aliqua.

Lorem ipsum dolor sit amet, consectetur adipisicing elit, sed do eiusmod tempor incididunt ut labore et dolore magna aliqua.

Lorem ipsum dolor sit amet, consectetur

Lorem ipsum dolor sit amet, consectetur adipisicing elit, sed do eiusmod tempor incididunt ut labore et dolore magna aliqua. Ut enim ad minim veniam, quis nostrud exercitation ullamco laboris nisi ut aliquip consequat. Lorem ipsum dolor sit amet, consectetur adipisicing elit.

Lorem ipsum dolor sit

Lorem ipsum dolor sit amet, consectetur adipisicing elit, sed do eiusmod tempor incididunt ut labore.

Lorem ipsum dolor sit amet, consectetur adipisicing elit, sed do eiusmod tempor incididunt ut labore.

Lorem ipsum dolor sit amet, consectetur adipisicing elit, sed do eiusmod tempor incididunt ut labore.

Lorem ipsum dolor sit amet, consectetur adipisicing elit, sed do eiusmod tempor incididunt ut labore.

Lorem ipsum dolor sit amet, consectetur adipisicing elit, sed do eiusmod tempor incididunt ut labore et dolore magna aliqua. Ut enim ad minim veniam, quis nostrud exercitation ullamco laboris nisi ut aliquip consequat. Lorem ipsum dolor sit amet, consectetur adipisicing elit, sed do eiusmod.

Lorem ipsum dolor sit amet, consectetur

Lorem ipsum dolor sit amet, consectetur adipisicing elit, sed do eiusmod tempor incididunt ut labore.

Lorem ipsum dolor sit amet, consectetur adipisicing elit, sed do eiusmod tempor incididunt ut labore.

Lorem ipsum dolor sit amet, consectetur adipisicing elit, sed do eiusmod tempor incididunt ut labore.

Lorem ipsum dolor sit amet, consectetur adipisicing elit, sed do eiusmod tempor incididunt ut labore.

Lorem ipsum dolor sit amet, consectetur adipisicing elit, sed do eiusmod tempor incididunt ut labore.

Lorem ipsum dolor sit amet, consectetur

Lorem ipsum dolor sit amet, consectetur adipisicing elit, sed do eiusmod tempor incididunt et labore et dolore magna aliqua. Ut enim ad minim veniam, quis nostrud exercitation ullamco laboris nisi ut.

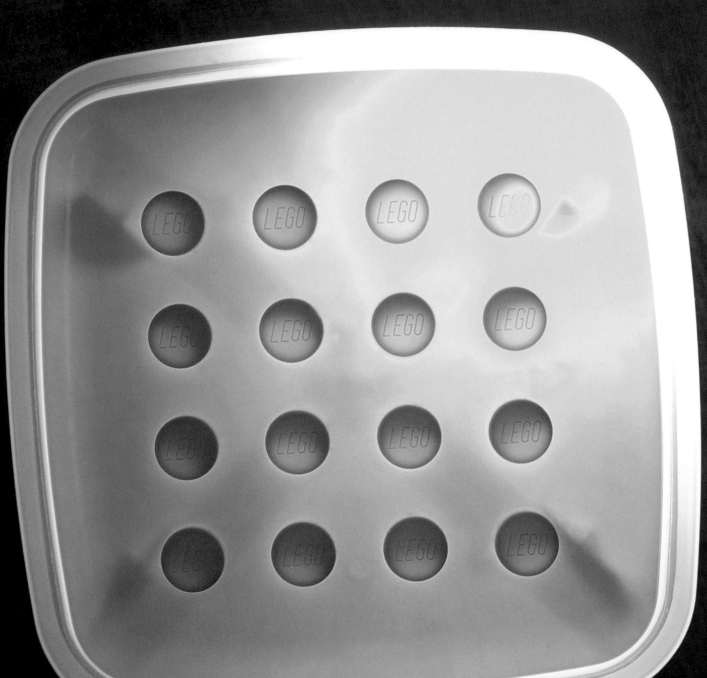

Bringing New Grids to Web Design

You have learned the importance of grids in creating visual order. Rather than leading to repetitive designs, they can inspire a wide variety of designs that present information in a structured way while at the same time maintaining the designer's ability to surprise the reader. It is important to remember that no matter how detailed the grid, it is always the designer who is in control, whether the end result of the design is a personal Web site, blog, portfolio, or a widely circulated newspaper that is read by hundreds of thousands of people.

So far you have been concerned with the use of grids in traditional news media. What about news outlets on the Web?

Breaking news

Launched in 2005, Newsvine (**Figure 3.31**) has become a popular news outlet with more than 400,000 unique visitors per day reading and discussing its news. Newsvine's topics include politics, sports, and technology. Its sources include mainstream news agencies such as Associated Press and its own member-contributed links to stories, articles, and blog posts.

The designers of Newsvine's homepage have succeeded in bringing a large amount of information and links into the site's layout, which is fixed and centered at 932 pixels.

I was interested to see the effect that bringing a popular, contemporary newspaper grid to Newsvine would have. In this section, you will dissect the layout of the current Newsvine homepage design, modify and remake the design, and see the effects of merging it with some common newspaper layout techniques. You will see the results of the following:

- Setting a baseline grid
- Creating columns, supercolumns, and gutters
- Using microgrids to give balance to design details
- Making images flexible in size

3.31 www.newsvine.com

Highlighting columns and gutters in the current Newsvine homepage

First, let's break down the layout of the homepage by overlaying a semitransparent layer to highlight its columns and gutters (**Figure 3.32**).

The proportions of this layout and the center column are dictated by the size of the lead story's image. The left column is sized to suit the minimal content that it contains, and the right column fills the remaining horizontal space. "Below the fold," only the center and right columns are combined, and they have been divided to form two more symmetrical columns that hold categorized links to other parts of the site.

Leading with the grid

Designing with grids is more than simply creating columns; it is about the horizontal as well as the vertical. Whereas in print design, this horizontal baseline grid will often be determined by the size and leading of your text, on the Web the fluidity of layout and text sizes make it difficult to control every aspect of a grid in both dimensions.

When you do establish a series of horizontal baselines, you can improve the horizontal flow of your content and create a cleaner, more constant feel. For this realign of Newsvine, I have chosen a contemporary five-column grid that would be ideally implemented using a flexible, liquid layout. I have deliberately chosen to work on a wider-format canvas because I find I am less tempted by the urge to shoehorn content into a narrow width that might be better suited to a fixed-pixel design.

The baseline grid I have chosen to use has been set to 100 pixels between each horizontal line; it's not too detailed to be restrictive or too open to be of less use in aligning the design elements. It is this five-column layout and the baseline grid that will provide the backbone of the design (**Figure 3.33**).

> **Note:** I prefer using Macromedia Fireworks for designing my page layouts and for its "pages" feature, enabling me to store variations of my design in a single file.

This completed grid can be combined with a colored overlay to show the structure of the columns more clearly. For the area that will contain the lead story, two of the columns will be combined to form one supercolumn (**Figure 3.34**).

In a slight departure from the existing Newsvine design, I have chosen to feature the full text of the lead story plus more information from two further articles. This content will also span two columns. The next task is to block out these areas and add gutters where the supercolumns will be subdivided (**Figure 3.35**).

Blocking out different types of content by using varying opacities to indicate their relative importance or hierarchy is a useful way to create a diagram of a visitor's possible path around a page. In the illustration shown here, I have blocked out the branding and navigation areas in black, and stronger colors indicate the most important content. This provides a highly visual structure into which to flow text and images. It also helps illustrate which content will likely appear above the fold, the point where a visitor might start to scroll, which I have indicated by a dotted white line (**Figure 3.36**).

Note: Judging the precise position of the fold is an almost impossible task. The height of the *viewport* (the area of a Web browser through which you view the page), and therefore the fold, will vary with so many factors, including the screen resolution and window size and the size and quantity of an open browser's toolbars. If it is important that particular content appears above the fold for most users, it is important to test your design in as many different browsing environments as you can.

3.33 Providing the backbone with a baseline grid

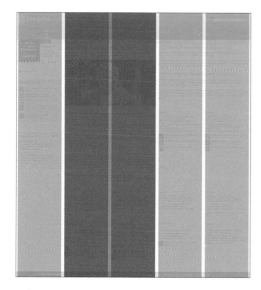

3.34 Combining columns

3.35 Blocking out content areas

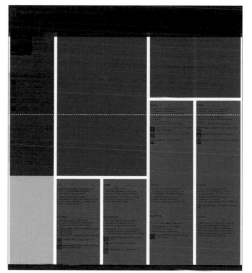

3.36 Indicating the fold with a dotted line at 700px

With the content areas now mapped out, it is time to import the content. I have used actual text and images from Newsvine as they appeared on the site at the time so you can compare the grid-based design and the live site with less difficulty.

Using column overlays as a guide takes the guesswork out of aligning content to a grid, and the baselines makes it far easier to create a more balanced vertical alignment of the elements (**Figure 3.37**).

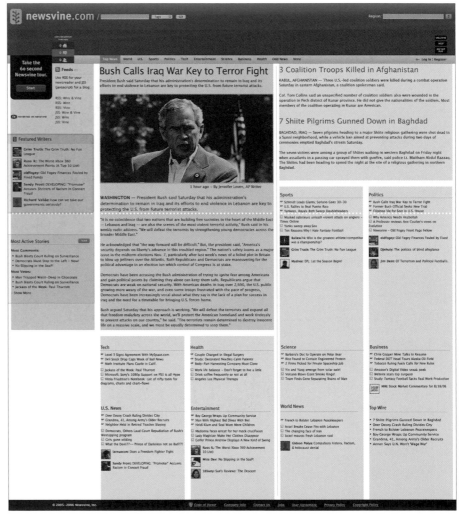

 Laying column structure over the design

Exposing dirty little secrets

The devil is in the detail, or so some say. With the main content flowed into the grid, it is time to learn more about how working with a grid can help you with many of the fine details of your designs.

When you have established the main proportions of a grid, you can further subdivide each of its modules, using either the same proportions or perhaps the divine proportion or the rule of thirds, if you prefer. This lets you precisely position elements within each module inside microgrids, which will help you keep your designs balanced right down to the finest details.

Zoom into the branding area at the top of this design. By overlaying the grid onto the design, you will see how a simple microgrid has helped to neatly arrange the various tools under the logo (**Figure 3.38**).

To achieve this, I have divided this module into four evenly spaced columns. These microcolumns not only ensure that the conversation tracker and the Take the 60 Second Newsvine Tour panel are well positioned, but they also influenced their widths (which are slightly different from how they appear on Newsvine) so they match this new grid.

You may also have noticed that the size of the logo has increased to match the width of the grid module containing it.

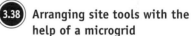
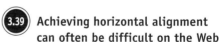

3.38 Arranging site tools with the help of a microgrid

Engaging in news manipulation

Having brought the full content of the lead story onto this page, I had to find a new position for the story's summary. Taking inspiration from newspaper design, the main headline and the summary now appear above the main image. This works especially well in leading your eye to the story and brings content above the fold.

Zooming back into the design, you will see how working with a baseline grid can be extremely effective for working with the horizontal alignment of your elements. For example, the paragraph of text to the right is aligned with the top of the main image, creating balance within the design. Although horizontal alignments can be difficult to maintain when the quantity and size of text in the browser window are likely to vary, striving to achieve good horizontal as well as vertical structure should be an important part of your design (**Figure 3.39**).

3.39 Achieving horizontal alignment can often be difficult on the Web

(3.40) **Using backgrounds to create elastic images**

Keeping you in the picture

If you have been paying really close attention, you may have noticed that in this realign, the lead-story image is wider than in the original. Like Newsvine, many sites are developed with fixed-pixel widths, mainly because they use either inline images or branding graphics that are a fixed size. In flexible, liquid layouts, fixed-sized images can cause headaches for designers because they remain of a fixed size no matter what the flexible layout is doing around them. Unlike vector graphics, bitmap images rarely scale effectively and although you can resize images with percentages or em units, none of the current techniques for flexible images is perfect in every respect. To obtain a wider image for a flexible layout at a larger window width and a narrower image at smaller window sizes, try this CSS background-image workaround technique.

For this example, I have placed the image as the background to an added <div> element. The width of this division remains flexible, with only its height and margins set:

```
div.lead_image {
height : 300px;
margin : 0 10px; }
```

To make this technique effective, create an image that is slightly wider than will be needed. It is important to ensure that its main focus remains in the center. You can attach this image as a background image using CSS; it should be positioned centrally (note that if the browser window is enlarged, such as it is in Figure 3.40, more of the background image is revealed):

```
div.lead_image {
height : 300px;
margin : 0 10px;
background : #fff url(lead_image.jpg) no-repeat center; }
```

If the browser window is enlarged, more of the background image is revealed (**Figure 3.40**).

In sites where these images may change dynamically and may even be populated from a database, attaching a background image to a <div> element in an external style sheet might not be possible. You can still utilize this technique by using a combination of external and inline CSS. (Although I would ordinarily advise that you remove all styling information from your document and place it in external CSS files, this is one situation where you can justify using inline styles.):

(3.41) Completing the Newsvine realign

```
<div class="lead_image" style="background : #fff url(lead_image.jpg)
no-repeat center;">

div.lead_image {
height : 300px;
margin : 0 10px; }
```

Hold the front page

With all the pieces in place, the press is gathered in the briefing room, and fingers are poised over camera shutters. The grid-based realign can be revealed (**Figure 3.41**). This reworking of the already impressive Newsvine demonstrates that creating a solid grid and using it for the basis of your page layouts down to the smallest of details will pay real dividends. For more experiments in flexible width and elastic image techniques, go to www. clagnut.com/blog/268/ and www.htmldog.com/articles/elasticdesign/demo.

In the next section, I share some of my favorite techniques, including how to set the mood for your designs, use paper and virtual scrapbooks, work more efficiently with photos and images, and extend your browser with helpful tools. Perhaps most important, I'll encourage you to look outside the Web for your design inspiration.

Finding Inspiration
in Unexpected Places

Last year, I was visiting the Tate Modern art gallery in London with a friend who is a fellow Web designer. Walking the galleries and browsing the shelves of the Tate's bookshop, I was surprised to learn from him that he rarely looks beyond the Web for his design inspiration. Instead, he keeps a bookmarks folder full of sites he admires for their layouts, navigation, and other design details. Later, munching a muffin in the gallery's café and musing over what he told me, I realized my friend might not be uncommon among Web designers in his approach.

Doing a homepage makeover

One late night last year, finding it hard to go to sleep, I sat up watching reruns of home-decorating shows on UKTVStyle, a UK satellite TV channel that shows wall-to-wall, floor-to-ceiling home makeovers.

On the schedule that night there was the glossy and extravagant *Extreme Makeover: Home Edition*, which was more about demolishing and rebuilding than making over. There was *Changing Rooms*, where two couples decorate a room in each other's houses, with the help of designers who have not spoken to the couple for whom they are designing. And lastly there was *House Invaders*, a typically British low-budget affair where the team decorates your entire house in one day using only leftover materials you have stored in your shed.

In between all the paint effects, MDF (a.k.a. particle board), and cans of frosting spray, I spotted a show presented by a flamboyant interior designer, Lawrence Llewellyn Bowen. Unlike many of its rivals, this makeover show took the viewer through the process of designing the room; they started with the client brief, visited inspirational locations, explained design decisions, and finally performed the "reveal"—that moment where ordinarily sane people leap up and down whooping (in the United States) or quietly sobbing "It's so lovely; isn't it, Norman?" (in Britain).

After several hours of nonstop designing, painting, whooping, and sobbing, I spotted several parallels between these home makeover shows and Web design.

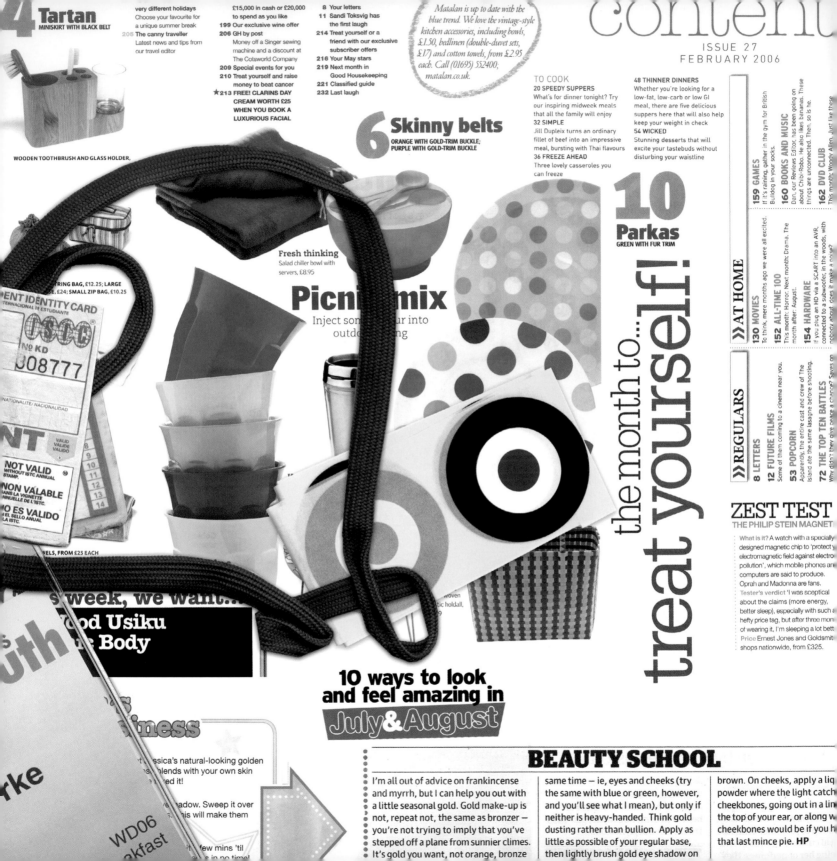

Matalan is up to date with the
blue trend. We love the vintage-style
kitchen accessories, including bowls,
£1.50, bedlinen (double-duvet sets,
£17) and cotton towels, from £2.95
each. Call (01695) 552400;
matalan.co.uk.

WOODEN TOOTHBRUSH AND GLASS HOLDER,

6 Skinny belts
ORANGE WITH GOLD-TRIM BUCKLE;
PURPLE WITH GOLD-TRIM BUCKLE

Fresh thinking
Salad chiller bowl with
servers, £8.95

Picnic mix
Inject some colour into
outdoor dining

10 Parkas
GREEN WITH FUR TRIM

ENT IDENTITY CARD

RING BAG, £12.25; LARGE
...E, £24; SMALL ZIP BAG, £10.25

No KD
008777

VALID
VALIDE
VALIDO

NOT VALID
WITHOUT ISTC
STAMP.

NON VALABLE
...ANS LA VIGNETTE
...NNUELLE DE L'ISTC.

...O ES VALIDO
...N EL SELLO ANUAL
...LA ISTC.

VELS, FROM £25 EACH

the month to... treat yourself!

ZEST TEST
THE PHILIP STEIN MAGNET

What is it? A watch with a specially
designed magnetic chip to 'protect y...
electromagnetic field against electro...
pollution', which mobile phones an...
computers are said to produce.
Oprah and Madonna are fans.
Tester's verdict 'I was sceptical
about the claims (more energy,
better sleep), especially with such a
hefty price tag, but after three mon...
of wearing it, I'm sleeping a lot bett...
Price Ernest Jones and Goldsmit...
shops nationwide, from £325.

s week, we want...
...ood Usiku
...e Body

...uth

...ke

...iness

10 ways to look
and feel amazing in
July & August

...t ...ssica's natural-looking golden
...es ...s ...lends with your own skin
... ...ed it!

...e ...adow. Sweep it over
... ...his will make them

WD06
...akfast

...it ...few mins 'til
...s in no time!

BEAUTY SCHOOL

I'm all out of advice on frankincense
and myrrh, but I can help you out with
a little seasonal gold. Gold make-up is
not, repeat not, the same as bronzer —
you're not trying to imply that you've
stepped off a plane from sunnier climes.
It's gold you want, not orange, bronze

same time — ie, eyes and cheeks (try
the same with blue or green, however,
and you'll see what I mean), but only if
neither is heavy-handed. Think gold
dusting rather than bullion. Apply as
little as possible of your regular base,
then lightly brush gold eye shadow on

brown. On cheeks, apply a liq...
powder where the light catch...
cheekbones, going out in a lin...
the top of your ear, or along w...
cheekbones would be if you h...
that last mince pie. **HP**

Extreme Makeover: Home Edition

Most Web site redesign projects follow a similar approach to *Extreme Makeover: Home Edition*: "This site is not good enough anymore," shouts the client. "Let's tear it down and rebuild it bigger, glossier, and with more appliances than we had before!"

You can start whooping now if you like, but this approach is really rather sad. There are probably at least a few good features of your old site that you will lose in your desire for something new. There is also the high cost of bulldozing the site and rebuilding it, not to mention the inconvenience and hard work involved.

And don't forget your visitors; they will be more than a little confused when they turn up to your house and find that it is unrecognizable from the last time they visited. They might even drive straight by and mistakenly pull up outside your neighbor's property, the house farther down the street, without concrete Roman pillars.

Changing Rooms

Watching the shocked faces of *Changing Rooms* contestants as they see their cozy living room transformed into an airport lounge or Spanish-style bar has a curious appeal. In contrast, the idea of a designer creating a new look without considering what is best for a client does not.

I can imagine that in the commercial real world away from the telly, few of the *Changing Rooms* designers would be asked back to decorate another room if they worked in that way. Designers should never stick to their own preconceived ideas of what would be best for a client. They should always consider their client's needs and the needs of the people who will use that room regularly. Then again, you may have clients or managers who are like those on *House Invaders*—clients who expect you can create an entire site for very little money using leftover markup and CSS!

After several hours on the sofa in the company of carpenters, decorators, and electricians, not forgetting of course the ever-smiling hosts, I drifted off to sleep thinking about whether some of the processes that I had seen could be effective in Web design.

Facing page: Magazine cuttings from my scrapbook containing inspiration for interfaces and layouts

Introducing mood boards

One of the techniques that interested me while watching Bowen's show was that in the weeks *before* redecorating, Bowen asked his clients to make a mood board to help in designing their new room.

In interior design, *mood boards* can be a highly effective way to bring together inspirational images, ideas, and materials on a large piece of mat or mounting board and to see how well they work in combination. It asks that the client consider the mood they want to create for their room, considering not only the visual aesthetic but also the emotions that the colors, lighting, and textures can create. An interior designer might ask his client, "Are you looking for a modern, high-tech look with stripped floors, minimal décor, and hard, shiny surfaces? Or are you aiming for a warmer, more organic feeling, with warm colors and a range of soft textures?"

The benefits of client and stakeholder participation can be enormous in any design process. If you are able to involve the key people for whom you're designing a site, actively challenging them to participate in the predesign phase, creating mood boards for their project can help reduce your time spent on exploratory ideas.

Working closely with the client or stakeholders will also help you reduce the risk of them getting a nasty *Changing Rooms*–style surprise. It has been my perhaps refreshing experience that helping everyone understand the benefits of creating a mood board and then encouraging them to participate in making one has always paid dividends.

Using mood boards for Web design

Mood-board design elements can come from almost anywhere. If the goal is a modern, high-tech look, the mood board might contain cuttings from magazines, such as adverts for shiny cars, high-tech gadgets, or brushed stainless steel appliances. Participants might have glued scraps of shiny fabrics or aluminum foil to the mood board. There may even be photographs of giant silver robots from 1950s sci-fi movies.

On the other hand, if the aim is for a fresh pastel look, the mood board might be filled with photographs of cottage gardens, a pastel paint chart from a hardware store, or soft cotton fabric samples. You might even encourage participants to make creamy marks on the board using oil pastels to see how well the different colors and textures combine.

Facing page: A mood board containing magazine cuttings from my scrapbook

2

e sold off the roll, and
on of lighting and
s is also available.

from original
ours by Joanna Twinn,
eetings cards show
cenes of a vegetable
potting shed, doorstep
ntry kitchen, among

shioned **milk paint** is
ith traditional materials
hods that predate the
etrochemicals, making
ironmentally friendly

ntents

Keeping a design scrapbook

Many of my art-school friends kept their scrapbooks chock-full of design inspiration as obsessively as I sharpened my pencils. It was only much later in my design career that I realized how important it is to keep a design scrapbook.

Like many designers, I now keep paper scrapbooks that are filled with cuttings from magazines or newspapers, photographs, postcards, and even old chocolate wrappers—anything that catches my eye because of interesting typographic treatments, unusual shapes, or color combinations.

Keeping a paper scrapbook, rather than an electronic one, can be useful not only for collecting scraps of design inspiration that can suggest new ideas for Web page designs but can also result in the often accidental and random combination of elements that can sometimes occur. For example, mixing and matching cuttings from classical broadsheet newspapers with snippets from children's comics or teenage magazines can lead to some surprising results. This is an effect that rarely happens when you scan design elements and store them on your computer.

Designers, developers, and everyone involved in the creative and technical process of creating a Web site should find that keeping a design scrapbook of their own can be useful, often in several ways.

Scrapbooks for developers, am I serious?

Yes! It helps developers better understand the job of designers by making both think about aesthetics. Both know that their work will have a critical influence over the quality of the design final and that their combined efforts are the key to that quality.

Scrapbooks are tactile, solid explorations that can help us all better appreciate how important typography, white space, and even the simple alignment of elements inside a grid can be to the overall polish of a design. When everyone involved in the creative and technical processes thinks more about aesthetics, we will all take greater care to achieve that polish.

LET'S SEE ACTION

Fashion Week special

liverpool biennial
16 Sept - 26 Nov 2006
www.biennial.com

GET INVOLVED
OPEN MIC
EVERY SUNDAY

Welcome

Explore
Discover
Relax

Manchester
Art Gallery

carbon
MUSIC STORE

URBAN OUTFITTERS

FOR PEOPLE WHO LOVE GOOD MUSIC

We love Posters!

Poster makes

Get creative and try one of these cool ideas for using your posters!

Funky frame

Make your frame any shape you want!

It's cool to hang on your door or wall!

What you need:

pen ☐ poster ☐ glue ☐ foam ☐
scissors ☐ sellotape ☐ ruler ☐
fun shapes ☐ ribbon ☐

What to do:

Put your poster on the foam, draw around it with your pen, then draw a squiggly line a few centimetres away from the poster. Cut out the squiggly line and the middle shape to get your frame! Put the frame face down, put your poster over it (so you'll be able to see the pic) and tape it down. Glue on some funky shapes and tape on ribbon.

Sequins or fun look fab!

Psychic hotline

Our team of top psychics will give you a one-to-one consultation on what the future holds. Get the lowdown on love, money and health just about any...

Text Psy RPLPS

Live Me

☎ 09064

I wanna be a GG Club Covergal!

Name: _____
Date of birth: _____
Fave celebrity: _____
Fave animal: _____
Fave film: _____
Fave TV prog: _____
Fave fashion item: _____
Fave GG page: _____

I'm _____ years old
Don't forget to send us you then ask Mum or Dad to si here: _____

My fave thing to do is

☐ Read Go Girl
☐ Watch DVDs
☐ Log on to GG site
☐ Have a sleepover
☐ Hit the shops
☐ Something else:
_____

My

because _____

wanna see poster of:

because _____

in this form, cut it out a d it with your address Go Girl Club, PO Box 51,

---

C·O·D·E CRACKER

This is a crossword without clues. Each number represents a different letter of the alphabet and all 26 letters are used. We've given you the first three letters: T = 17, E = 8, X = 19.
Write these on the grid opposite. Then start working out which numbers represent the other letters. Use the smaller grid and the alphabetical list underneath it to keep track of the letters you've identified. When you've finished, a mystery word will appear in the shaded squares.

Keep track of your letters here

| 1 | 2 | 3 | 4 | 5 | 6 | 7 | 8 E | 9 | 10 | 11 | 12 | 13 |
| 14 | 15 | 16 | 17 T | 18 | 19 X | 20 | 21 | 22 | 23 | 24 | 25 | 26 |

A B C D E F G H I J K L M N O P Q R S T U V W X Y Z

WRITE THE MYSTERY WORD ON THE COUPON ON PAGE 36 AND YOU COULD BE A W

Find the phrase

Ooh, I think I've finally got it! Have you?

Look closely at the clues below. Some make a catchphrase, others a common word. Got 'em? Answers on page 36.

WEEK 10: £50,000

herring

can can

somewhere

rainbow

bjaockx

just for fun

WIN £50,000 JACKPOT!

Plus £1,000 every week

WEEK 10: £50,000
WEEK 9: £45,000
WEEK 8: £40,000

It's week 8 of our ackpot game. With only three re weeks to go, including this e, be sure to try your luck at ning. This week, the jackpot is a huge £40,000. Good luck!

STEP 1 — THE O WK GAME
his week and for the next two eeks, five different numbers will e printed on the Lucky Numbers age. You need to match your five umbers (see step 3) to win.

STEP 2 — JACKPOT JOY
This week's jackpot is £40,000 and it grows by another £5,000 every week. So by the end of the 10 week run, the jackpot prize could be a whopping £50,000.

STEP 3 — TEXT OR PHONE
Text LUCKY8 or call 3058). You'll receive five numbers per entry. If they match those printed, then you may have won!

STEP 4 — £1,000 BONUS
n addition, there's one bonus £1,000 to be shared between all winners who match that week's £1,000 number. This number gives you another

STEP 5 — GET YOUR WEEKLY PICK ME UP
You need to keep buying your Pick Me Up every week to match the new numbers and find out the text and phone lines that change every week.

STEP 6 — THE RULES
You must be 18 or over and each call or text costs £1 (ROI 150c per call and 2 euros per text). Each week's game starts Thursday and lasts until midnight Wednesday.

Yes! I would l

Quarterly every three

One-year Get your fo FREE to yo

Two-year Get your fo FREE to yo

Your detai

Name: _____
Address: _____
Postcode: _____
Telephone: _____
Email: _____
Date of birth: _____
Parent's signat

Postag

FRUITY FUN!

just for fun

Tell us which su fruit isn't hidd this grid to be i a chance of win an iDrop MP3 p

P	S	D	U	E	L	V	G	S	Z	Y	E	Z	Y
A	I	M	Q	F	J	X	J	M	A	N	I	S	P
V	L	N	Y	S	W	K	J	E	Y	P	L	E	K
Q	Q	J	E	F	L	M	L	R	K	T	V	O	Q
C	R	Z	E	A	V	A	R	Z	T	O	N	X	X
E	A	A	S	E	P	E	A	E	R	C	D	O	X
H	P	B	Q	H	B	P	N	F	R	T	N	X	X
Q	P	O	T	W	O	I	L	A	T	H	J	Q	X
V	L	T	A	D	R	R	M	E	P	Q	J	Z	T
X	E	R	B	A	P	U	A	P	S	F	F	S	D
F	T	Y	T	A	S	E	O	N	L	N	H	X	L
S	F	C	W	T	J	C	A	M	G	Z	Q	C	W
L	E	Z	A	N	G	B	L	R	S	E	O	K	J
N	B	S	X	W	Q	D	B	E	N	U	A	K	Y

♥ Apple   ♥ Pear
♥ Nectarine   ♥ Orange

How to enter

Send your answer, nam address in a sealed en

WI

PLAY

Looking at magazines for interface inspiration

Next time you are in the supermarket queue or in line to buy a pack of twenty Rothmans at your local newsagent, pick up a magazine at random. Don't worry too much about the subject matter or the looks you may get from fellow customers; just pick it up and flick through its pages.

Whatever you find yourself flicking through, you will almost always find an interesting idea for the layout of an interface element, perhaps a form on a puzzle page or maybe even a different treatment for a sidebar. If you don't feel like splurging on *Woman's Weekly* or the latest copy of *Celebrity Tittle Tattler*, don't worry—you can always find magazine inspiration for free.

Once the inspiration bug has bitten you, tearing pages out of the magazines left in doctors' waiting rooms can become quite a habit. I have found that if my kleptomania raises eyebrows among fellow patients, saying, "It's OK, I'm a designer" keeps the tutting noises to a minimum. Wherever you can find magazines, looking at the page designs, from the front contents pages to the small ads at the rear, can inspire you to think differently about various elements in your designs.

Getting typography inspiration

Newspapers and magazines can inspire not only new ideas for grid layouts; they can also be an amazing source of inspiration for typography. But inspiration for type is not only confined to the printed page; you can find it all around you. Whether you are stacking your supermarket trolley with everyday essentials or flipping CDs in your local music store, you will find hundreds of type design ideas in one store alone. If you are a scrapbook and chocolate junky like me, pasting your empty chocolate bar wrappers into a scrapbook can often provide not only new ideas for type but also some interesting juxtapositions of different but complementary styles.

Typography and lettering styles make up so much of the world that we see around us everyday. Walk outside your front door, and it will be only seconds before your eyes will fall on typographic design. Shop signs may have become familiar, but they are also often some of the most varied forms of typographical design you will encounter; posters and advertising billboards jostle for our attention, and when they have been exposed to the ravages of the weather, they will take on new characters as they degrade.

Typography resources

Particletree's Kevin Hale has compilied a list of some great typography resources in his Typography Crash Course Roundup at http://particletree.com/notebook/typography-crash-course-roundup/.

Andy Hume has also written a comprehensive article called "The Anatomy of Web Fonts" at www.sitepoint.com/article/anatomy-web-fonts.

PRIMAL SCREAM

"DAMAGED? WE NEARLY DIED!"

RIX

THE TRUE STORY OF HIS ROCK REVOLUTIO

SPECIAL ANNIVERSARY EDITION!

NOVEMBER 2006 £4.10 US$8.99 CAN$12.95

9 771351 019119

HELLO DARKNESS MY OLD FRIEND

"KIDS ARRIVED WITH **LONG HAIR** REALISED THEY WEREN'T PUNK AND STARTED CUTTING THEIR HAIR OFF"

...INTO SWINGING LONDON, HE LED ... REVOLUTION. FORTY YEARS ... ETERNAL POWER OF ... ENCE. "GENIUS!" ... HENOMENAL!" ... ODS JEFF BECK.

Mecca for mods"

It is the TV stronghold of mods, the frighteningly clean, sharply-dressed arbiters of tomorrow's tastes in practically everything

Bordermne
OFF MANETTE ST, SOHO

RIZL

THURSDAY 5th OC
EILEEN RO
FRIDAY 6th OC
LARRY MILLER
+Nell Bryden +Derwent
MONDAY 9th OCTOBER
RADNEY FOSTER
TUESDAY 10th OCTOBER
WE
WEDNES
THE BAS
THURS
KEVIN
FRI
DA
MO
KRIS DEL
TUE
WILLY CLAY BAND
+Southpaw +Thomas Heyman
FRIDAY 27th OCTOBER
PETER BRUNTNELL BAND
MONDAY 30th OCTOBER
AUSTRALIAN ROCKERS RETURN
THE SAINTS
WEDNESDAY 1st NOVEMBER
SINGER SONGWRITER NIGHT
KRISTINA OLSEN & PETER GRAYLING
FRIDAY 3rd NOVEMBER
THIS IS THE BOB DYLAN TRIBUTE BAND!
SCARLEY RIVERA ON FIDDLE AND ROLLING THUNDER BASS PLAYER
HIGHWAY 61 REVISITED

THE JAM

40 YEARS OF MAXIMUM R&

MONDAY 20th
THE RESEN
TUESDAY 21st
MONDAY 4th
FRED EAGL
FRIDAY 8th DE
THE FRANK &
FRIDAY 15th
THE INMATES CHR
SATURDAY 16th
THE PIR

Theories rants, etc

OCEAN COLOUR SCENE • QUADROPHENIA • THE CREATION • READY STEADY

AFTERWORD

Using sIFR for fine typography for the Web

Typography has long been a source of frustration for visual designers working on the Web. The limited set of fonts you can rely on to be installed across a range of platforms and operating systems have meant that little progress has been made in creating attractive typography.

In the past few years, designers have been working hard to overcome many of these limitations by creating new techniques and workarounds that provide more control over typographical style. One of those techniques, sIFR (scalable Inman Flash Replacement), achieves fine typography through a combination of CSS, JavaScript, and Macromedia Flash.

In the absence of font embedding, sIFR enables you to embed any font in a Web page by including it within a Flash movie. Whereas in the past, Flash was criticized for its lack of accessibility, sIFR uses Flash in combination with meaningful markup to preserve the structure, meaning and accessibility of your document. sIFR works by enhancing only the design of the page and leaves the document itself untouched, maintaining wide accessibility and not impacting search engine optimization.

sIFR can be particularly effective when used to style headings, such as <h1> or <h2> elements inside your designs. When JavaScript is available in a visitor's browser, a customizable JavaScript file parses the content of your page, looking for the specific elements or class or id attributes you have earmarked for replacement. The script measures and extracts the content of these elements and in a split second creates a Flash file for each one containing the extracted content, rendered in any typeface you have chosen. This Flash file is then overlaid on top of the original elements.

The inventors of sIFR have created an elegant solution using a combination of standards-based technologies that degrade well under a variety of conditions. If either JavaScript or Flash is unavailable in their browser, visitors will see the standard browser text in the element, styled with CSS. This transcendent approach provides a more advanced design to visitors with browsers that support the full range of sIFR technologies.

> **Note:** You can read about the background to sIFR at www.mikeindustries.com/sifr/ and download the latest sIFR source files and documentation from developer Mark Wubben at http://novemberborn.net/sifr3/alpha.

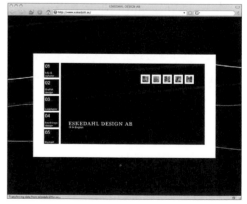

Reexamining Flash design

Flash design has not undeservedly been criticized in recent years for its long download times, its poor general usability, and its lack of accessibility. Many designers passionate about standards-based design have largely dismissed Flash and have concentrated instead on what is and is not possible with CSS.

CSS design galleries multiplied because designers have been hungry for new inspiration and examples of good CSS-based design. In the process, many of these galleries have concentrated on particular design trends or techniques such as dark color schemes or flexible layouts, and others such as Stylegala have grown to include articles on design and forums for discussing design or CSS.

Outside the world of CSS, Flash-based design has continued to be a dominant force, and many of the sites showcasing the work of graphic designers or illustrators continue to be made almost entirely in Flash. As a technology, Flash not only includes its own powerful scripting and behaviors but it also largely frees designers from many of the constraints placed upon them by the grid-like constructs of HTML tables and a conventional approach to CSS. It can be no accident that many designers have chosen to work with Flash.

Flash has liberated them from worrying about browser compatibility issues and the typographical limitations of standard browser text. As a technology specifically designed for presenting rich graphic and media content, it provides the perfect playground for creative ideas.

However, many of the designs that are implemented with Flash could just have easily have been produced using meaningful markup and transcendent CSS, albeit without some of the slick motion effects and interactivity that are some of Flash's fortes. Looking outside the narrow field of the CSS design galleries to what is being created in the industry at large can be a powerful source of creative inspiration, and Flash and design showcases such as Netdiver are packed with creative ideas, with many—but not exclusively—created using Flash.

Note

As interest in the creative possibilities of CSS has increased, online galleries of CSS-based designs have become popular destinations, both as wider sources of inspiration and also as references of specific design topics including dark/light, high-contrast designs and flexible layouts. Although most of these sites now feature much of the same examples, others surround their galleries with discussions, forums, and community news. Two of the CSS gallery sites that remain in my bookmarks include Stylegala (www.stylegala.com) and CSS Beauty (www.cssbeauty.com).

Working with images and photos

It was not so many years ago that the photography process was complicated, inconvenient, and expensive. It involved the agony of choice: "Do I buy a 24-or a 36-shot reel?" This was closely followed by the agony of indecision: "Should I take another one in case the last one won't come out?" Then after an encounter with the white-coated teenager in charge of the automatic-processing machine at Boots or Walgreens, it involved the disappointment of finding only three photos worth saving. The rest would be stored in boxes in the attic to be uncovered centuries later. That was certainly my experience; I hope yours was better and hope, in several hundred years, your descendants won't find your boxes and wonder why some of their ancestors in the late twentieth century had no heads.

Thank heavens for the inventors of digital cameras and also the clever people who invented free photo storage and sharing services such as Flickr and Yahoo! Photos and who made photography so much easier and more fun (**Figure 3.42**).

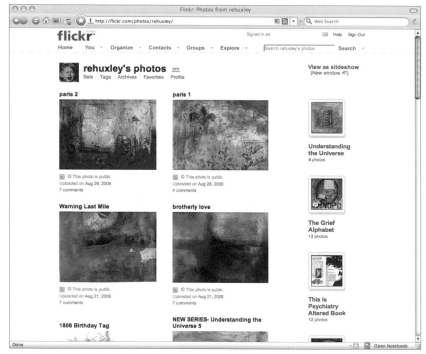

3.42 www.flickr.com

Photos are a great place to look for inspiration for your Web designs. Whether you are looking for layout ideas, color schemes, or simply a new starting point for a new creative concept, flickering through Flickr can be an enjoyable and productive way of finding that spark for new ideas.

Flickr for inspirational photos

If you ever need a quick inspiration fix but your coffee-table magazines are all used up and a walk to the local newsagent is out of the question, Flickr and similar photo storage and sharing sites are an amazing source of new inspiration for design ideas (**Figure 3.43**).

One useful tip for finding the most unexpected combinations of images is to search for general terms such as *red*, *grid*, and *shiny*, rather than for specific topics. Because its many thousands of contributors constantly update Flickr, even a wait of a few minutes can give you a totally new set of inspirational results.

3.43 Sourcing inspiration from Flickr

Note

Please check for copyright and Creative Commons licensing. Many people using Flickr share their photos quite freely, but not everyone does. Fortunately, Flickr lets you search within a particular Creative Commons license, including licenses that allow you to reuse images without permission or attribution. In some cases, if there are restrictions, you can write to the photographer, who may give you permission based on your need.

Creating color palettes

When designing a color scheme, the colors I find in photography and fine art often influence me. One of my favorite techniques creates a selection of complementary tones from just two or more sampled colors. I love Fireworks and prefer to design my Web graphics with it, but you can easily adapt these steps to the imaging program of your choice:

1. Start by making a white canvas (usually 250 × 100 pixels), and then add a 250 × 50 pixel black rectangle to that base layer:

2. Sample one color from the photograph of the painting:

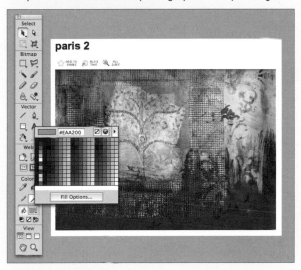

3. Create two 50 × 50 pixel squares, and fill them with that color. Place one colored square over the black rectangle and the other over the white base:

4. Duplicate both squares four times, and then arrange them horizontally across the canvas:

5. Finally, adjust the opacity of each square (usually 100%, 75%, 50%, 25%, and 10%) to allow progressively more of the base color to show through the squares. This will create ten tones from a single color and is easy to replicate for additional base colors:

Note: If you would prefer a more automated way of using this technique, Steve Chipman has created a JavaScript-powered Color Palette Creator, which is available on his Web site at http://slayeroffice.com/tools/color_palette/.

Flock for photo research

Once you start using Flickr on a regular basis to look for inspiration from its millions of images, you might find it helpful to use some of the photo integration features of Flock, a browser based on Firefox that is available for both Windows and Mac OS.

Flock integrates with Flickr and Photobucket, another photo service, to help you work with these sites from inside your Web browser (**Figure 3.44**). Flock's photo "topbar" contains a handy set of tools for searching both sites.

When you have found inspiring images, Flock's photo tools make it easy for you to drag images into a snippets bar and save them for later. When you have finished searching, you can use the uploader to store your found images on Flickr, perhaps in a "Found Inspiration" set.

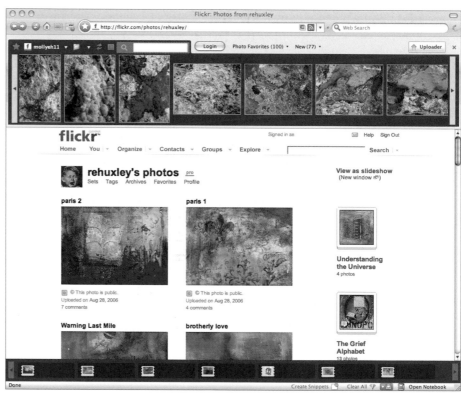

3.44 **Saving photos in Flock**

iPhoto scrapbooks

The habit of keeping paper design scrapbooks is less common among Web designers than it is among traditional graphic designers. If paper, tape, or glue sounds too messy for you, then you do have less sticky alternatives.

For example, designer Jon Hicks chooses to store scans of his design ideas, paper sketches, and found inspirational type styles and colors in folders he creates within the Apple iPhoto photo application for OS X (**Figure 3.45**). You could easily do the same in the imaging and photo applications of your choice.

3.45 **Storing inspiration using iPhoto**

FINDING EXTREME PLEASURE
WILL MAKE YOU
A BETTER PERSON
IF YOU ARE
CAREFUL ABOUT
WHAT THRILLS YOU

TOCCA

Pressing My Lips Against Yours

PURE GRASS

This being human is a guest-house
Every morning a new arrival

DRAW YOUR TOMORROW

StyleCity
LONDON

Fine Art Activities

Many discussions about standards-based design revolve around the technologies you use: markup, CSS, or JavaScript. Other common conversations cover best practices for how you use these technologies. These conversations are important, because striving to develop new techniques and sharing ideas on how best you can use them will benefit not only designers and developers but also the visitors to the sites you create.

That these conversations have focused on technology is not surprising. In the move from using old-fashioned methods to standards-based methods, both visual designers and developers have had to learn a great deal, not least about each other and how they can better work together.

Technology is only part of the story, and markup, CSS, and other languages are only some of the tools you have in your toolbox. In fact, they are only a means to an end and should never be an end in themselves. When you remove beauty and aesthetics, code is simply something to be read by machines. It is only in combination with design that they can make an end result that people will enjoy using.

Designing is more than creating attractive visuals

It is easy to think visual design is about making attractive-looking interfaces. But design is more than that; it is about evoking feelings and emotions in the people who visit a Web site. Create the right mood, and visitors are more likely to want to interact with your site, no matter how much Ajax or other interactivity you have used in creating it.

Design helps convey brand values in ways that are just as important as usability or the slickness of an interface's operation. A well-crafted design provides a framework in which interaction can operate, never the other way around, and it is important to always keep in mind how a visual design can add meaning to a site that goes far beyond the pixels drawn on the screen.

Taking the focus off technology

I know few designers or technical developers who have been formally educated in the broad spectrum of Web skills. Many designers have learned about the nuances of markup and CSS through reading and their own experimentation, and few developers have gone to art schools where the teaching is largely focused on concepts rather than techniques. It is now critical that designers have a better understanding of technical issues while they are designing and that developers look outside their areas of interest to get a different perspective on the work of visual designers.

In this section, it is time to take a break from thinking about technologies and how and where to apply them. It's time to put the various techniques and inspirational sources you have seen together in a short series of activities that have been designed to broaden your creative thinking.

If you are a developer who is more at home in a text editor or even a command-line tool, right about now you might be thinking about fast-forwarding to the next part where you can get your hands dirty with CSS selectors. But hold it right there; an element of creative thinking pops up in every activity related to Web development, and developers can learn much from understanding the creative process of designers.

If you are a visual designer, you may already be working with some of these techniques in your work; however, just like taking a holiday in the sun, it can never hurt to recharge your creative batteries and possibly gain a new perspective on the methods you use.

CSS hasn't revolutionized web design.

The reason lies not with the technology (which

is revolutionary), but with the designers using

it. Most designers have simply swapped the

old technology (tables and font tags) for

the new technology, without fully exploring

what's so completely new.

—JEREMY KEITH
http://adactio.com/journal/1149/

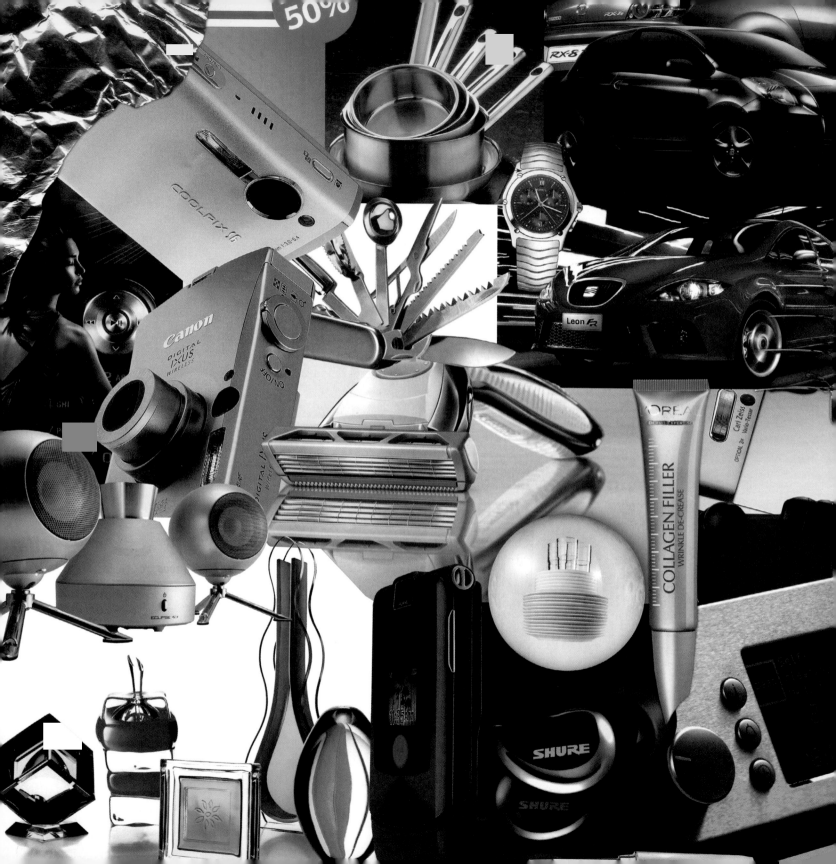

Enhancing the mood

If you were expecting that this part of the book came with a free holiday in the sun, sorry, but I lied. But never mind—holidays can be overrated, and you still need to collect materials for your mood board. You shouldn't have to look too far; you can find a wealth of inspiration without even leaving your home. You can collect these inspirational materials from everyday items, and you can combine them on a mood board in interesting ways.

Please don't imagine this book as your art teacher. I might have grown a beard long enough for a badger to live in while writing it, but I have not worn sandals and have never, ever listened to the Grateful Dead. Think of it more like a client who has come to you with a need for a Web site to promote a shiny new kitchen gadget. Your first task is to collect materials for a mood board that you can show to your client before you start work on your computer. The aim is to find the right tone for the site by looking at examples of shininess.

Your first stop might be the stack of magazines that have been piling up in the corner of your room. The more varied your reading material, the better. Flicking through their pages, you might find advertisements for everything from shiny kitchen appliances to shiny cars, perhaps starkly lit in the photo studio to show off their curves and angles. Magazine advertising can be a terrific source of ideas. Look for examples where the highly reflective surfaces have been polished or perhaps where the colors have been muted to give a minimal, high-tech feel.

Where better to look for inspiration for a shiny new appliance than in the kitchen itself? It's time to raid those kitchen cupboards and drawers and dig out the shiny packaging you will find. Chocolate bars and crisps are not only great for eating; they can also be colorful and reflective. Open the wrappers and slide out the contents; the wrappers will be easier to stick onto your mood board without their contents, and if you don't feel like adding a few extra pounds, you can always have someone else eat them for you.

Aluminum foil is not only great for roasting chickens; it can be crumpled up and then smoothed to create some amazing reflective patterns. Experiment by sticking the foil onto your mood board, both shiny and matte side up, and look at the ways it reflects the room around you and the other elements of your mood board.

Creating a mood board can be a fun and informative way of testing what your client likes to see without looking at other Web sites from a similar field. The combinations of imagery and materials can help spark new ideas, and in some cases they can even become pieces of interesting art in their own right.

Looking for a different perspective

When I first started art school, the first few weeks were different from what I had ever experienced. Whereas during high-school art lessons the emphasis was on technique and the end result of achieving a qualification, at art school we were encouraged to unlearn much of what we had been taught. Here the emphasis was on thinking differently, and the early weeks contained various activities designed to help the students break away from old-school thinking.

One of the first activities that the unsuspecting students were asked to enter into and one that I still love to inflict on unsuspecting conference audiences, involved nothing more than standing on the nearest chair or table to get a different perspective on the space around us. If you don't feel too much like getting strange looks from your colleagues at work or maybe your fellow passengers if you are reading on a bus, you can look at the world around you in other ways without too much embarrassment.

It really was not that long ago that the Web was new and exciting. For many people the Web has largely become an everyday tool to get things done: buy a book, book a flight, or pay off your credit card account. These were all activities that only a few years ago you would have accomplished by a trip into town. Just like the town or city where you live, the Web has become familiar.

It is often true that when you see something regularly enough, you become desensitized to it. When you drive or walk around the town or city where you live, you will probably already be familiar with most of its visual landmarks. You might already hardly notice the fronts of office buildings, banks, cafés, and shops you see every day.

On your next journey to work, take your eyes off your newspaper or iPod screen and look around you for things that are different. These things don't have to be new additions to the urban landscape; they might just be new to you because you haven't gone looking for them.

If you live in most parts of Europe or in much of the central and eastern United States, many of the buildings around you will have stood for almost a century or sometimes even much longer. Where I live, in the north of England, many older buildings have survived both World wars and the overzealous urban planners of the 1960s, and in one form or another, they retain some of their original character.

At ground level, many of these older buildings in cities such as Manchester or Liverpool have been redeveloped to accommodate modern shop fronts or offices with large areas of glass and modern signage. But up above, you'll often still see glimpses of what was there before.

Your own town or city may have a wealth of architectural history only a few feet above your eye level. This might include details in stonework or windows, which you might easily miss when you are focused only on getting to where you are going. The next time you are traveling to work, look up above eye level to get a different view of what you thought you knew. (Just be sure to keep half an eye on where you are going to avoid walking into a lamppost or falling over the newspaper seller on the corner.)

You can also get a different perspective by climbing the fire escape to the roof of your building or lying down on a bench and looking up at the buildings around you. You will see a different view of what you thought was so familiar.

Many of the sights in an urban environment can provide new and interesting ideas. By looking at the grid designs of many buildings, you may get ideas for innovative new grids for your Web page layouts that you may not have seen otherwise. Whereas you have seen that many newspaper designs are based on symmetrical grids, the proportions of buildings from different angles may inspire you to take a different approach. Where a building's grid has been softened by nature taking back control, perhaps where trees have softened the view or ivy has grown on the face of a building, you might be inspired to make designs that have a much more asymmetric feel.

All it takes to find inspiration is for you to go looking, and when you find something new or different that motivates you, share it by uploading photos of what you have found online to inspire others.

LITTLE MANHATTAN

DETAILS PG/90 mins, June 30
DIRECTOR Mark Levin
STARRING Josh Hutcherson, Bradley Whitford, Cynthia Nixon

YOUNG LOVE BLOSSOMS IN MODERN-DAY
Manhattan, but don't vomit just yet: this observational teen comedy has just enough sass to win over young adults. Much like TV's The Wonder Years (which director Mark Levin also story-edited and produced), it's narrated by 11-year-old Gabe (Josh Hutcherson), who recalls the summer he started to look at schoolmate Rosemary (Charlie Ray) in a new light. Romantic obstacles include her flowergirl duties and his shyness over kissing, but by using Gabe's POV, this depicts the uncertainties, agonies and ironies of first love with accuracy, affection and wry humour. Some points are laboured, and the build-up of Gabe's crush is overlong, but this remains an unexpectedly enjoyable little film that found one better at the US box office. **ANNA SMITH**

★★★

LOBO

DETAILS 15/125 mins, June 16
DIRECTOR Miguel Courtois
STARRING Eduardo Noriega, Silvia Abascal, Patrick Bruel

BASED ON TRUE EVENTS IN '70S SPAIN,
in which "El Lobo" ("The Wolf") infiltrated the higher echelons of terrorist group ETA, this taut political thriller – an award-winning smash hit in Spain – crackles with edginess, energy and contemporary frisson in precisely the same way that The Interpreter didn't. As a friend of several ETA activists, "Txema" (Eduardo Noriega) was well-placed to infiltrate the Basque separatists, but soon found himself at odds with both the rival factions of the group and the demands of his secret-service paymasters. Though set during the dying days of Franco's dictatorship, Courtois' film has plenty to say about such timely issues as the blurred lines between freedom fighter and terrorist, activism and anarchism.
DAVID HUGHES

★★★

ThinkPink hair straighteners. Glam up your hair in style!

Kittens. Is there anything cuter?

School holidays. Six weeks of no homework and no stress. Yay!

Losing your earring backs. Why don't they come with spares?

The World Cup Now it's over, who'd have thought we'd miss watching footie?

Sunburn. Lobster red is not a good look, plus it's dangerous.

MIDSUMMER ORGANIC SUNFLOWER OIL

GLAM BAND ALERT!

Keep an eye out for The Puppini Sisters – a '40s-inspired trio, who perform classic pop songs like *I Will Survive* in their own unique style! Their album *Betcha Bottom Dollar* is out on July 19th and will add a touch of glamour to the music scene! Go to www.thepuppinisisters.com.

expert

Nutritionist Julie Dean answers your questions.

Why is it so important for children to drink water?
● Dehydration can affect children's development, and can cause lethargy and constipation. Children who are drinking enough water will feel healthier, have more energy and find it easier to concentrate, too.

How much water should my child be drinking?
● Just like adults, children need around six to eight glasses of fluid a day. More fluids are required in hot weather and after exercise.

How do I know if my child is drinking enough water?
● Check the colour of their urine, which should be very pale. When

WISH LIST

1 Last-minute present hint to our loved ones – this DAB digital radio has been designed by the king of glam prints himself, Matthew Williamson, and is therefore Very Desirable Indeed. It's available from branches of John Lewis, all of which are open until at least 4pm today; £125, 08456 049049 (johnlewis.com).

2 Mug trees are inexcusable. Mug racks, on the other hand, are rather a good idea since they take storage pressure off shelves and cupboards. This one comes with four colour-toning mugs. One for the must-buy list, we reckon; £25, by Joseph Joseph, 020-7261 1800 (josephjoseph.com).

3 Come January, the design world will be focusing on all things Chinese, so why not get ahead of the trend by knocking yourself up a cushion in one of John Stefanidis' new Beijing fabrics? Pricey, but so right for 2006. Ladakh silk taffeta in Dusky Blue (W: 130cm), £129.95 a metre, from John Stefanidis, 020-7808 4700 (stefanidisfabrics.com).

4 This is the perfect stocking. Made from folksy American fabrics, it has the family heirloom feel that's so important at Christmas, but without any of those nasty, musty smells. If you can't make it to London EC1 today, at least you can phone up and reserve one for next year. Patchwork stocking, £35, by Chica Wixon, from Saloon,

BRAZILS
A study from the University Of Illinois suggests brazils might help prevent breast cancer, thanks to their high selenium content. They give you an energy buzz, too.

ALMONDS
These are real heart savers, as they're rich in a form of vitamin E called alpha-tocopherol, which lowers your risk of cardiac disease.

MACADAMIAS
University Of Hawaii found that people who ate high-fat macadamias had the same cholesterol levels as those on a low-fat diet.

Overheard
YouTube popularity is hell unless you're a fucking saint with nothing to hide, or you have indestructible confidence levels.
Emmalina, 18-year-old YouTube star
tinyurl.com/nnzeu

5 Balance scales
Spring balance scales,

Store in a cool, dry place and reclose the inner pack to prolong product life.

This pack is sold by weight and not volume. Some settling of contents may have occurred during transit. To redistribute the nuts before opening, turn box on side and shake gently.

↗ **Non GM**
↗ **Source of fibre**
↗ **No artificial flavourings, colourings or preservatives**

ALLERGEN INFORMATION
CONTAINS: Oats, Barley, Almonds, Hazelnuts, Brazil Nuts, Pecans
MAY CONTAIN: Wheat, Rye, Milk, Sesame Seeds, Other Nuts

INGREDIENTS
Conservation Grade Wholegrain Oat Flakes, Raw Cane Sugar, Nuts (16.5%), (Flaked Almonds, Roast Hazelnuts, Flaked Brazil Nuts, Pecans), Conservation Grade Barley Flakes, Vegetable Oil (Rapeseed Oil, Palm Oil), Rice Flour, Desiccated Coconut, Conservation Grade Wholegrain Oat Flour, Sea Salt, Natural Hazelnut Paste.

AtHome/DVD Club
FURTHER VIEWING
Run out of Woody? Try these...

DUCK SOUP (1933)
The Marx Brothers' unique mix of cerebral wit and perfect slapstick is a huge influence on Woody, and in Groucho he found a way into his own on-screen comic persona: a smart-arsed wiseacre, fuelled by nervous energy, forever chasing after unattainable women.

8 1/2 (1962)
Fellini's masterpiece is an autobiographical drama lifted

BEST SELLERS
The big make-up houses produce bucket-loads of their best-selling bases – here are their most popular.
1 Bobbi Brown Stick Foundation, £24 (16 shades): the original stick foundation and still one of the best.
2 Yves Saint Laurent Radiance Smoothing Foundation, £26.50 (eight shades): contains light-reflective particles to give tired skin a glowing boost.
3 Lancôme Adaptive, £20.50 (nine shades): mattifies and moisturises at the same time.
4 Diorskin Pure Light, £22 (six shades): gives an oil-free, reflective finish.

NEW BOOKS
Switch off your telly and read something instead!
The Story Of Film
By: Mark Cousins
Supplied by: Pavilion
Price: £25.00
Film history is no simple thing. It is filled with more twists than an M Night Shyamalan picture, more nuances than *Citizen Kane* and more stories than there could ever be time to tell. Giving anything more than a whistle-stop tour is a laborious undertaking for both writer and reader, however, Mark Cousins stations through the silent era, Hollywood and the European avant-garde to Japanese and other non-Western filmmaking. At every turn he is incisive, colourful, provocative and probing. This is a truly important piece of history literature. Read it now.

THE STORY OF FILM

Laun Platfo
New webs challenge
URL www.adob flash/special/fla
Designed by Bl
What would the without Flash? N isn't it? To celeb anniversary, Ado interactive timeli previews with son Adobe's chief of Lynch), and plen

The Chosen Ten

OFFIC FAVO
The DVD colleagu pinching

1 HOU FLYIN DAGG 20TH C

2 MEE FOC SEM

to mum

I hated gory walking it has been I

Scrapbooking with a goal in mind

I always recommend designers look for inspiration wherever they go without an end result in mind. By keeping an open mind to whatever you see around you, you will not be limited by the practicalities of how useful an item might be or how you can use it. Sometimes you are looking for a specific spark to add something different to a design, and you will need to set out to look for that special something.

If you are as bored as I am with the traditional arrangements of many online stores and the way they present their products and you are hungry for something a little different, go looking for the many different ways products are presented in different forms of print. In magazines, products are arranged in hundreds of ways, and many of those ways can make for unusual product displays if adapted for the Web.

Magazine Contents pages from different types of publications can also provide clues to new ways to present content on a site's homepage. All the key elements are there: summaries and links to pages inside the magazine, featured or lead stories, and often a letter from the editor that could so easily become a company's key message to their customers. These pages are full of content and links that when transposed to become Web pages can provide highly useful content to readers and also enhance a site's search engine visibility.

Of course, slavishly copying a design or layout from one medium into another is never going to achieve the full benefits of that new medium. The Web is not print, and a Contents page is not a homepage; yet we can be inspired by looking for creative opportunities in similar or related places. You can even give the most common Web interface elements a new lease on life by bringing in ideas from unexpected places. The humble sidebar, common to most Web pages, can benefit from techniques more commonly found in print. Images that break out of their columns to add a more organic visual flow can help Web designs avoid looking too structured or boxy. You can give form elements, very difficult to present in new and interesting ways, a new twist by adding graphic details that may be inspired by a teenage magazine's puzzle page.

Looking at the design elements you create time and time again in different ways can be creatively liberating, and with today's techniques of using CSS, JavaScript, Flash, or a combination of all three, you now have fewer restrictions on what you are able to achieve creatively on the Web.

Magazine cuttings from my scrapbook suggest new and interesting ways to design for the Web

Product
Brownie
Prep Date
3/11/05

Initials
JM

Discard Date
3/14/05

THURSDAY
10
MAR 05

NOT FOR SALE

KEEP

THIS TRANSFER/
FARE RECEIPT
AS PROOF
OF PAYMENT

USE FOR
TRAVEL IN ANY
DIRECTION UNTIL
TIME INDICATED

The Fine Art of Web Design

In this part, you have seen how important it is for designers to look outside to both new and established media and bring some of those ideas to the Web. You have also seen how you can bring new life to your designs without thinking first about the constraints of implementing those designs in legacy browsers.

Today, thousands of sites—from blogs to designer portfolios and from small businesses to multinational corporations—all rely on CSS. This has caused even experienced Web designers to wonder whether we can learn much more about Web design and about CSS. In 2006, Australian developer and cofounder of the Web Standards Awards gallery site, Cameron Adams, wrote about closing the gallery:

> Now we've arrived at a situation where beautiful sites with beautiful code are being produced by the hundreds; every month, every week, every day. It's no longer a myth that you can produce a stunning site with Web standards. We feel that our mission is complete, that standards have now ensured their rightful place in the process of Web design. So, it's time to hang up our spurs.
>
> —Cameron Adams (http://webstandardsawards.com)

Along with other online galleries showcasing CSS design, the Web Standards Awards site (**Figure 3.46**) succeeded in demonstrating that using valid, meaningful markup and CSS can result in highly creative sites. But I question Adams's notion we have reached the limits of what we can learn or should aim to achieve. Should we accept that we have taken CSS design as far as we can? Are we prepared to believe that there is little more we can do?

Designers should do more

We have not reached the pinnacle of what we can achieve with CSS-based design. Even though the Web is still relatively young, we have already been told what good Web design should be. Usability specialist Jakob Nielsen has repeatedly said that good design is about conventions and about following rules: typically his rules.

One of Nielsen's central themes is that visitors have been taught what to expect from the Web sites they visit regularly, and therefore this familiarity creates conventions Web designers should follow when creating usable Web sites.

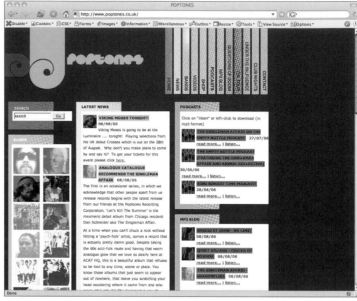

 Taking CSS to new heights

I'm not dismissing Nielsen's respected ideas out of hand. But I do take issue with his notion that just because visitors are familiar with a convention, that makes it right in all cases. After all, how can you know yet what is good Web design when the Web as a mainstream, commercial medium is still only a decade old?

Throughout the history of art, successive generations have often rejected the conventions of the past and invented new rules to challenge the old. In modern times, the cubists, abstract expressionists, and pop artists of the 1950s and 1960s looked at what went before, assimilated some ideas, and rejected others. They often looked to the modern world for their inspiration and incorporated modern ideas and materials to create new and exciting work.

Popular music takes inspiration from what has gone before, but when done well, it is not afraid to adapt to modern tastes and prides itself on making previous generations uncomfortable with new sounds. Without the Beatles there may not have been the Jam; without the Jam there may not have been Oasis—or the Brit pop bands that followed them.

You can and should be continually making and breaking rules as you learn more about the Web and how people use it. Now is not the time to stop. Much of the recent buzz over Web 2.0 solutions assumes we have learned something from Web 1.0. I believe the Web is far from version 2.0; it is barely into the alpha version, and I see many of the mistakes of the past being repeated again, this time with the added gloss of big footers, rounded corners, and often inappropriate uses for Ajax and related technologies.

We must ask ourselves, have we really understood everything there is to know about what makes a well-designed Web site? Is the layout and structure of Amazon the pinnacle of what can be achieved with e-commerce? Does the simplicity of Google's antidesign mean that search interfaces have reached their minimalist best? When we look at the Web today, it's clear we have so much more to experiment with and to learn.

It is important to remember that the Web is a creative industry and visual designers and developers should not solely focus on technologies; instead, you should focus on what you want to achieve creatively. Only then should you use the most appropriate technologies to accomplish your creative goals. The world around us is a collage of inspiration, and the Web is a collage of technologies. The key to success is knowing when and how to best use those technologies: This is what makes Web design a fine art.

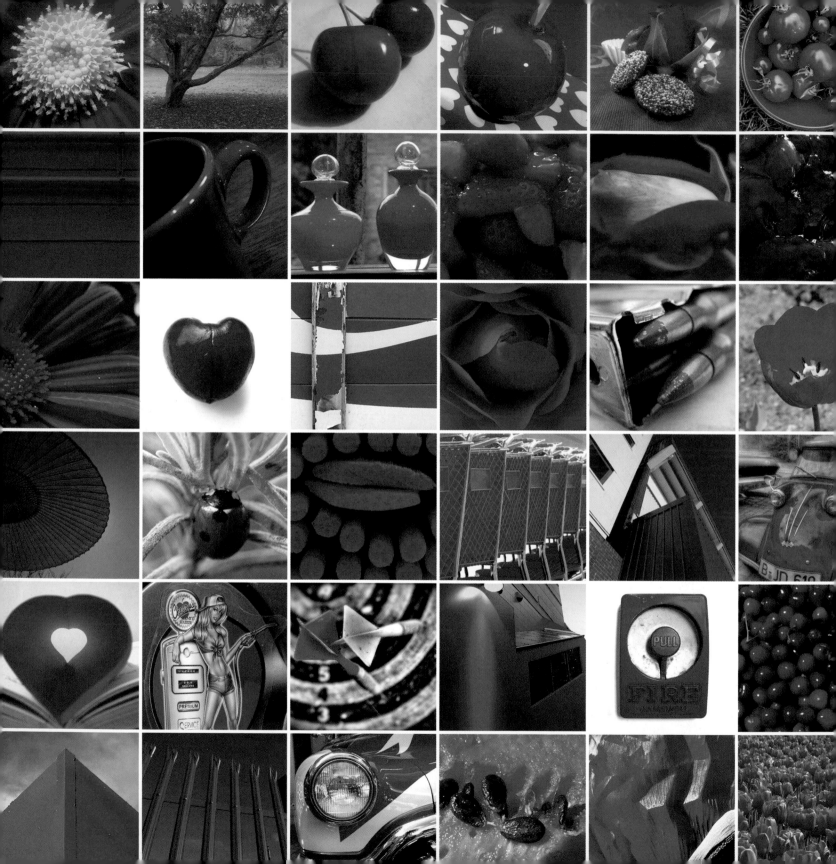

4

Transcendence

Work with CSS positioning and floats

Explore the developments in CSS3

Create with the Absolute Layout Module

Transcendent CSS

So, you're nearing the end of this book, but the fat lady isn't singing just yet. In this final part, you'll bring together all the principles and approaches you have learned this far. You'll focus on using meaningful markup and Transcendent CSS to create a series of new designs for layouts and interface elements. These have all been inspired by different sources from the pages of my own scrapbook.

> **Note:** Rather than taking a more conventional book approach, each of the examples focuses not on a single technique but on how to combine techniques to create inspiring results.

Not all the techniques that I'll cover, or all the examples you will develop, will work or look the same across all browsers; some will, and some won't. Don't worry; this is intentional because this book is concerned with what is possible within today's standards-aware browsers. So, I will not attempt to cover hacks, patches, or workarounds to create pixel-perfect rendering across all browsers or attempt to deal with older browsers.

If you are working in an agency or consultancy environment, saying "To hell with bad browsers" may be a more realistic option than if you are working within a larger organization or perhaps even a government department where it may be more difficult to convince your managers of the need to move forward.

Fortunately, certain solutions make it possible for you to fully adopt CSS2.1 and have it work in what is today the most used browser on the Web.

Absolute positioning

CSS positioning has fallen a little out of favor in recent years. Where once it provided the backbone to many early CSS layouts, designers have largely given up positioning for layouts and instead have concentrated on floated layouts. This is unfortunate because positioning is one of the most powerful design tools you will find in CSS.

CSS has four positioning values:

- **Relative**: Better described as *offsetting*, relative positioning moves an element from where it would usually appear in the normal flow. For example, an offset of top : 1em; will move an element up a distance of 1 em but will leave a ghosted space behind where the element would have been before offsetting.

- **Absolute**: Absolute positioning positions an element according to its closest positioned containing block within the document tree. In the absence of a positioned containing block, an absolutely positioned element will take its position from the root element, <html>. Throughout this book, I will refer to a positioned containing block as an element's *positioning context*.

- **Fixed**: An element that is positioned with a value of fixed is always positioned in respect to the viewport of the browser window and stays in position, even when the visitor scrolls the document. Fixed positioning is considered a type of absolute positioning.

- **Static**: This is an element's default position in the normal flow of the document. The static value is useful really only for overriding any previous positioning rules.

> **Note:** For a more detailed look at the differences in positioning schemes, Tommy Olsson has written a fantastic introduction on his now sadly defunct Web site at www.autisticcuckoo. net/archive.php?id=2004/12/07/relatively-absolute.

On the opposite page (**Figure 4.1**) is the visual design you are aiming to achieve for this first example, plus the elements you will use to convey the meaning of your content. You will create the design using only this minimal, but highly meaningful, markup. This design could have several uses, from a small interface panel to a whole new way of arranging products on an e-commerce Web site.

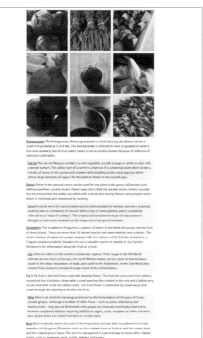

4.1 The inspiration for the design (top), the final layout (bottom), and the markup (right)

List items, list anything

It might at first seem strange to see headings and paragraphs enclosed within a list item. Unordered lists and their ordered counterparts are two of the most useful and flexible elements available in XHTML and you can use them to present a wide variety of content when a series of content elements forms a list, such as a list of product names and descriptions, a list of addresses, or even a list of specification tables.

Note

What? No alternative text in the `alt` attribute? No. In this context where the images immediately precede their descriptive text, I have chosen to set an empty alt "string" on each image, which is perfectly valid and accessible. You don't need to force users of a screen reader to hear the same word twice.

Before you start working with CSS, you'll see how just the "naked" document appears in a browser, which will help you understand the order of the content and how it might appear to a visitor for whom the style sheet might not be available (**Figure 4.2**).

The markup you need to accomplish this design is about as simple as it gets: just one unordered list. Each of the named list items contains a heading, an anchor, an image, and a paragraph of descriptive text:

```
<li id="pomegranate">
<h3><a href="#pomegranate">
<img src="1-1.jpg" alt="" />Pomegranate</a></h3>
<p>Descriptive text</p>
</li>
```

Setting the stage

You'll set the stage for this design by giving the `<body>` element a fixed-pixel width, centered in the browser window. At this point, it is also a good idea to set basic `<font>` and `<color>` values:

```
body    {
width : 500px;
margin : 0 auto;
background-color : #fff;
font : 72%/1.6 "Lucida Grande", Verdana, sans-serif;
color : #333; }
```

This design relies on positioning that takes the images out of their usual position in the normal flow of the document and places them at the top of the window. But before you can position the images, you need to establish the positioning context for these positioned images by adding `position : relative;` (with no offsets) to the unordered list.

Remember the explanation of the four types of positioning? An absolutely positioned element takes its position from its most recent positioned containing block. This containing block can have any of the positioning methods but static applied to it, including `position : relative;`. In this example, the positioning context has no offsets applied to it and will stay in its calculated position in the normal flow of the document. It will, however, become the positioning context for any of its positioned children.

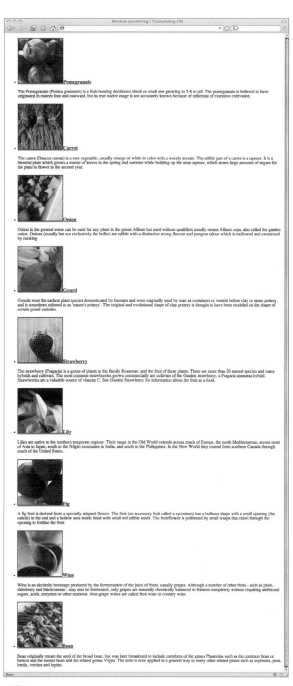

- **Pomegranate**

The Pomegranate (Punica granatum) is a fruit-bearing deciduous shrub or small tree growing to 5-8 m tall. The pomegranate is believed to have originated in eastern Iran and eastward, but its true native range is not accurately known because of millennia of extensive cultivation.

- **Carrot**

The carrot (Daucus carota) is a root vegetable, usually orange or white in color with a woody texture. The edible part of a carrot is a taproot. It is a biennial plant which grows a rosette of leaves in the spring and summer while building up the stout taproot, which stores large amounts of sugars for the plant to flower in the second year.

- **Onion**

Onion in the general sense can be used for any plant in the genus Allium but used without qualifiers usually means Allium cepa, also called the garden onion. Onions (usually but not exclusively the bulbs) are edible with a distinctive strong flavour and pungent odour which is mellowed and sweetened by cooking.

- **Gourd**

Gourds were the earliest plant species domesticated by humans and were originally used by man as containers or vessels before clay or stone pottery, and is sometimes referred to as 'nature's pottery'. The original and evolutional shape of clay pottery is thought to have been modeled on the shape of certain gourd varieties.

- **Strawberry**

The strawberry (Fragaria) is a genus of plants in the family Rosaceae, and the fruit of these plants. There are more than 20 named species and many hybrids and cultivars. The most common strawberries grown commercially are cultivars of the Garden strawberry, a Fragaria ananassa hybrid. Strawberries are a valuable source of vitamin C. See Garden Strawberry for information about the fruit as a food.

- **Lily**

Lilies are native to the northern temperate regions. Their range in the Old World extends across much of Europe, the north Mediterranean, across most of Asia to Japan, south to the Nilgiri mountains in India, and south to the Philippines. In the New World they extend from southern Canada through much of the United States.

- **Fig**

A fig fruit is derived from a specially adapted flower. The fruit (an accessory fruit called a syconium) has a bulbous shape with a small opening (the ostiole) in the end and a hollow area inside lined with small red edible seeds. The fruit/flower is pollinated by small wasps that crawl through the opening to fertilise the fruit.

- **Wine**

Wine is an alcoholic beverage produced by the fermentation of the juice of fruits, usually grapes. Although a number of other fruits - such as plum, elderberry and blackcurrant - may also be fermented, only grapes are naturally chemically balanced to ferment completely without requiring additional sugars, acids, enzymes or other nutrients. Non-grape wines are called fruit wine or country wine.

- **Bean**

Bean originally meant the seed of the broad bean, but was later broadened to include members of the genus Phaseolus such as the common bean or haricot and the runner bean and the related genus Vigna. The term is now applied in a general way to many other related plants such as soybeans, peas, lentils, vetches and lupins.

4.2 Viewing the "naked" document

 Adding top padding for creating space in which to position images

 Absolutely positioning images into the created space

Also, clear 510 pixels of space for the images by applying top padding to the list that is equal to the height of three rows of images (**Figure 4.3**). Because nothing is as boring as looking at an empty space, I have added a dotted, red border around the space where the images will appear.

```
ul {
position : relative;
padding-top : 510px; }
```

Positioning the images

The real magic in this design (**Figure 4.4**) occurs when you move the images from their position in the normal flow and position them in the space you have created:

```
h3 img {
position : absolute; }

#pomegranate h3 img { top : 0; left : 0; }
#carrot h3 img { top : 0; left : 170px; }
#onion h3 img { top : 0; left : 340px; }
#gourd h3 img { top : 170px; left : 0; }
#strawberry h3 img { top : 170px; left : 170px; }
#lily h3 img { top : 170px; left : 340px; }
#fig h3 img { top : 340px; left : 0; }
#wine h3 img { top : 340px; left : 170px; }
#bean h3 img { top : 340px; left : 340px; }
```

While I'm on the subject of images, you can also add some subtle styling to the images by giving them padding and a 1-pixel outline:

```
h3 img {
position : absolute;
padding : 1px;
outline : 1px solid #ccc; }
```

Playing with your food

If the Web were a food, then I'd like it not to be as dull as instant mashed potatoes, so your next job will be to add a little gravy in the form of behaviors, enabled not by JavaScript but by CSS.

You can begin tidying up the typography by adding padding and a subtle, alternating color scheme. To target the list items that will receive the different `background-color` attributes, you will use the elements' unique `id`:

```
li { margin-bottom : .5em; }

li#carrot, li#gourd, li#lily, li#wine {
padding : .5em;
background-color : #fcf3ea; }

h3, p { display : inline; }
h3 { font-weight : normal; }
p { color : #666; }
```

One of the most important differences between the Web and a printed page is the ability to make your designs interactive for your visitors. Sometimes this will involve scripting; other times you can use CSS to add subtle behaviors. Of course, some designers might argue that JavaScript, not CSS, is the rightful home of behaviors, but that is an argument best left for a walk along Brighton Beach.

You'll start by adding a subtle `:hover` behavior to your images for when the visitor's mouse passes over them:

```
a:hover img { outline : 1px solid #000; }
```

The interaction need not stop there. Remember that you placed each image inside an anchor?

```
<a href="#pomegranate"><img src="1-1.jpg" alt="" />Pomegranate</a>
```

Now you can put those anchors to work by using the `:target` pseudo-class. When your visitors click an anchor, they will be taken directly to the named list item (**Figure 4.5**). You'll then give this targeted list item a different background color, a border, and higher-contrast text:

```
li:target {
margin : .5em 0;
padding : .5em;
border : 1px solid #dab69c;
color : #000; }

li:target p { color : #000; }
```

Note

Because of a lack of implementation, you may not have previously used the `outline` property, which specifies an outline for a box. Drawn around the outside of the border and on top of a box, the outline does not affect the height or width of a box.

Note

If you haven't had the time yet to cook up this design for yourself, don't worry; I have saved you the trouble. You can find all the files you need for this tasty example at www.transcendingcss.com/support/.

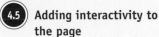

4.5 Adding interactivity to the page

Same design, different markup

I am sure the debate over how to mark up this type of content will rumble on long after I have ridden my scooter into the sunset. Some Web designers and their developer counterparts will insist that an unordered list containing headings and paragraphs is best; others will argue the case for a definition list.

When using CSS to the fullest, it matters little which markup solution you prefer—each is just as valid. To accomplish your design, CSS does the presentational hard work, whatever the markup.

Look at the screenshots shown here (**Figure 4.6**). On the left is the visual result of using an unordered list, and on the right is a definition list complete with definition terms and descriptions. Can you see a difference?

4.6 Showing that the same visual design can be achieved even when different markup is used

CSS image zoom sidebar

When it comes to writing markup, I am fundamentally lazy. I much prefer sorting through my record collection than rewriting lines of code several times. When you need to re-create this design as a sidebar, what could be better than reusing the markup from the previous example?

For this design, you will transform the same unordered list into a sidebar—but this is a sidebar with a difference. Your first job is to make several minor changes to the CSS, which sets the stage for your sidebar and any content that sits alongside it. You are opting here for a flexible content area that will expand to fill 80 percent of the width of the browser window:

```
body    {
width : 80%;
margin : 0 auto;
padding : 40px 0;
background-color : #fff;
font : 72%/1.6 "Lucida Grande", Verdana, sans-serif;
color : #333; }
```

In this design, a single unordered list is all it takes to create the sidebar; an outer, container division is not required. Start by floating the list to the left and styling it to match this new design. Then add a background color, a border, and space at its top into which to position the images:

```
ul {
position : relative;
float : left;
width : 316px;
margin-right : 20px;
padding : 350px 10px 40px 10px;
background-color : #fcf3ea;
border : 1px solid #dab69c; }
```

Finally, style the text and the images. If your images are larger than 100 pixels, give them a display size of 100 pixels by 100 pixels. Under regular circumstances, resizing images using either HTML or CSS is not recommended. Enlarging an image will often result in pixilated results, and reducing the display size of a large image will increase the time it takes for an image to download. In this example, the minor changes to the image sizes will create the zoom effect using a single set of images:

```
li, h3, p { display : inline; }
li p { color : #666; }

h3 img {
position : absolute;
padding : 1px;
height : 100px;
width : 100px;
outline : 1px solid #ccc; }
```

Position each image in a grid design by using absolute positioning (**Figure 4.7**):

```
#pomegranate h3 img { top : 10px; left : 10px; }
#carrot h3 img { top : 10px; left : 115px; }
#onion h3 img { top : 10px; left : 220px; }
#gourd h3 img { top : 115px; left : 10px; }
#strawberry h3 img { top : 115px; left : 115px; }
#lily h3 img { top : 115px; left : 220px; }
#fig h3 img { top : 220px; left : 10px; }
#wine h3 img { top : 220px; left : 115px; }
#bean h3 img { top : 220px; left : 220px; }
```

4.7 Using absolute positioning for the grid design

Image zoom with CSS

Using CSS can help you create interactive, unconventional designs without scripting. For this design, your aim is to create an image-zooming feature by using CSS dynamic pseudo-classes. You need only one set of images to create the effect.

Start building the zooming effect by defining a style for the images only for when a visitor's mouse hovers over them. This new style changes the display size of the images and adds padding and a higher-contrast border:

```
a:hover img {
width : 160px;
height : 160px;
padding : 5px;
background-color : #fff;
border : 1px solid #333; }
```

This simple CSS should be all you need to create the zooming effect, but it has a "gotcha." If you do not give a positioned element a specific z-index value, the last element in the document source appears closest to the viewer. This will result in your cunningly repositioned images staying behind those that follow them in the source order of the document. This is hardly the effect you want (**Figure 4.8**).

Adding a high z-index value to all your images will ensure that these hover images stay in front of their neighbors:

```
a:hover img {
z-index : 100; }
```

Excited? Fire up your nearest Web browser to see the effect of your CSS image-zooming interface in action (**Figure 4.9**).

4.8 **Without a z-index value, images remain behind those that follow in the source order**

Pomegranate The Pomegranate (Punica granatum) is a fruit-bearing deciduous shrub or small tree growing to

Pomegranate The Pomegranate (Punica granatum) is a fruit-bearing deciduous shrub or small tree growing to

Pomegranate The Pomegranate (Punica granatum) is a fruit-bearing deciduous shrub or small tree growing to

Pomegranate The Pomegranate (Punica granatum) is a fruit-bearing deciduous shrub or small tree growing to

4.9 By setting a z-index value, the rollover effect is created

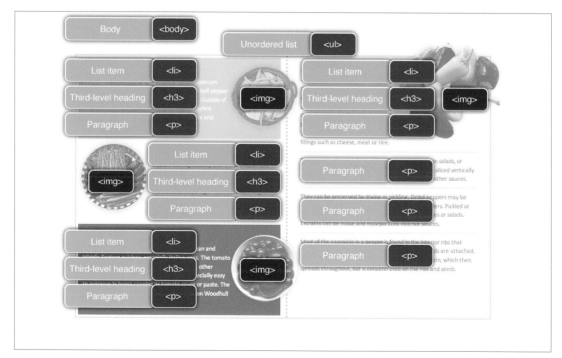

(4.10) The inspiration for the design (left), the final layout (right), and the markup (bottom)

Relative positioning

One of the main principles of the Transcendent CSS approach is the separation of meaning and presentation not only in your markup but also in your mind.

Look at the following example, and remember the content-out approach you learned in Part 1, "Discovery." The markup is essentially the same as the examples you worked with earlier, although the visual design and layout are different (**Figure 4.10**).

Set the stage for this flexible layout, a design that will expand to 92 percent of the browser window width but will never go smaller than 770 pixels:

```
body    {
width : 92%;
min-width : 770px;
margin : 0 auto;
padding : 100px 0;
background-color : #fff;
font : 88%/1.4 Calibri, "Lucida Grande", Verdana, sans-serif;
color : #333; }
```

You should add `position : relative;` to establish the unordered list as the positioning context for any of its positioned descendents:

```
ul { position : relative; }
```

Add a `border` and a dotted `background-image` property that will repeat vertically in the center:

```
ul {
border : 2px solid #96b440;
background : url(ul.png) repeat-y 51% 0; }
```

Each list item will expand to fill half the width of your list. To give each item its own distinctive styling, target it by using its `id` attribute value:

```
li {
position : relative;
width : 49%;
padding bottom : .5em; }
```

```
#pepper {
margin : 5px;
background : #96b440; color : #fff; }

#tomato {
margin : 5px;
background : #a00100;
color : #fff; }

#cuisine {
position : absolute;
top : 0;
right : 0; }
```

Styling the headings

Each of your list items contains the following: a third-level heading, a paragraph of text, and an inline image.

Your first task is to style each of the headings with unique margins, padding, and subtle control over typography:

```
h3 {
margin : 0 10px;
padding : 10px 0;
font : 160% Constantia, Verdana, sans-serif;
letter-spacing : 1px; }
```

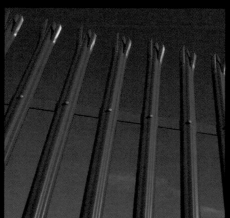

```
#asparagus h3 {
margin-right : 0;
padding-left : 160px; }

#cuisine h3 {
margin : 0 20px 10px 30px;
padding-bottom : 10px;
font-size : 200%;
border-bottom : 1px solid #333; }
```

Paragraphs

The key to making this layout break away from a rigid, box-based design is a combination of positioning and alpha-transparent PNG images. These images break out of their containers to give the design a more organic feel. You should start by applying right and left margins and some bottom padding to add white space around your text and give it room to breathe:

```
p { margin : 0 10px; padding-bottom : 10px; }
```

You will soon be giving each image its own position. Right and left padding within the paragraphs that contain them will create the space into which these images will then be positioned (**Figure 4.11**):

```
#pepper p {
margin-right : 0;
padding-right : 110px; }

#asparagus p {
margin-right : 0;
padding-left : 160px; }
```

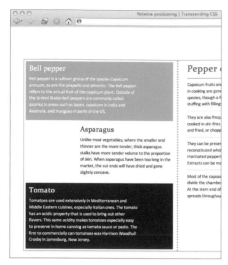

4.11 Creating padding around the paragraphs gives needed space for images

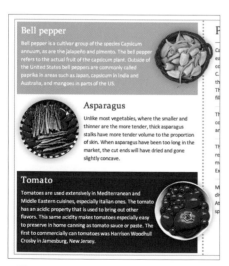

4.12 Positioning images absolutely

```
#tomato p {
margin-right : 0;
padding-right : 110px; }

#cuisine p {
margin : 0 30px 10px 30px;
border-bottom : 1px solid #ccc; }
```

Positioning the images

Now you can absolutely position three of the images into the spaces you have created (**Figure 4.12**):

```
li img { position : absolute; }

#pepper img {
top : 10px;
right : -50px;  }

#asparagus img {
top : -5px;
left : 0; }

#tomato img {
top : 10px;
right : -50px; }
```

The image within the `id` of `cuisine` demands special treatment. You will use a combination of techniques to achieve the visual effect you are looking for in this design.

Adding `float : right;` to this image enables its neighboring text to flow around it:

```
#cuisine img {
float : right; }
```

By positioning the image relatively, offset from its position in the normal flow, you can move the image outside the confines of both the list item and the unordered list (**Figure 4.13**):

```
#cuisine img {
position : relative;
top : -100px;
right : -60px; }
```

Negative margins

What about all that white space? It's not quite the desired visual effect you were looking to achieve. It is important to remember that when an element is relatively positioned, it is visually offset from where it would ordinarily appear within the normal flow, and the Web browser reserves that space and does not allow other elements to flow into it.

The answer to this unwanted white space comes from using negative margins on this offset image. By setting a negative top margin value, the following text is effectively moved up over the space where the image would have been displayed before it was offset (**Figure 4.14**):

```
#cuisine img {
margin : 0 0 -100px -70px; }
```

Note: You can find all the files you need for this example at www.transcendingcss.com/support/.

With this sound knowledge of how positioning works, you will find that you have even greater confidence to turn the humblest meaningful markup into striking designs that break away from common Web design conventions (**Figure 4.15**).

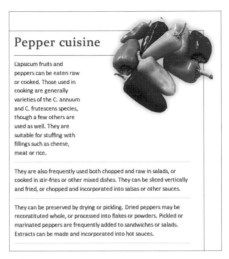

 Adding a sophisticated look by positioning images outside the list item and ordered list

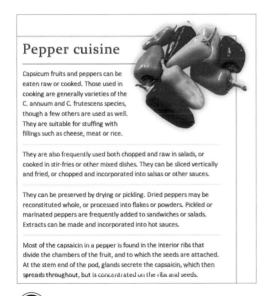

4.14 **Using an effective negative top margin value**

4.15 **Accomplishing a rich Web design using relative positioning**

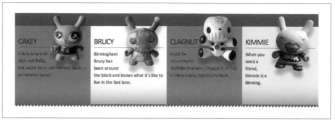

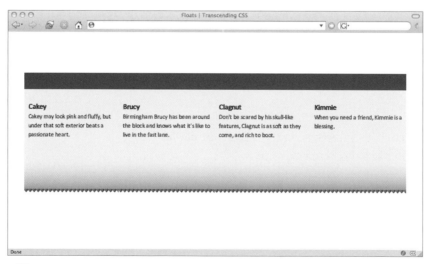

4.16 The inspiration for the layout (left), the final design (right), and the markup (bottom)

4.17 Floating the listed items

Creative floating

For the next example (**Figure 4.16**), I have already made an interface element for a toyshop Web site. You will use a combination of floats and percentage measurements to create a flexible and distinctive product layout.

Look closely, and you will see that a single ordered list is the most appropriate element to choose. What you can't see, but is equally as important as the design, is that the combined total weight of markup and CSS is a tiny 4 KB.

Start implementing the design by setting a few basic styles for the <body> of your page:

```
body    {
background-color : #fff;
font : 82%/1.4 Calibri, "Lucida Grande", Verdana, sans-serif;
color : #333; }
```

In many lists that display products or are used for navigation, items are listed in no particular order, so an unordered list is the most appropriate element. For this example, imagine that the items are listed in order of their popularity, meaning an ordered list would be most appropriate.

First define the width of your list, up to a maximum of 92 percent of a containing element and down to a minimum width of 950 pixels:

```
ol {
width : 92%;
min-width : 950px;
margin : 0 auto;
border-top : 40px solid #e94c92; }
```

A thick pink border tops off the design. With the styling for the ordered list now defined, it is time to float each of its items. Because this design has four items, set a symmetrical width of 25 percent on each (**Figure 4.17**):

```
li {
float : left;
width : 25%;
padding-top : 2em;
background : #f6ecf5 url(li.png) repeat-x 0 100%; }
```

Dean Edwards's IE7 scripts

In 2005, with browser development at Microsoft stalled at Internet Explorer 6 and with no plans to release an updated browser before the Windows Vista operating system, Web designers and developers had grown increasingly frustrated at Internet Explorer's lack of development.

Dean Edwards, a UK-based developer with a Web server in his kitchen and a passion for standards and for scripting, decided to take matters into his own hands and advance IE through the use of clever scripting. Edwards's solution uses JavaScript to parse style sheets into a form that Internet Explorer 6 and older versions can understand.

Dean Edwards's IE7 scripts allow you to use CSS2 and even some CSS3 selectors in your style sheets to transform legacy versions of Internet Explorer into a shiny new browser capable of interpreting the following:

- Child selectors

- Adjacent sibling selectors

- Attribute value selectors

- `:first-child`, `:last-child`, `:only-child`, and `:nth-child` structural pseudo-classes

- `:before` and `:after` generated content

The scripts enable `:hover`, `:active`, and `:focus` dynamic pseudo-classes on all elements, not just on links, and they make fixed positioning possible. Dean Edwards's IE7 scripts also add support for PNG alpha-transparency within older versions of Internet Explorer.

> **Note:** You can download all the necessary Dean Edwards IE7 files along with the full implementation instructions at http://dean.edwards.name/IE7/.

CONDITION IS EVERYTHING

Microsoft engineers have suggested that designers and developers abandon their use of CSS hacks and switch to using Microsoft's proprietary conditional comments. *Conditional comments* are supported only by Internet Explorer for Windows, and they make it simple to target versions of Internet Explorer by placing comments in the `<head>` portion of your document. Although the most common use for these comments is to serve specific style sheets to work around bugs and rendering errors in legacy Internet Explorer versions, you can just as easily use them to serve Dean Edwards's IE7 scripts only to browsers that need them. For example, this comment will serve the ie7-standard-p.js file only to versions of Internet Explorer 6 and older.

```
<!--[if lte IE6]>
<script src="ie7-standard-p.js" type="text/javascript">
</script>
<![endif]-->
```

Attribute and child selectors

For this example, you will use attribute selectors in place of the more normal id selectors (i.e., #cake) to bind the styling to each element and to give three of the four list items their own distinctive background color.

Attribute selectors are amazingly powerful; they offer ways to style an element either based on whether an element has an attribute name such as href or based on the attribute value.

You will also be using *child selectors*. These offer you the ability to style elements based on their parent element.

For this example, you'll use both attribute selectors and child selectors to give three of the four list items their own distinctive background color:

```
li[id="cake"], li[id="clagnut"] {
background-color : #e185bb; }

li[id="brucy"] {
background-color : #fff; }
```

Now style each of the headings and paragraphs that are children of the list items, transforming their typographic style and giving each a 1-pixel bottom border:

```
li > h3 {
margin : 0 10px 10px 10px;
font-size : 160%;
font-weight : normal;
text-transform : uppercase;
letter-spacing : -1px;
border-bottom : 1px solid #e94c92;
color : #a6376a; }

li > p { margin : 0 10px; }
```

Once again, by floating images you allow the text to wrap around them. By offsetting the images using negative positioning and then by using a negative bottom margin, which allows any text to move up into the space left behind, the design takes on a more fluid feel, free from the confines of conventional boxes (**Figure 4.18**):

```
h3 > img {
position : relative;
top : -100px;
float : right;
margin-bottom : -120px; }
```

Playing with the layout

You could choose to alter this design in a host of different ways, all without making
any changes to your meaningful markup. For example, try floating the images to the left
and then use relative positioning to visually place the images between the list items
(**Figure 4.19**):

```
li { position : relative; }

li > p { margin : 0 40px 0 10px; }

h3 > img {
float : left;
position : relative;
top : -10px;
left : -50px;
margin-right : -50px; }
```

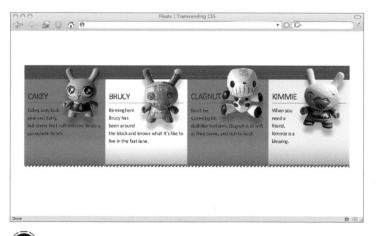

4.18 Using negative positioning and a negative bottom margin
gives a more fluid look and feel

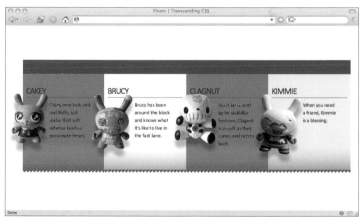

4.19 Visually place the images between list items by
floating and using relative positioning

Making a sidebar

If sidebars are what you are seeking, look no further. You can easily transform the same markup from the previous example into a sidebar. In the grand tradition, apply basic styles to the <body> element and list:

```
body      {
background-color : #f9e6f6;
font : 92%/1.4 Calibri, "Lucida Grande", Verdana, sans-serif;
color : #333; }

ol {
width : 300px;
margin : 0 auto; }
```

Add a fat border to the list and a background-image property at the top to give an extra level of cuteness that matches the characters on display. Note that the 150-pixel top padding matches the height of the background image. This padding moves the list items down to allow the image to show:

```
ol {
float : right;
width : 300px;
margin : 0 auto;
padding-top : 150px;
background : #fff url(ul.png) no-repeat;
border : 5px solid #e94c92; }
```

Now pull those attribute selectors out of the bag one more time to create the striped, alternating background on every second item (**Figure 4.20**):

```
li {
clear : both;
padding : .5em 10px; }

li[id="cake"], li[id="clagnut"]{ background-color : #f185bb; }
```

4.20 **Creating alternating backgrounds on the sidebar**

Relatively position and float your images, and use negative margins to suck the neighboring text into the space created by their offset (**Figure 4.21**):

```
h3 {
text-align : right;
font-size : 160%;
font-weight : normal;
text-transform : uppercase;
border-bottom : 1px solid #e94c92;
color : #a6376a; }

h3 > img {
position : relative;
top : -60px;
left : 0;
float : left;
margin : 0 0 -70px -50px; }
```

4.21 Using negative margins for neighboring text

Remember Part 2, "Process," where you learned about wireframing with XHTML and CSS? What if your client asks you to switch the position of your swanky new sidebar from the right of the page to the left? With some minor edits to your CSS, you are ready to go (**Figure 4.22**):

```
h3 {
text-align : left;
font-size : 160%;
font-weight : normal;
text-transform : uppercase;
border-bottom : 1px solid #e94c92;
color : #a6376a; }

h3 > img {
position : relative;
top : -60px;
right : 0;
float : right;
margin : 0 -50px -70px 0; }
```

4.22 Switching the positioning of the sidebars

£18.00 PER BUNCH

£4.00 EACH

£10.00 PER STEM

£6.00 PER STEM

Flowers in my garden

Purple Tulip

The national flower of Iran and Turkey, and tulip motifs feature prominently.

The European name for the flower comes from the Persian word for turban, a origin probably originating in the common Turkish custom of wearing flowers in the folds of the turban.

Lily

Martagons appreciate some shade, and are quite decorative in the garden.

Along with the earliest of the asiatics, blooms another entirely different group called the martagons, or martagons hansonii hybrids. These are tall lilies with many little down-facing flowers and whorled leaves.

Pear blossom

Pears are native to temperate regions of the Old World, from western Europe and north Africa east right across Asia.

The flowers are white, rarely tinted yellow or pink, 2-4 cm diameter, and have five petals. Like that of the related apple, the pear fruit is a pome, in most wild species 1-4 cm diameter.

Sunflower

While the vibrant sunflower is a recognized worldwide for its beauty, it is also a source of food.

Sunflower oil is a valued and healthy vegetable oil and sunflower seeds are enjoyed as a healthy, tasty snack and nutritious ingredient to many foods.

 Combining techniques for a dynamic page

Combining techniques

Why stick with just positioning or floats alone? When you combine many of these techniques, you can achieve amazing possibilities from the simplest of markup (**Figure 4.23**).

Opposite, you can see the static design for an interface for a flower seller's Web site. One of the aims of this design is to create a flexible layout that adapts to wider window widths and also allows a visitor to increase the default text size in the browser without the layout falling apart.

At first glance, you might imagine that implementing this design will need multiple divisions—perhaps one for the images at the top, possibly another for the main content, and still more for the columns. Think back to the content-out approach, and what do you see?

Although this design might at first appear complex, the markup you will use is not; it includes only one division, a heading, and an unordered list. As in previous examples, each item in the list contains a heading, two paragraphs of content, and an image:

```
<div id="content">

<h2>Flowers in my garden</h2>

<ul>
<li id="tulip">
<h3>Purple Tulip <span>£10.00 per stem</span></h3>
<p><a href="#tulip"><img src="tulip.png" alt="" /></a>
First paragraph.</p>
<p>Second paragraph</p>
</li>
</ul>

</div>
```

The key to implementing this design with so little markup is understanding that CSS gives you the ability to think outside the conventional rows-and-columns approach. By using CSS positioning, you can offset an element to a new position within its parent container or anywhere on the page.

Start by adding a few basic styles to the `<body>` element of your page, and then add `position : relative;` (but no offsets) to the content division to establish it as the positioning context for its positioned descendents:

```
body    {
width : 80%;
min-width : 800px;
margin : 0 auto;
background-color : #f5efff;
font : 88%/1.4 Cordoba, Verdana, sans-serif;
color : #000; }

div#content {
position : relative; }
```

Creating the floated columns

To create the effect of symmetrical columns from the items in the list, give the items a width of 25 percent, and float each to the left. The result isn't going to be stunning in an instant, but you'll be fixing that in just a moment (**Figure 4.24**):

```
li {
float : left;
width : 25%; }
```

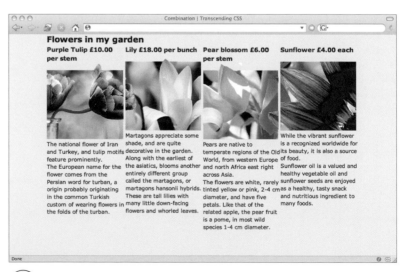

(4.24) **Creating an effect of symmetrical columns**

Now that the list items have become columns, you should style each one by giving it a unique background image:

```
li {
float : left;
width : 25%;
background-repeat : no-repeat;
background-position : 10px 10px; }

#tulip { background-image : url(1-1_tbn.png); }
#lily { background-image : url(1-2_tbn.png); }
#blossom { background-image : url(1-3_tbn.png); }
#sunflower { background-image : url(1-4_tbn.png); }
```

Because the background images are all 200 pixels high, clear enough space for them to show through by adding 200 pixels of top padding to all the list items (**Figure 4.25**):

```
li {
float : left;
width : 25%;
padding-top : 200px;
background-repeat : no-repeat;
background-position : 10px 10px; }
```

4.25 Adding top padding to the list items

Active branding

It is common for sites to use horizontal banners or mastheads for site identity. These often look attractive, but they rarely contain any useful features, with the possible exception of a link to a homepage.

When you add navigation and other functionality to a branding area, you make it active and more useful for your visitors.

Making the masthead active

The design is starting to shape up, but you still have more to do. Your next task is to use absolute positioning to move the inline images out of the normal flow of the document and up to the top of the design.

First, you'll need to clear some room up there by using top padding on the content division to push its content downward:

```
div#content {
position : relative;
padding-top : 200px; }
```

Next, you can now move your inline images to the top of the design by positioning the anchors that enclose them. This forms what on first glance might look like any common or garden-variety branding area or masthead, but this is a masthead with a difference in that it contains links to content elsewhere on the page (**Figure 4.26**). You will be using these links in just a little while:

```
p a { position : absolute; top : 0;}

#tulip p a { left : 0; }
#lily p a { left : 200px; }
```

4.26 **Creating a masthead with links to content on the page**

```
#blossom p a { left : 400px; }
#sunflower p a { left : 600px; }
```

With your images in place and the design coming together nicely, it is time for you to add some finishing touches to the unordered list (**Figure 4.27**):

- A graduated background that helps define the content area
- A fat 5-em top border onto which to position your heading
- A 1-pixel bottom border that stops your eyes from wandering off the bottom of the page

Here's the code to add these touches:

```
ul {
background : url(ul.png) repeat-x;
border-top : 5em solid #f5efff;
border-bottom : 1px solid #999;
overflow : hidden; }
```

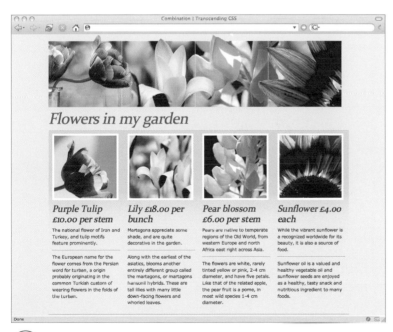

4.27 **Adding some finishing touches**

Clearing floats without added markup

You may have spotted in the previous code that I added `overflow : hidden;` to the rules for the unordered list. You might be wondering why. When you float an element either left or right, you remove it from the normal flow of the document. In this example, I have floated both the list items. Because the list now visually has no children, it collapses in on itself and has no height, which is not handy when using a background image that you want to wrap around your columns (**Figure 4.28**).

In the past, many designers added clearing elements to their markup—breaks and divisions—to help create the visual effect they wanted to achieve. This extra, presentational markup should not be part of any meaningful document; in fact, you have other ways to resolve this issue without resorting to hacks using markup. One of the simplest, and my current preferred solution, is to use the `overflow` property.

For a more detailed explanation about clearing floats without structural markup, see Peter-Paul Koch's article at www.quirksmode. org/css/clearing.html.

 4.28 Top: Collapsing list hides the background image. Bottom: Using the overflow property to show the background image.

Working with type

With the structural parts of the design now implemented, it is time for you to concentrate on typography. Your first task will be to position the second-level heading and give it a classic feel with italics, letter spacing, and Constantia (one of the new fonts designed by Microsoft that comes with the Windows Vista operating system):

```
h2 {
position : absolute;
z-index : 3;
top : 210px;
font : italic 340% Constantia, Palatino, Times, serif;
letter-spacing : -1px;
line-height   : 100%;
color : #4e5812; }
```

Add margins and padding to the headings and paragraphs inside your list items using a child selector:

```
li > h3 {
padding : 0 10px;
font : italic 200% Constantia, Palatino, Times, serif; }

li > p {
margin : .5em 0;
padding : 0 10px; }
```

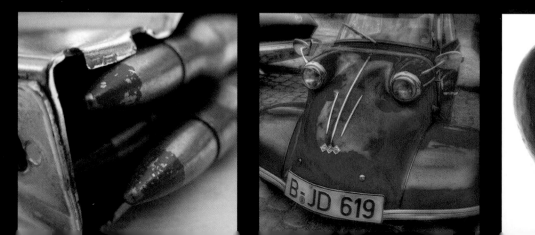

Add distinctive styling to the second paragraphs that follow third-level headings by targeting them with an adjacent sibling selector. You will notice that I have used two + combinators within the selector. This selects the second paragraph following the heading:

```
h3 + p + p {
margin : .75em 10px 0 10px;
padding : .75em 0;
border-top : 1px solid #999; }
```

Putting spans to work

By now I hope you realize the tremendous creative opportunities that positioning offers you, for large-scale layouts down to the subtlest of design details. It is with one of these details that you can add an extra level of sparkle to this design.

Remember when you started by looking at the markup underpinning this design? Each heading contains the price of that flower, wrapped in shiny paper. Actually, the price was wrapped in a <span> element, but the result will be just as attractive:

```
<ul>
<li id="tulip">
<h3>Purple Tulip <span>£10.00 per stem</span></h3>
<p><a href="#tulip"><img src="tulip.png" alt="" /></a>
First paragraph.</p>
<p>Second paragraph</p>
</li>
</ul>
```

Note

The :target pseudo-class is currently
supported only by Firefox and its
siblings, OmniWeb and Apple Safari.
Opera and Internet Explorer users
will stay blissfully unaware that this
feature exists in your design, but Mark
Wubben has developed a JavaScript
solution to emulate the :target
pseudo-class in Internet Explorer.
See his nifty solution at http://
tests.novemberborn.net/javascript/
emulate-css-pseudo-class-target-
in-ie.html.

Glance back at the static design. These prices appear not next to the name of the flower
but at the top of the design, overlaid on the images at the top of the page.

You will give these <span> elements a style that will set them apart from the images
behind them by using a background color, a border, and fonts that all work well at smaller
sizes:

```
h3 span {
position : absolute;
z-index : 2;
padding : .15em .3em;
background-color : #f3f4e4;
border : 1px solid #4e5812;
color : #333;
font : bold 52% "Lucida Grande","Lucida Sans Unicode", Verdana, sans-serif;
font-variant : small-caps;
text-align : center; }
```

Next, you should give each <span> element a unique position, placing them complementary to the images behind them. You can experiment with different compositions and even
place some of the <span> elements outside their parent containers (**Figure 4.29**):

```
#tulip h3 span { top : 160px; left : -20px; }
#lily h3 span { top : 40px; left : 220px; }
#blossom h3 span { top : 150px; left : 440px; }
#sunflower h3 span { top : 60px; left : 780px; }
```

 Placing the <span> elements inside and outside their parent containers

Hearing the fat lady warming up

The design layout is complete, but you don't want to stop there, do you? One of the reasons why the Web is such an exciting medium to design for is that, unlike a printed page, a Web page can and often should include interactive features to help visitors accomplish their goals on your site.

CSS can provide many interactive effects without needing to resort to scripting techniques. For the final part of this example, you'll add some subtle interactivity to this design.

The inline images you previously positioned at the top of this design are each wrapped in an anchor that contains a fragment identifier that points to its parent, a named list item:

```
<a href="#tulip"><img src="tulip.png" alt="" /></a>
```

Now it is time for you to put those fragment identifiers to good use by employing the CSS3 `:target` pseudo-class. This handy pseudo-class enables you to alter the styling of any element that is the target of a link. For this design, you will reverse the contrast of a targeted list item by changing its background and text color (**Figure 4.30**):

```
:target {
background-color : #4e5812;
color : #fff; }
```

Ride of the Valkyries

So now that the lights have dimmed and the orchestra is playing, the fat lady is on her way to the stage. If the prospect of listening to an opera that lasts several days has little appeal to you, don't run for cover. CSS3 is about to take you on a ride that will be far more exciting than *Ride of the Valkyries*.

In the next section, you'll learn about CSS3 and many of the cool features it will bring to your design for the Web. "Ah!" you might be thinking, "I can stop reading here, because CSS3 will be a long time coming." Well, put that thought out of your mind because not only will you learn how some of the most interesting new design possibilities will work with CSS3 but you'll also see solutions to emulate them in your work today.

 Using the pseudo-class to change the styling of an element

CSS3 (Third Time Lucky)

As Web designers turn their backs on old-fashioned, presentational layout methods and see the advantages of minimal, meaningful markup and CSS, they recognize that to achieve more complex, rich interfaces, they need more from CSS. Not only should the new CSS specification build on what has gone before, making it easy to learn and more backward compatible, but it should also provide new features for designers to solve their everyday problems. The journey to improved CSS, however, has not been an easy one.

The first CSS specification, CSS1, was published in 1996. Its successor, CSS2, was published less than two years later, and an updated CSS2.1 followed to address a number of errors and inconsistencies. CSS2.1 still remains, at the time of writing, a candidate recommendation despite that many browsers now support most of its features, and standards-savvy designers and developers have long been using CSS2.1 in their daily work.

Work on CSS3 started in 2000, but the progress of the World Wide Web Consortium (W3C) has seemed painfully slow. For Web designers and developers who have realized that CSS2.1 cannot easily accomplish the visually rich, complex interfaces and layouts that modern Web sites need, watching this slow process has been maddening. This is something that, as a recently invited expert to the CSS Working Group, I hope to influence for the better.

The sum of its parts

One of the major differences between CSS3 and earlier versions is that CSS3 is a modular specification. Because so many new features have been requested, the W3C's CSS Working Group decided to break down work on CSS3 into a number of separate modules:

Module name	Description
Selectors Module (www.w3.org/TR/css3-selectors/)	New, refined selectors will make it easier to target an element based on its attributes and position in the document flow. New pseudo-classes and pseudo-elements will make it possible to achieve more typographic effects without adding presentational elements to your markup.

continues

Module name	Description
Paged Media module for printed publications (www.w3.org/TR/css3-page/)	CSS was always intended to do more than simply style the appearance of a document in a Web browser. Generated content for paged media focuses on styling documents for paper publishing and uses generated content to add notes, leaders, markers, and footnotes. Although many modern browsers support generated content, it is missing from Internet Explorer 7 and may not be a priority for implementation in a future version 8.
Backgrounds and Borders module (www.w3.org/TR/css3-background/)	The Backgrounds and Borders module offers designers new ways to style any box's background or borders. It includes a new way to attach more than one background image to an element and to use images to create borders.
Multi-column Layout Module (www.w3.org/TR/css3-multicol/)	Flowing text into multiple columns is a technique more familiar in print than on the Web. The Multi-column Layout Module is designed to make it simpler to create columns without additional markup by using column counts, gaps, and rules.
Advanced Layout Module (www.w3.org/TR/css3-layout/)	The Advanced Layout Module is designed to solve many of the common layout problems that Web designers and developers face. It also aims to fully separate the visual layout order from a document's content.
Media Queries module (www.w3.org/TR/css3-mediaqueries/)	Screen, print, and handheld are three media types that should already be familiar to Web designers and developers. Media queries extend the functionality of these media types when used in combination with other information, such as the width or height of a browser and even the aspect ratio of a screen; this is useful for developing for sites that will be viewed on a TV.

These modules are currently being worked on individually and are at different stages of completion. It is the Working Group's intention that browser makers will be able to choose which modules they will support and when they will implement them.

Getting involved in making new standards

Not only is progress on CSS3 slow, but another problem for those who are interested in helping shape the future of CSS is that the working drafts and documents for CSS are almost impenetrable to Web designers.

Web designers are mostly visual thinkers, and they focus on what they can achieve when using CSS, rather than on the intricate technicalities of the specifications. Much of the language used in specifications, and other W3C documentation, is scientific and complicated and does not lend itself to being easily understood by those without a background in science or academia.

> *The layout algorithm distinguishes the case of an element of a-priori known width and a shrink-wrapped element. In the former case, the target width of the template is the width of the element itself; in the latter case, the target width is the width of the initial containing block (often the viewport).*
>
> —The Advanced Layout Module working draft (www.w3.org/TR/css3-layout/#colwidth)

Hmmm. Answers on a postcard to...

Another problem with the specifications is that without clear examples of the visual effects that CSS3 is designed to accomplish, Web designers have a difficult job in visualizing how new selectors and properties will apply in their work. Many of the current examples used throughout the various modules have little in common with practical realities.

In fairness to the W3C, specifications are technically designed to be read and understood by browser makers and other implementers, rather than to act as training manuals for Web designers or developers. However, strong visual examples would not only help implementers understand how a feature should be implemented, but they would also serve as visual aids for designers and developers who may struggle to understand much of the specifications' complex terminology.

The W3C should not develop ideas for the specifications without input from working designers and developers who use their tools every day. Specification development should be a three-way partnership between designers, implementers, and the W3C. But if more Web designers and developers are going to help the W3C's CSS Working Group create tools that will be useful in their everyday work, the W3C must start working hard to write documentation that can be more widely understood.

Note

You can read more about the new CSS3 selectors in my article "A Tribute to Selectors" at www.stuffandnonsense. co.uk/archives/css_a_tribute_to_ selectors.html and in Roger Johansson's excellent article "CSS3 Selectors Explained" at www.456bereastreet. com/archive/200601/ css_3_selectors_explained/.

Back to the future

CSS3 offers many tools to enable Web designers and developers to create highly visual designs without needing presentational markup.

It is understandable that browser makers have been reluctant to implement much of CSS3 until either the specifications have been finalized or there is widespread demand for them to do so. However, some parts of CSS3 are already supported, albeit in a limited capacity, by certain browsers. Where it is relevant and possible, you should take advantage of these tools now, if only so you can become familiar with how they work.

Not enough pages are available in this book to cover all the exciting developments in CSS3, so I have chosen to concentrate on some of the most interesting design opportunities in CSS3: selectors, background images, columns, and finally the Advanced Layout Module, one of the most exciting and intriguing developments to come out of the CSS Working Group.

Designing with the CSS3 Selectors Module

Web designers and developers have been asking for more efficient ways to target either an element or a node in the document tree for styling, and the CSS3 Selectors Module certainly does not disappoint. CSS3 offers so many new and powerful selectors that understanding how and when to use them can be daunting. The new selectors include the following:

- New attribute selectors that will enable you to target an element based on only part of its attribute, including `href`, `src`, `alt`, and `title`
- New dynamic pseudo-classes, including `:target` and `:lang`
- New structural pseudo-classes, including `:nth-child`, `:last-child`, `:only-child`, and even `:first-of-type` and `:last-of-type`

I can see ways that almost all the new CSS3 selectors will improve the lives of Web designers and developers in the future. In the following section, you'll learn how to work with one of the most helpful new selectors to solve an alarming common problem. No, it's not what to do when your Apple iPod runs out of battery; it's how to make zebra-style striping to tables and lists.

Improving readability with zebra stripes

When you leave tables for layout behind and use them only for presenting tabular information, you emphasize their meaning. Many designers choose to help the readability of this tabular information by giving different styling to alternate rows, often simply by changing the color of the background. In the past, this simple design device would have required you to add a presentational `class` attribute to every other table row:

```
<table class="discography">
<thead>
<tr>
<td>Album</td>
<td>Year</td>
<td>Chart position (<abbr title="United Kingdom">UK</abbr>)</td>
</tr>
</thead>

<tbody>
<tr class="odd">
<td>Paul Weller</td>
<td>1992</td>
<td>8</td>
</tr>

<tr class="even">
<td>Wild Wood</td>
<td>1993</td>
<td>2</td>
</tr>

<tr class="odd">
<td>Live Wood</td>
<td>1994</td>
<td>13</td>
</tr>
</tbody>
</table>
```

And the CSS would be:

```
tbody > .odd { background color : #fff; }
tbody > .even { background-color : #000; color : #fff; }
```

Plugging the holes in :nth-child support with JavaScript and the DOM

With browser support for `:nth-child` structural pseudo-classes still rare (at the time of this writing, only Konqueror 3.52 for Linux supports them), many Web designers and developers have turned to DOM scripting to emulate them.

Using JavaScript, you can insert a `class` attribute of `even` on even-numbered items in a series and style that element using a simple CSS class selector:

```
li.even {
background-color : #d0d0b0;  }

li.even img {
position : relative;
left : -50px;
margin-right : -40px;  }
```

Until more browsers support the `:nth-child` pseudo-classes, DOM scripting can be an effective method of creating striping and other visual effects without resorting to presentational markup.

Note: Aaron Gustafson has written a flexible and easily updatable script for striping table rows and list items. Download the script and all supporting files exclusively at http://easy-designs.net/code/stripey/.

Album	Year	Chart position (UK)
Paul Weller	1992	8
Wild Wood	1993	2
Live Wood	1994	13

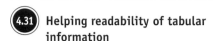

4.31 Helping readability of tabular information

SUNFLOWER

The family Asteraceae or, alternatively, Compositae, known as the aster, daisy or sunflower family, is a taxon of dicotyledonous flowering plants.

COMPOSITAE

The family name is derived from the genus Aster and refers to the star-shaped flower head of its members.

ASTERACEAE

The Asteraceae is the second largest family in the Division Magnoliophyta, with some 1,100 genera and over 20,000 recognized species.

4.32 Alternating-color list items

Not only can this quickly become tedious to edit manually, it can also be a difficult effect to achieve when the information in the table is dynamically generated.

This effect is not appropriate only for table rows. Perhaps you would like to style every other product in an online store's product page or even every second link in a sidebar (**Figure 4.31**).

The :nth-child() pseudo-class

CSS3 provides a way for you to target odd and even table rows, list items, or other elements in a series by using :nth-child pseudo-classes. These are highly useful when you are designing for a series of items on a page and you need to provide a way to separate them visually.

For this example, you'll create an attractive sidebar with alternating-color list items (**Figure 4.32**). By thinking first about content and meaning, you can keep the markup for this sidebar minimal and meaningful. Because the items in the sidebar list will be ordered by their popularity, an ordered list is the most appropriate element to choose. Each list item contains the name of the featured item, a short summary of it, and an image:

```
<ol id="nav_sub">
<li>
<h3>Sunflower</h3>
<p><img src="item-1.png" alt="" />
The family Asteraceae or, alternatively, Compositae, known as the aster, daisy
or sunflower family, is a taxon of dicotyledonous flowering plants.</p>
</li>
</ol>
```

Simple top and left borders on this ordered list separate the sidebar content from other elements on the page, and they also visually emphasize the effect of the images breaking free from their containers:

```
ol {
list-style-type : none;
width : 400px;
border-top : 3px solid #3f080a;
border-left : 3px solid #3f080a;  }
```

Floating and setting a right margin on each image will enable the text within each of the list items to wrap around them:

```
li { clear : both;  }

li img {
float : left;
border : none;  }
```

Adding styles for the headings and paragraphs in the list will complete the basic sidebar:

```
h3, p {
margin : 0;
padding : .5em 20px;  }

h3 {
font-size : 110%;
text-transform : uppercase;  }
```

CSS3 :nth-child structural pseudo-classes enable you to style odd and even items without attaching any presentational class attributes in your markup. As is often the case with CSS, you have more than one way to accomplish the same goal, but by far the simplest method is to use :nth-child(odd) and :nth-child(even) selectors.

The following rule applies a background color only to even-numbered list items, creating the strong horizontal bands that are important in this design:

```
li:nth-child(even) {
background-color : #d0d0b0;  }
```

Finally, you can create the effect of the images breaking out of their boxes by using relative positioning to move every image in an "even-numbered" list item 50 pixels to the left. Adding a negative right margin will suck the surrounding text into the space that this image would have occupied:

```
li:nth-child(even) img {
position : relative;
left : -50px;
top : -20px;
margin-right : -40px;  }
```

CSS computation

If, after reading this, you feel a strong urge to dive into the specifications for structural pseudo-classes, you might soon be wondering if you have stumbled across a lesson in mathematics by mistake. As well as the more self-explanatory :first-child, :last-child, and :nth-child pseudo-classes, you can target specific elements based on the number of siblings that have come before them.

Imagine you have a long table of data with more than fifty rows; it will be difficult for a visitor to scan this table to find the specific piece of information he needs.

tr:nth-child(10n-1) will count the number of rows in increments of 10 (10, 20, 30, and so on) and target the rows that come immediately before (-1), enabling you to style the 9th, 19th, 29th, and so on, rows. You might choose to add a thick bottom border and extra white space to break the table into sections to help readability.

Designing with the
Backgrounds and Borders Module

I've been working hard, all hours of the day and night. My eyes are bloodshot, and my fingers are raw, all because I want to invent a time machine—not your average time machine, no twinkling lights or shiny buttons for me (although a time machine that is shaped like a blue police box would be cool). I want a CSS time machine.

Where or when would I go? To the future perhaps, to find out the results of next year's racing results or the winner of the 2010 World Cup (actually I know that already)? No, I would return to 1996 and insist that the CSS Working Group add multiple background images to CSS1.

Attaching more than one background image to any element is on the wish list of almost every CSS-savvy designer I know. Alas, until CSS3 it has been possible to use only a single image per element.

Web designers and developers have worn their fingers to the bone concocting ways to implement even the simplest design element that requires more than one image. For such a simple effect, these solutions have become increasingly complex.

Like three-button jackets with side vents, fishtail parkas, and Fred Perry shirts before them, rounded corners are the fashionable must-have for many a "mod"ern Web site or application.

Adding rounded corners to a fixed-pixel-width element using CSS1 and CSS2.1 has been relatively straightforward; you do it usually by attaching a top image to one element and a bottom image to another. Creating a resizable box with rounded corners, custom borders, or drop shadows has always been a more complex affair, usually requiring additional <div> or <span> elements to be added to your markup.

For example:

```
<div class="content_introduction">
<div class="bi">
<div class="bt">
<div></div>
</div>
<p>A flexible box with rounded corners</p>
<div class="bb">
<div></div>
</div>
</div>
</div>
```

This is hardly the most semantic use of divisions and one where the calorie count of your markup can easily weigh down the amount of content. CSS3 puts this markup on a diet by enabling you to attach more than one image to the background of an element. Your new, slim markup is as follows:

```
<p class="content_introduction">A flexible box with rounded corners</p>
```

Plugging the holes in multiple background images using JavaScript and the DOM

Rounded corners have become almost a standard design element in Web sites and application design; square corners just don't cut it anymore.

Rounded corners are not the only use for multiple background images, and to make them a possibility in a wider range of browsers, designers and developers have been turning to JavaScript to simulate multiple background images.

Among the many JavaScript solutions, one developed by Roger Johansson solves many problems by inserting additional elements into a document via the DOM. You can find Johansson's solution at www.456bereastreet.com/archive/200505/transparent_custom_corners_and_borders/.

That's it! It's lighter, healthier, and with almost 100 fewer characters. The CSS, on the other hand, is a little fatty. You can add several background images to your division, separating each image with a comma (**Figure 4.33**):

```
div.content_introduction { background-image :
url("top_left.png"),
url("top_right.png"),
url("bottom_right.png"),
url("bottom_left.png"),
url("top_center.png"),
url("middle_right.png"),
url("bottom_center.png"),
url("middle_left.png"); }
```

You can also set the repeat properties, taking care to use the same order for the repeat as for your list of images:

```
div.content_introduction { background-repeat :
no-repeat, no-repeat, no-repeat, no-repeat, repeat-x,
repeat-y, repeat-x, repeat-y }
```

Finally, you can position each background image to create the effect of a flexible, resizable box (**Figure 4.34**):

```
div.content_introduction { background-position:
top left,
top right,
bottom right,
bottom left,
top left,
top right,
bottom right,
bottom left; }
```

Phew! It's not quite the slimmest CSS, but it keeps the presentation information where it belongs, in a style sheet rather than in your markup, bulking it up with high-calorie "divness."

Note: At the time of writing, only those health-conscious folks at Apple have made multiple backgrounds available in Safari and other browsers based on the WebKit engine.

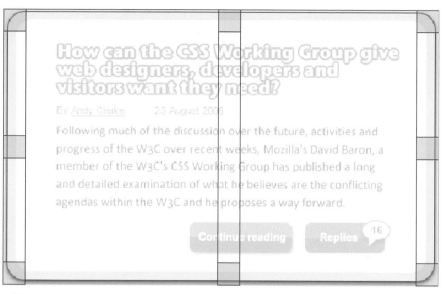

(4.33) Adding multiple background images

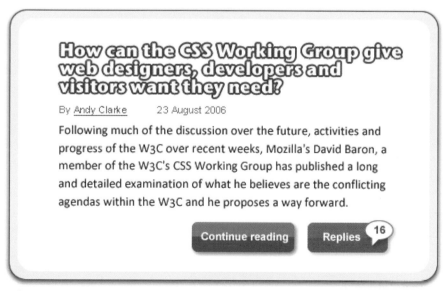

(4.34) Creating a flexible box

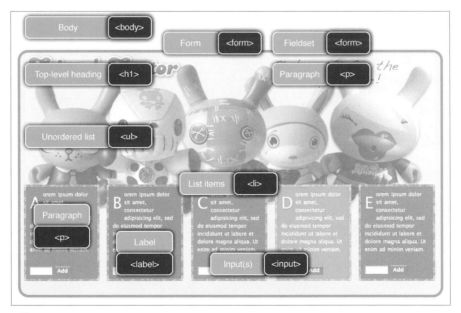

4.35 The final layout (top) and the markup (bottom)

Designing with multiple background images

Whatever platform you are working on—Windows, OS X, or Linux—you will be able to work along with most of the techniques in the next example (**Figure 4.35**). However, as this book goes to press, only Mac users running Safari and other browsers based on WebKit will be able to see the full benefits of multiple background images. If that's not a good enough reason to switch to a Mac, I don't know what is.

For this example, you're designing an interface element for a gift site that has been inspired by a teen magazine. You will use percentage and em measurements to create a flexible design and use positioning, image replacement, and multiple background images to create a different type of e-commerce layout.

On the opposite page is the static design you are aiming to achieve, plus the meaningful elements you will use to mark up your content. Look closely, and you will see you need headings, paragraphs, a form, and a single unordered list. Look Ma, no divisions! What you can't see, but is important for e-commerce stores, is that the total combined "weight" of the markup and CSS is only 8Kb.

Before you get carried away with this design, you'll preview the naked document in a browser (**Figure 4.36**).

You'll set the stage for the design by applying some simple rules to both the root <html> and <body> elements. Because this design will be flexible, all the measurements you'll use are based on em:

```
html    {
padding : 2em 0;
background-color : #fff;
color : #333; }
```

4.36 Previewing the naked document first

Note

Windows users, you can test your own examples in Safari and just about any other browser by using BrowserCam, a subscription service that takes screen shots of your pages in just about any browser and operating system combination. Find out more at www.browsercam.com.

```
body {
font : 78%/1.5 "Lucida Grande","Lucida Sans Unicode", Verdana, sans-serif;
width : 66em;
min-width : 710px;
margin : 0 auto; }
```

Because you'll use absolute positioning to place the top-level heading and tagline, you will need to add position : relative; to the <body> element to establish it as the first positioning context:

```
body {
position : relative; }
```

Positioning and z-index

Positioning and z-index are two of the main techniques making this design possible. The first part of the positioning process is to place the top-level heading and tagline in position. You will then use the Phark image replacement technique discussed in Part 2, "Process," to replace the browser text with graphic images (**Figure 4.37**):

4.37 **Placing the top-level heading and tagline before replacing the browser text with images**

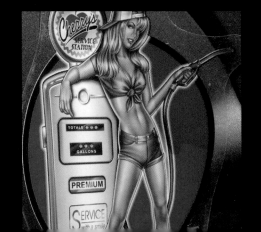

```
h1 {
position : absolute;
z-index : 2;
top : 10px;
left : 10px;
width : 375px;
height : 65px;
background : url(h1.png) no-repeat 0 0; }

h1 + p {
position : absolute;
z-index : 2;
top : 20px;
right : 0;
width : 395px;
height : 70px;
background : url(p.png) no-repeat 0 0; }

h1, h1 + p {
text-indent : -9999px; }
```

Because you will position many of the elements within the form, the form must also become a positioning context by adding position : relative; but no offsets:

```
form {
position : relative;
z-index : 1;
padding : 0 1em;
min-height : 38em;
background-color : #f9e6f6; }
```

Z's not dead, baby; Z's not dead

In combination with alpha-transparency in PNG images, stacking elements with `z-index` is a powerful creative tool. Remember geometry at school? The *x*-axis represents the horizontal; the *y*-axis represents the vertical. In CSS, the *z*-axis represents depth. Elements that are stacked using `z-index` are arranged from front to back. It is also important to understand that `z-index` is applied to only those elements with a `position` property and a value—in other words, no positioning property and value, no `z-index`.

`z-index` values can be either negative or positive, and the element with the highest value appears closest to the viewer, regardless of its order in the source. If more than one element has the same `z-index`, the element that comes last in the source comes out on top of the pile.

Note: For a more detailed examination of `z-index`, read my article at http://24ways.org/advent/zs-not-dead-baby-zs-not-dead. More about complex `z-index` relationships from Aleksandar Vacic at http://aplus.co.yu/css/z-pos/.

You will now position the unordered list 10 pixels from the top of the form and use a combination of minimum height and padding to allow room for the montage of characters:

```
ul {
position : relative;
top : 10px;
min-height : 80px;
padding-top : 300px; }
```

It's time to complete the unordered list by attaching the characters image to its background. Because this image sits behind the positioned list items, the design takes on an unusual out-of-the-box appeal (**Figure 4.38**):

```
ul {
background : url(ul.jpg) no-repeat 50% 0; }
```

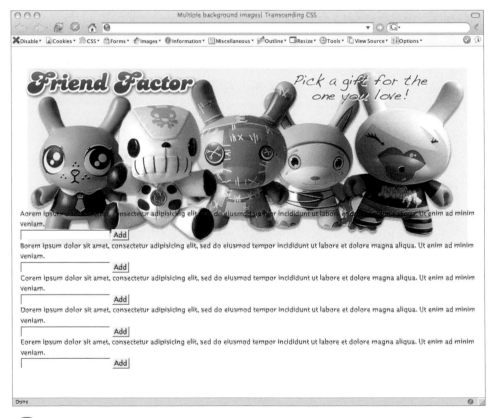

 Attaching the characters image to its background

You'll now position each of the five list items to create the appearance of five columns. I have calculated their positioning to add a small gutter between them:

```
li {
position : absolute;
width : 10em;
padding : 1em;
background-color : #f9496b;
color : #fff; }

li[id="a"] { left : 0; }
li[id="b"] { left : 13em; background-color : #f185bb; }
li[id="c"] { left : 26em; }
li[id="d"] { left : 39em; background-color : #f185bb; }
li[id="e"] { left : 52em; }
```

The layout of this design is beginning to take shape, so press on and preview the design in your browser (**Figure 4.39**).

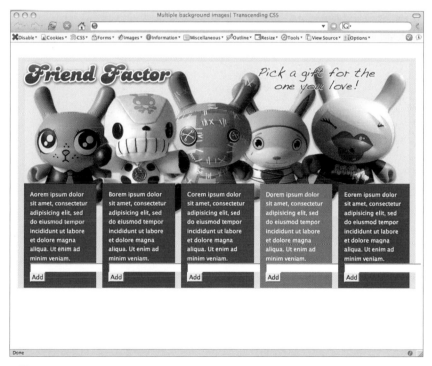

4.39 Previewing the design

Note

For more on styling form buttons, see Aaron Gustafson's "Push My Button" article for *Digital Web* Magazine at www.digital-web.com/ articles/push_my_button/.

Form element styling

To add a little flair to each of the form elements, it is time to pull out one of the most flexible selector types in the CSS designer's toolbox, an attribute selector. Peeking into the markup, you will see that each of the list items contains a text input for the quantity and an "Add to cart" button:

```
<label for="a_qty"><span>Add to cart</span>
<input type="text" id="a_qty" />
<input type="submit" value="Add" />
```

Without attribute selectors, you would need to target each form element either by using its id (requiring multiple CSS selectors) or by adding a class attribute such as this:

```
<label for="a_qty"><span>Add to cart</span>
<input type="text" id="a_qty" class="qty" />
<input type="submit" value="Add" class="submit" />
```

Attribute selectors remove the need for this extra markup. They target inputs based on their type and their value (**Figure 4.40**):

```
input[type="text"] { width : 4em;
font : 82% "Lucida Grande", "Lucida Sans Unicode", sans-serif; }
```

```
input[value="Add"] {
padding : 0 .25em;
color : #fff;
border : 2px double #9c2f45;
border-top-color : #fff;
background-color : #f9496b;
font : bold 82% "Lucida Grande", "Lucida Sans Unicode", sans-serif; }
```

Typographic flair

One of the aspects from the inspirational magazine design you are aiming to replicate in this interface is a drop cap. The :first-letter pseudo-element will style this first letter, enlarging the text size and floating it to enable the neighboring text to wrap:

```
li > p {
min-height : 14em;
font-size : 82%; }
```

Note

Need a reminder of the difference between a block and an inline element? Tommy Olsson has written an excellent tutorial at www.autisticcuckoo.net/archive.php?id=2005/01/11/block-vs-inline-1.

 4.45 Previewing the results of adding multiple backround images

Designing multicolumn layouts

As you saw in Part 3, "Inspiration," dividing text into columns has been a common technique in many forms of design. It is one that helps the readability of written content by limiting the length of lines of text.

On the Web, splitting large blocks of text into multiple columns has always been problematic and has so far required that Web designers break their text into extra divisions to form visual, rather than semantic, groupings of content:

```
<div id="content_main" class="column">
Main content
</div>

<div id="content_sub" class="column">
Additional content
</div>
```

```
<div id="content_supp" class="column">
Supplementary content
</div>
```

The CSS3 Multi-column Layout Module is attempting to rectify this problem by making creating columns easier. It introduces a new column box that you can apply to paragraphs, lists, divisions, and other block-level elements.

Column widths and count

You can implement multiple columns within a column box in two ways. The first is by dictating the number of columns you require using the column-count property:

```
div#content_main { column-count : 3; }
```

The width of all three columns will expand equally to fill the available horizontal space of the containing element. Alternatively, you can set your desired width for the columns, and the browser will calculate how many columns will fit into the available space:

```
div#content_main { column-width : 15em; }
```

The ability for content to flow from column to column and the ability for new columns to be created as the browser window expands are effects that have not yet been achievable using CSS alone.

Gutters, gaps, and rules

To improve readability and visual balance, the Multi-column Layout Module introduces two new properties, column-gap and column-rule. To use these features, you insert both *gaps* (gutters) and *rules* (dividers) between columns, and their heights will always be equal to the height of the columns.

You place a column rule in the middle of a column gap. These rules do not take up space. That is, the presence or thickness of a column rule will not alter the placement of either columns or gaps (**Figure 4.46**):

```
div#content_main {
column-gap : 1em;
column-rule : thin solid black; }
```

Rustic Cherry Pie	Rhubarb Scone Cake	Sesame Noodles with Cucumber
My mom isn't a cake person. Growing up, our celebration treats were always pies, cupcakes were the closest thing to a birthday cake that she'd attempt, and then only under duress.	These are scones for the person who can't be bothered to make cute little triangles. Simply roll the dough out flat, smear on the fruit, roll and bake. And, what do you get for being this lazy? Gorgeous swirls in a tender crumb.	I always forget about tahini. I'm not sure why, when I have it, I'm always fond of the mild but nutty flavor. Sure, it's a touch paste-like. But paired with the right herbs or some chili flakes, it's a fantastic lower note.
Hot Asparagus Dip	**Nancy's Pasta with Greens**	**Spring Veggie Tart**
Here's a little spin on artichoke dip. Use asparagus instead. The result? Still creamy, but a bit more pungent and green, nutritionally excellent and easier to prepare.	I was emotionally scarred by cooked greens. Greasy, mushy mustard and collard greens with overtones of lysol and sweat socks, any redeeming qualities long since boiled out.	It has been well over a month since I've posted about a tart! I am going through tart-withdrawl, so last weekend whipped up this simple spring vegetable tart

 Placing a column rule in the middle of the column gap

Note: At the time this book went to press, parts of the Multi-column Layout Module are supported only in the Firefox 1.5+ and its siblings using the standards-compliant prefix –moz-prefix. (According to the spec, proprietary CSS properties are allowed, but must be prefaced with a hyphen and an identifier; -moz, in this case. These include -moz-column-count, -moz-column-width, and -moz-column-gap.) Find out more about Multi-column Layout support in these browsers at http://developer.mozilla.org/en/docs/CSS3_Columns.

Multi-column thrills or spills?

I am definitely thrilled by certain aspects of the Multi-column Layout Module but am distinctly underwhelmed by others. The ability for content to flow from column to column and the ability for new columns to be created as the browser window expands make Multi-column Layout an exciting prospect when used under the right circumstances.

However, many parts of the current working draft are less than ideal, and a great deal of work needs to be done on the specification before it should become a recommendation.

From both the design and usability perspectives, the results of content reflowing can be unsatisfactory; for example, content can easily become separated from its associated headers, and images can be separated from their descriptions or other associated text (**Figure 4.47**).

Fortunately, a group of new properties determine where column breaks occur:

```
h1 { column-break-before : always; }
h2 { column-break-after : avoid; }
h1, h2 { column-break-inside : avoid; }
```

A gap in the proposals?

The current Multi-column Layout working draft allows only for the basic styling of column-rule including dotted and dashed styles and other values from the CSS2.1 border style list, including the unusable, ugly ridge and groove styles.

The CSS Working Group doesn't seem to be planning to implement a feature I imagine many designers would like to use: image rules. I can think of many instances where images would be the perfect choice for column rules. Perhaps the following *fictitious* syntax might be appropriate:

```
div#content_main {
column-rule-image : url(rule.
png); }
```

Even better would be the possibility of positioning these images either at the top, bottom, or vertical center of the column gap:

```
div#content_main {
column-rule-image : url(rule.
png);
column-rule-align : middle; }
```

Plugging the holes in the Multi-column Layout Module using JavaScript and the DOM

Designers and developers have turned to JavaScript to help them simulate some parts of CSS3, including the Multi-column Layout Module.

Developer and author of "Introducing the CSS3 Multi-Column Module" at A List Apart (www.alistapart.com/articles/css3multicolumn/), Cédric Savarese has developed an experimental JavaScript implementation of the CSS3 Multi-column Layout Module.

Find out more about Savarese's ingenious solution at www.csscripting.com.

 4.47 Column reflowing can result in undesirable results

4.48 Using column break properties can result in additional problems

Unfortunately, these too can introduce problems, including large amounts of unnecessary white space or ugly and uneven column lengths (**Figure 4.48**).

Earlier working drafts of the Multi-column Layout Module included the now missing in action `column-span` property that would have enabled elements, such as headings, to span across a designated number of columns to create the effect regularly seen in newspaper design. Later drafts are now lacking this way to stop and restart columns.

The Multi-column Layout Module is an exciting prospect for designers, but to be completely useful, the CSS Working Group must talk to working designers about the features they think are missing and how they would put these features into everyday use.

Too many designers value "creativity" above

readability, usability, and accessibility. Using

multiple columns in a print stylesheet may

be useful, but onscreen, for longer articles? No.

Face it, the Web is not a printed magazine.

—ROGER JOHANSSON
www.456bereastreet.com/archive/200509/
css3_multicolumn_layout_considered_harmful/

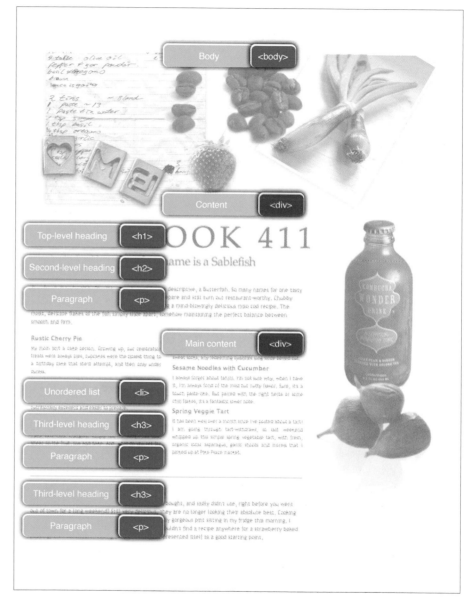

4.49   The design inspiration (top), the final layout (bottom), and the markup (right)

Designing with the Multi-column Layout Module

For the next example (**Figure 4.49**), you'll design an interface design for a cookery site. You will use percentage and em measurements to create a flexible layout, use a little background-image trickery, and use the Multi-column Layout Module to split the text content and create an attractive result.

On the opposite page is the static design you are aiming to achieve plus the meaningful elements you will use to mark up your content. Look closely, and you will see that you require headings, paragraphs, a single unordered list, and only two divisions. What you can't see is that the total combined weight of the markup and CSS is only 4Kb, hardly a heavyweight.

You should begin by setting the stage for the design by applying some simple rules to both the root <html> and <body> elements, allowing the design to fill 92 percent of the browser's width, down to a minimum of 640 pixels:

```
html     {
background-color : #fff; }

body {
font : 78%/1.5 "Trebuchet MS", "Lucida Grande","Lucida Sans Unicode", Verdana,
sans-serif;
width : 92%;
min-width : 640px;
margin : 0 auto;
color : #333; }
```

To allow room for the large product images at the top of the design, set padding-top to 360 pixels on the <body> element, and apply the image to the background. Setting its horizontal position at 50 percent ensures that it will always stay horizontally centered, no matter what the browser window size:

```
body {
padding-top : 360px;
background : url(body.png) no-repeat 50% 0; }
```

The design needs only two divisions: an outer container for the top-level heading and introduction text and a second for the main content that includes the all-important unordered list.

Note

If you haven't had the time yet to create this design for yourself, don't worry; I have saved you the trouble. You can find all the files you need for this example at www.transcendingcss.com/support/.

To make room for the image that runs down the right side of the page, set a right margin on the `#main-content` division to prevent its contents from overlapping this `background-image`:

```
div#content {
width : 100%;
background : url(content.png) no-repeat 100% 0; }

div#content_main {
margin-right : 320px; }
```

Now, with your layout complete, a little sprinkling of typographic style will complete the design (**Figure 4.50**).

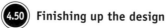 **Finishing up the design**

What about the multi-columns? Oops! I almost forgot. Creating these columns can't be much simpler. You will now apply the multi-column layout styles to the unordered list only so as not to affect any of the content that comes either before or after it in the document flow.

Because Gecko-based browsers have already implemented the new multi-column layout properties using the proprietary –moz– prefix, you will add two sets of style rules, one for today's Gecko browsers and one for other browsers when they begin supporting the Multi-column Layout Module:

```
ul {
padding : 1em 0;
column-width : 18em;
column-gap : 25px;

-moz-column-width : 18em;
-moz-column-gap : 25px; }
```

Now you have a flexible design with em-based column widths. Open the final result in a Gecko-based browser, and play with both the browser width and the text size. Watch as the list switches from a one-, two-, and three-column layout (**Figure 4.51**).

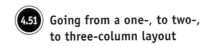

4.51 Going from a one-, to two-, to three-column layout

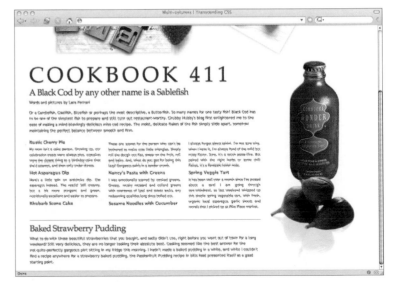

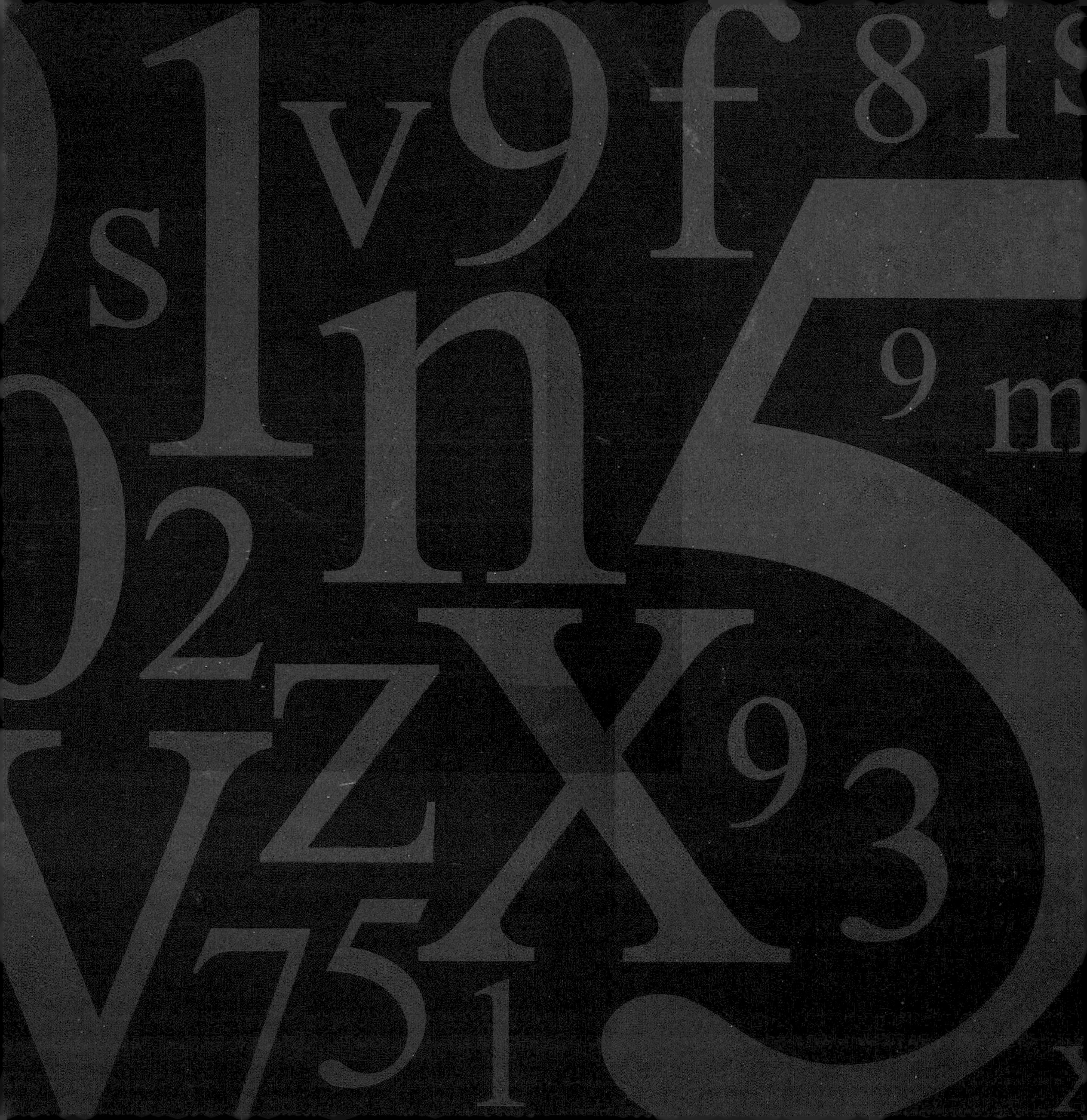

Advanced Layout

It has been ten years since the launch of CSS1, and visual designers have done more with CSS layouts than the early adopters ever would have thought possible. Compared to the earliest layout examples from The Noodle Incident and Blue Robot's Layout Reservoir, the designs featured every week on CSS gallery sites or planted in the CSS Zen Garden show just how far designers have taken CSS. In the hands of creative designers and Web developers, CSS is capable of producing stunning results.

Full CSS layouts have always been a compromise. The current CSS specifications were never designed to create the visually rich and complex interface layouts that the modern Web demands. The current methods—floats and positioning—were never intended as layout tools. The problems with using floats and positioning for layout go far beyond the fragility of floating an element to create a column and the fact that absolutely positioned elements are removed from the normal flow of a document. For a large part, both floated and positioned layouts depend on a document's source order. Although many designers have worked hard to create any-order columns, these types of layouts have almost always required a mass of additional divisions or hacks and filters to make them work reliably across different browsers.

Note: You can find many solutions to any-ordered columns at www.positioniseverything.net.

When a visual layout depends on source order, making larger changes to a design has always required changes to the underlying markup—hardly a true separation of content and style as promised by CSS. A full separation of content order from visual layout is not only desirable, but it is essential if designers are ever going to be able to move away from the familiar CSS layout with either two or three columns and create rich and inspiring designs without resorting to presentational markup.

Advanced Layout is one of the modules forming the CSS3 specification. It is being designed specifically to enable designers to break free of these conventions and many of the limitations of the past. It is perhaps one of the most interesting developments in CSS 3.

Acknowledging César Acebal

On a personal note, I would like to thank my co-contributor, César Acebal, and the University of Oviedo, Spain. Acebal is a member of the W3C's CSS Working Group and the author of the ALMCSS Advanced Layout proof of concept that made this section possible.

Back to the grid

The Advanced Layout Module builds on the concepts of grid design discussed in Part 3, "Inspiration." It establishes a new visual grid model that will enable designers to determine the layout of forms, navigation, content divisions, or even an entire page. Advanced Layout divides these elements into slots and uses a simple set of letters to position any child element inside a slot in the grid.

Advanced Layout introduces a new display-model property that defines the number of horizontal fields within the areas of the grid with strings of letters.

For example, the following code:

```
display:
"abc"
"def";
```

will create two horizontal grid fields, each with three vertical slots. Two other values (@ and .) define whether a slot is the default or contains only white space:

- **Slot letter.** This identifies the slot within the grid for any content that will be positioned within it.
- **@ (at symbol).** This identifies a default slot into which content that has not been situated can flow.
- **. (period).** This identifies a slot that can have no content inserted into it.

For more creative control over the grid, using the same letter more than once will force two or more slots to combine to form supercolumns. Any content placed inside them will span multiple columns, a design device that is common in newspaper layouts (**Figure 4.52**):

```
{ display:
"a a a"
"d e f"; }
```

In the next example, using floats to construct even this simple grid layout would require the elements to be ordered largely according to their visual layout. Using positioning would be a more reliable but more complex solution. Sadly, this solution could easily break if a visitor resized the browser window or changed the default size of the text.

Do you know the muffin man?

Photography by Eric Fung

Breads and desserts are often baked and baking is the primary cooking technique used to produce cakes and pastry-based goods such as pies, tarts, and quiches. Such items are sometimes referred to as baked goods and are sold at a bakery.

Eric Fung is a software developer on weekdays, aspiring baker all other times. His journal serves primarily to document the Bakery Arts classes he is taking at George Brown College in Toronto, Canada.

White peach jelly   Zucchini-walnut protein bread   Sweet and sour cherry choconut ice cream

 Spanning multiple columns

Using the Advanced Layout Module, you can keep the markup needed for this example lean and structural (**Figure 4.53, next page**):

```
<div id="biscotti">
<p><a href="#"><img src="one.png" alt="" /></a>
Moroccan Biscotti</p>
</div>

<div id="waffles">
<p><a href="#"><img src="two.png" alt="" /></a>
Yeasted Waffles</p>
</div>
```

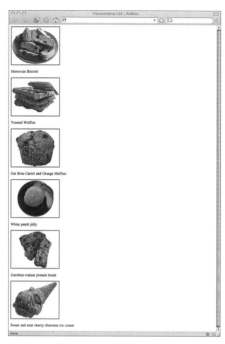

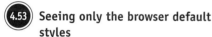

(4.53) **Seeing only the browser default styles**

```
<div id="muffins">
<p><a href="#"><img src="three.png" alt="" /></a>
Oat Bran Carrot and Orange Muffins</p>
</div>

<div id="jelly">
<p><a href="#"><img src="four.png" alt="" /></a>
White peach jelly</p>
</div>

<div id="bread">
<p><a href="#"><img src="five.png" alt="" /></a>
Zucchini-walnut protein bread</p>
</div>

<div id="icecream">
<p><a href="#"><img src="six.png" alt="" /></a>
Sweet and sour cherry choconut ice cream</p>
</div>
```

Also using Advanced Layout, you can define a grid either on a division or, as in this example, on the <body> element. Two strings will divide the <body> element into two fields, each containing three slots. You will also be able to dictate how the height of each slot will be defined: either by the height of the content inside it, termed *intrinsic height*, or by setting an explicit height in pixels or ems:

```
body { display:
"a b c (intrinsic)"
"d e f (intrinsic)"; }
```

With this simple CSS in place, each of the page elements will be situated in their slots by referencing each slot's identifying letter. The CSS is far less complex than any floating or positioning methods (**Figure 4.54**):

```
div#biscotti { position : a; }
div#wafles { position : b; }
div#muffins { position : c; }
div#jelly { position : d; }
div#bread { position : e; }
div#icecream { position : f; }
```

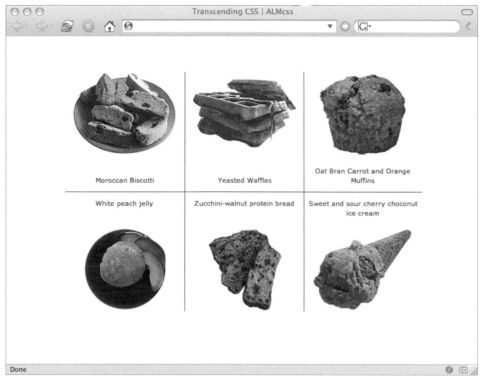

4.54 Situating content into slots

That's it! You don't have any floating worries or absolute positioning–clearing woes, just letters. It doesn't get much simpler than that.

The Advanced Layout working draft calls its grid-based approach *template-based positioning*, an unfortunate choice of words. Templating is rarely a concept that appeals to creative designers, but you should forgive the choice of name. Advanced Layout will allow a whole new realm of creative potential, not limit designers' creative options.

If you're hungry to see how easy it will be in the future to create layouts, check out the next section, where you'll see just how flexible the Advanced Layout Module will be.

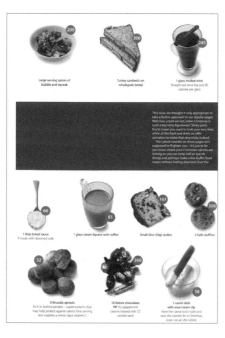

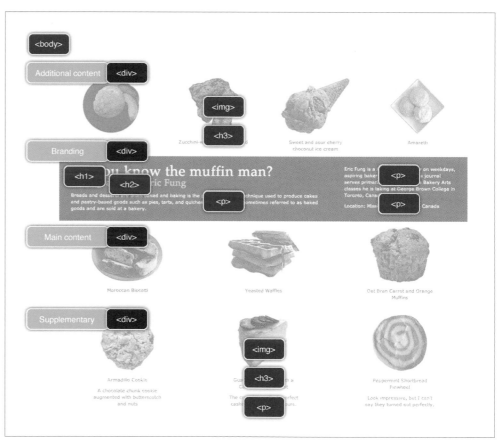

(4.55) **The inspiration for the layout (top), the finished design (bottom), and the markup (right)**

Designing with the Advanced Layout Module

On the opposite page (**Figure 4.51**) you can see the static design you are aiming to achieve using the Advanced Layout Module, plus the meaningful elements you will use to mark up your content.

Developing this layout using floats should, on the face of it, present few challenges; you would give each column an explicit width and float it inside its container division.

But what would happen if you needed to switch the position of any of the columns or perhaps even the vertical position of the fields? Most likely this would involve diving back into your markup and moving the elements so you could achieve the visual design. The Advanced Layout Module removes this necessity because it finally breaks any relationship between the visual design and the order of the content.

First, set up the four horizontal fields by creating four divisions. The order of these divisions should make sense to any visitor who is reading the content of the page without styles, and you should preview your document in a browser without styles to ensure that the order is logical:

```
<div id="branding">
Branding and introduction
</div>

<div id="content_main">
Main content
</div>

<div id="content_sub">
Additional content
</div>

<div id="content_supp">
Supplementary content
</div>
```

Note: César Acebal has made ALMCSS publicly available, and you can find links to all the files and Acebal's own examples at www.transcendingcss.com/support/.

The Advanced Layout Module is an exciting prospect, and many Web designers and developers (including me) have been aching to try it. Experimenting with new CSS features before the CSS Working Group has finalized a specification has been impossible until now.

As you might imagine, currently no browsers support any of the CSS for the Advanced Layout Module. This should come as no surprise because the module is, at the time of this writing, only a working draft. Fortunately, you can explore many parts of Advanced Layout by using ALMCSS, which is a proof of concept that uses JavaScript and CSS positioning to mimic how Advanced Layout will work.

As you will see in the following examples, to work around certain issues with CSS parsers in some browsers, ALMCSS uses a slightly different syntax than the proposals in the Advanced Layout Module: display becomes display-model and position becomes situated.

Note that the proposed syntax for the Advanced Layout CSS has been modified to work in this section's examples.

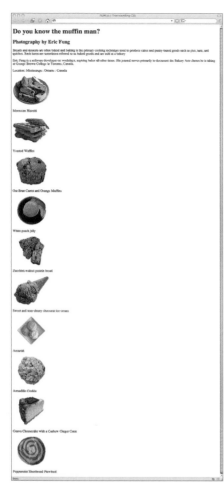

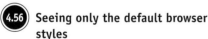

Seeing only the default browser styles

Second, in each of these divisions, create the columns using nested divisions that, in this example, contain a paragraph and an image but could just as easily contain any structural elements. For simplicity (some might say laziness), I have named these divisions *one*, *two*, *three*, and so on (**Figure 4.56**):

```
<div id="content_main">
<div class="one">
<img src="one.png" alt="" />
<p>Moroccan Biscotti</p>
</div>

<div class="two">
<img src="two.png" alt="" />
<p>Yeasted Waffles</p>
</div>

<div class="three">
<img src="three.png" alt="" />
<p>Oat Bran Carrot and Orange Muffins</p>
</div>
</div>
```

Whereas using floats or positioning to accomplish the design layout might be convoluted, with the Advanced Layout Module the CSS is simple. Next, define the display-model property on the <body> element:

```
body { display-model :
"a (intrinsic)"
"b (intrinsic)"
"c (intrinsic)"
"d (intrinsic)"; }
```

You can also create a microgrid by giving each field its own display-model property to divide it into varying numbers of vertical columns:

```
div#branding { situated : a; display-model : "112 (intrinsic)";
div#content_main { situated : b; display-model : "123 (intrinsic)";
div#content_sub { situated : c; display-model : "1234 (intrinsic)";
div#content_supp { situated : d; display-model : "123 (intrinsic)";
```

If you are watching closely, you may notice that the #branding division uses the same numbered identifier twice (122). This will allow its content to span across two of the three columns.

Lastly, you can position each of the nested divisions into any of the slots you have defined, but only inside their containing division:

```
div#branding div.one { situated : 1; }
div#branding div.two { situated : 2; }

div#content_main div.one { situated : 1; }
div#content_main div.two { situated : 2; }
div#content_main div.three { situated : 3; }

div#content_sub div.one { situated : 1; }
div#content_sub div.two { situated : 2; }
div#content_sub div.three { situated : 3; }
div#content_sub div.four { situated : 4; }

div#content_supp div.one { situated : 1; }
div#content_supp div.two { situated : 2; }
div#content_supp div.three { situated : 3; }
```

The result is a robust, flexible grid layout that can get smaller and bigger with the browser window and will accommodate changes in text size without breaking (**Figure 4.57**).

Have your cake, and eat it too

You have seen how simple it will be to create a complex grid design with the Advanced Layout Module. The flexibility of placing content into any slot without changing the source order of the content makes the Advanced Layout Module impressive, and it will liberate designers from presentational thinking about markup and CSS.

To demonstrate the layout flexibility of Advanced Layout, the next examples are all variations of the same markup. The Advanced Layout CSS appears with each variation (**next pages**).

4.57 Developing a layout that is flexible and robust

```
div#branding { situated : b; display-model : "112 (intrinsic)"; }
div#branding div.one { situated : 1; }
div#branding div.two { situated : 2; }

div#content_main { situated : a; display-model : "123 (intrinsic)"; }
div#content_main div.one { situated : 1; }
div#content_main div.two { situated : 2; }
div#content_main div.three { situated : 3; }

div#content_sub { situated : c; display-model : "1234 (intrinsic)";      }
div#content_sub div.one { situated : 1; }
div#content_sub div.two { situated : 2; }
div#content_sub div.three { situated : 3; }
div#content_sub div.four { situated : 4; }

div#content_supp { situated : d; display-model : "123 (intrinsic)";      }
div#content_supp div.one { situated : 1; }
div#content_supp div.two { situated : 2; }
div#content_supp div.three { situated : 3; }
```

```
div#branding { situated : a; display-model : "112 (intrinsic)"; }
div#branding div.one { situated : 1; }
div#branding div.two { situated : 2; }

div#content_main { situated : b; display-model : "123 (intrinsic)"; }
div#content_main div.one { situated : 1; }
div#content_main div.two { situated : 2; }
div#content_main div.three { situated : 3; }

div#content_sub { situated : c; display-model : "1234 (intrinsic)";      }
div#content_sub div.one { situated : 1; }
div#content_sub div.two { situated : 2; }
div#content_sub div.three { situated : 3; }
div#content_sub div.four { situated : 4; }

div#content_supp { situated : d; display-model : "123 (intrinsic)";      }
div#content_supp div.one { situated : 1; }
div#content_supp div.two { situated : 2; }
div#content_supp div.three { situated : 3; }
```

```
div#branding { situated : b; display-model : "112 (intrinsic)"; }
div#branding div.one { situated : 1; }
div#branding div.two { situated : 2; }

div#content_main { situated : c; display-model : "123 (intrinsic)"; }
div#content_main div.one { situated : 1; }
div#content_main div.two { situated : 2; }
div#content_main div.three { situated : 3; }

div#content_sub { situated : d; display-model : "1234 (intrinsic)";      }
div#content_sub div.one { situated : 1; }
div#content_sub div.two { situated : 2; }
div#content_sub div.three { situated : 3; }
div#content_sub div.four { situated : 4; }

div#content_supp { situated : a; display-model : "123 (intrinsic)";      }
div#content_supp div.one { situated : 1; }
div#content_supp div.two { situated : 2; }
div#content_supp div.three { situated : 3; }
```

```
div#branding { situated : d; display-model : "112 (intrinsic)"; }
div#branding div.one { situated : 1; }
div#branding div.two { situated : 2; }

div#content_main { situated : a; display-model : "123 (intrinsic)"; }
div#content_main div.one { situated : 1; }
div#content_main div.two { situated : 2; }
div#content_main div.three { situated : 3; }

div#content_sub { situated : b; display-model : "1234 (intrinsic)";      }
div#content_sub div.one { situated · 1; }
div#content_sub div.two { situated : 2; }
div#content_sub div.three { situated : 3; }
div#content_sub div.four { situated : 4; }

div#content_supp { situated : c; display-model : "123 (intrinsic)";      }
div#content_supp div.one { situated : 1; }
div#content_supp div.two { situated : 2; }
div#content_supp div.three { situated : 3; }
```

```
div#branding { situated : b; display-model : "112 (intrinsic)"; }
div#branding div.one { situated : 1; }
div#branding div.two { situated : 2; }

div#content_main { situated : d; display-model : "123 (intrinsic)"; }
div#content_main div.one { situated : 1; }
div#content_main div.two { situated : 2; }
div#content_main div.three { situated : 3; }

div#content_sub { situated : a; display-model : "1234 (intrinsic)";       }
div#content_sub div.one { situated : 1; }
div#content_sub div.two { situated : 2; }
div#content_sub div.three { situated : 3; }
div#content_sub div.four { situated : 4; }

div#content_supp { situated : c; display-model : "123 (intrinsic)";       }
div#content_supp div.one { situated : 1; }
div#content_supp div.two { situated : 2; }
div#content_supp div.three { situated : 3; }
```

```
div#branding { situated : b; display-model : "122 (intrinsic)"; }
div#branding div.one { situated : 2; }
div#branding div.two { situated : 1; }

div#content_main { situated : d; display-model : "123 (intrinsic)"; }
div#content_main div.one { situated : 3; }
div#content_main div.two { situated : 2; }
div#content_main div.three { situated : 1; }

div#content_sub { situated : a; display-model : "1234 (intrinsic)";       }
div#content_sub div.one { situated : 4; }
div#content_sub div.two { situated : 3; }
div#content_sub div.three { situated : 2; }
div#content_sub div.four { situated : 1; }

div#content_supp { situated : c; display-model : "123 (intrinsic)";       }
div#content_supp div.one { situated : 3; }
div#content_supp div.two { situated : 2; }
div#content_supp div.three { situated : 1; }
```

```
div#branding { situated : c; display-model : "122 (intrinsic)"; }
div#branding div.one { situated : 2; }
div#branding div.two { situated : 1; }

div#content_main { situated : a; display-model : "123 (intrinsic)"; }
div#content_main div.one { situated : 3; }
div#content_main div.two { situated : 1; }
div#content_main div.three { situated : 2; }

div#content_sub { situated : d; display-model : "1234 (intrinsic)";      }
div#content_sub div.one { situated : 3; }
div#content_sub div.two { situated : 2; }
div#content_sub div.three { situated : 4; }
div#content_sub div.four { situated : 1; }

div#content_supp { situated : b; display-model : "123 (intrinsic)";      }
div#content_supp div.one { situated : 2; }
div#content_supp div.two { situated : 3; }
div#content_supp div.three { situated : 1; }
```

```
div#branding { situated : a; display-model : "122 (intrinsic)"; }
div#branding div.one { situated : 2; }
div#branding div.two { situated : 1; }

div#content_main { situated : c; display-model : "123 (intrinsic)"; }
div#content_main div.one { situated : 1; }
div#content_main div.two { situated : 3; }
div#content_main div.three { situated : 2; }

div#content_sub { situated : d; display-model : "1234 (intrinsic)";      }
div#content_sub div.one { situated : 1; }
div#content_sub div.two { situated : 2; }
div#content_sub div.three { situated : 4; }
div#content_sub div.four { situated : 3; }

div#content_supp { situated : b; display-model : "123 (intrinsic)";      }
div#content_supp div.one { situated : 1; }
div#content_supp div.two { situated : 3; }
div#content_supp div.three { situated : 2; }
```

Concluding Remarks

So, here you are at the end of the book. What's next?

The future.

If you enjoy designing for the Web as much as I do, you'll find that there will be very exciting times ahead of you. You will have many opportunities—ones that only a few short years ago were unimaginable—to create great-looking sites that people will love to use.

In just a few years since CSS was born, the Web design industry has changed significantly: Accessibility, meaningful markup, and presentation with CSS are now a reality in the Web professional's daily life. A true professional never stops learning and CSS would not be used so widely today had it not been for the hard work and generosity of the many men and women who struggled to find solutions and who then shared their work with the rest of us. I hope that as CSS develops in the future and even more exiting solutions are reached, you will follow in their footsteps and share what you have learned.

Designing and developing for the Web should be a process filled with creativity and whether you write code, create databases, or are a visual designer, there is creativity in everything that you do. As part of my role as an invited expert to the W3C's CSS Working Group, I help to bring a creative designer's voice to the table and I welcome your thoughts. If future versions of CSS are to meet the needs of visual designers and developers then it is up to all of us to help shape its future by becoming involved in the discussions and debates over how and where it is to go next. So I urge you to become involved in whatever capacity you can, no matter how big or how small your contribution.

Now it's time to stop listening to me and time to start designing the future.

Credits

Page 13, Figure 1.2, Opera software, www.opera.com

Page 19, Figure 1.3 CSS Zen Garden designs: Shaun Inman, www.shauninman.com; Mike Davidson, www.mikeindustries.com, and Egor Kloos, http://dutchcelt.nl/

Page 25, Figure 1.5 Jon Hicks, www.hicksdesign.co.uk

Page 26, Figure 1.7 John Oxton, www.joshuaink.com

Page 26, Figure 1.8 Jeremy Keith, www.adactio.com

Page 27, Figure 1.9 Andy Budd, www.andybudd.com

Page 27, Figure 1.10 Andy Budd, Jeremy Keith, and Richard Rutter, www.clearleft.com

Page 28, Figure 1.11 Jon Hicks, www.hicksdesign.co.uk

Page 28, Figure 1.12 Andy Budd, Jeremy Keith, and Richard Rutter, http://2006.dconstruct.org/

Page 29, Figure 1.13 Richard Rutter, http://clagnut.com

Page 29, Figure 1.14 Tomas Caspers, www.webkrauts.de

Page 30, Figure 1.15 and Figure 1.16 Mark Boulton, www.markboulton.co.uk

Page 38, Figure 1.18 Douglas Bowman, www.stopdesign.com, and Dave Shea, www.mezzoblue.com

Page 39, Figure 1.19 Jeffrey Zeldman, www.alistapart.com, and Ryan Carson, www.thinkvitamin.com

Page 48, Figure 1.20 CSS Reboot design rebooters, at www.cssreboot.com

Page 80, "Read 'em and Weep," by Peter Austin, http://flickr.com/people/53366513@N00/

Pages 82–83, Dave Shea, www.mezzoblue.com

Pages 89–95, Figures 1.26, 1.27, 1.29, 1.30, 1.31 (photos), Molly Holzschlag, www.molly.com

Page 116, Jason Santa Maria, www.jasonsantamaria.com

Page 187, Figure 3.2, 3.3, and 3.4 Jeffrey Zeldman, www.alistapart.com

Page 194, Figure 3.10 CSS Zen Garden, www.csszengarden.com, Patrick Griffiths, www.htmldog.com

Page 195, Figure 3.11 www.mozilla.org

Page 199, Figure 3.12 http://web.burz.hr/

Pages 201–203, Figures 3.13, 3.14, 3.15, 3.16, 3.17 Khoi Vinh, www.subtraction.com

Pages 204–205, Figures 3.18, 3.19, 3.20, 3.21, 3.22, Greg Storey, Airbag Industries, www.airbagindustries.com

Pages 206–207, Figures 3.23, 3.24, 3.25, 3.26 Jeff Croft, www2.jeffcroft.com

Pages 208-209, Figures 2.27, 3.28, 3.29, 3.30 Veerle Pieters, http://veerle.duoh.com

Pages 225–231, Figures 3.31 through 3.41 Mike Davidson, www.newsvine.com

Page 246 www.naho.com, www.elisasassi.com, www.jennysrealm.com, www.glu-glu.org, http://exptypo.com, www.mirada.it/satrapi, www.dzinenmotion.com, www.mondotrendy.com

Pages 248, 250-252, 266 Ron Huxley, http://flickr.com/people/rehuxley

Page 249, Figure 3.43, Flickr, www.flickr.com

Page 253, Figure 3.45 Jon Hicks, www.hicksdesign.co.uk

Page 254 –Kariann, http://flickr.com/people/dailypoetics

Page 268, Figure 3.46 Web Standards Award, http://webstandardsawards.com, www.poptones.co.uk, www.jasonsantamaria.com, www.bearskinrug.co.uk

Photography credits

Many of the photographs and artistic works in this book are from Flickr and are published under a Creative Commons license or are published with the artist's consent. Many of the food images used in the examples in Parts 2 and 4 are by Lara Ferroni, www.platesandpacks.com, and Eric Fung, http://flickr.com/people/gnuf.

The following talented artists' photography is featured in this book. To learn more about them, point your browser to www.flickr.com/people/... and add their Flickr name (in parentheses):

H. Alexander (barto), J. Armstrong (shutupyourface), H. Bernard (cygnoir), Bialy-Fox, Sharon (10939571@N00)W. Boyd (wetsun), cobalt (cobalt), dailypoetics, Kariann (dailypoetics), R. y Dani (78453948@N00), David (funkblast), B. Dimmick (dimmick), Dudu P (dudup), Dusk Rude boy (methad), L. Elkind (wurzle), L. Ferroni (laraferroni), E. Fung (gnuf), V. J. Fungo (fungo), C. Glass (chrisglass), T. Hawk (thomashawk), R. Holland (robh), M. Holzschlag (mollyeh11), W. R. Howell (wrhowell), O. Ingrouille (82705724@N00), S. Isaacs (stefanisaacs), J. Ito (joi), Jen (jcm), L. Jones (lizjones), R. Keefe (robinkeefe), J. Keith (adactio), P. Keleher (pkeleher), Indenture, Kim (40389360@N00), A. Koskinen (ansik), T. Krech (extranoise), P. Lindberg (plindberg), D. Marsh (hotmedia), A & W Mc (indigogoat), M. McCauslin (michale), T. McCullough (idletype), Metha-D Davide (methad), V. Miettinen (wili), S. Morales (selva), T. Morgan (trevormorgan), Muffet, Liz (calliope) Nancycallahan, Kristina (nancycallahan), ohsleepless1, Lisa (54998840@N00), Omnia, Brenda (omnia), C.G. Palmer (cgp314), Pikaluk (pikaluk), D. Pontes (dudup), R. Rizk (tempest), Saffanna, Carolyn (mamabarns), Sally (sallypics), A. Sampson (adrian_s), T. Sapateiro (tatianasapateiro),

A. Saunders (kaptainkobold), D. Shea (mezzoblue), M. Sheehan (finsterbaby), Sister 72, Jackie (sis), J. Soni Neto (jamilsoni), B. Sparkle (beesparkle), M. Spasoff (clownfish), M. Spolin (automatt), J. F. Stuefer (josefstuefer), H. Sudoneighm (striatic), Sysy8, Silvia (sysy81), tanakawho (28481088@N00), Thomas (onkel_wart), J. van Wunnik (artlantis), visualpanic (visualpanic), P. Vora (payalvora), wermsrus, Jacki (werms), D. Wilson (iboy_daniel), J. Wilson (hive), E. Yang (midweekpost), R. Zebrowski (firepile), Züleyha (zulzul),

The following talented artists' photography courtesy of iStock is also featured in this book. To learn more about them, visit www.istockphoto.com:

Christine Balderas, Galina Barskaya, blackred, John Clines, Jorgé Delgado, Erin Derkatz, Diane Diederich, Elena Eisseva, fitzer, Nicole Gawron, Jon Helgason, javarman, javarman3, Ljupco, Jason Lugo, Marek Pawluczuk, Denis Pepin, Alexis Puentes, John Rodriguez, fanelie rosier, Andrey Prokhorov, Dustin Steller, UteHil

Index

: (colon) combinator, 27
, (comma) combinator, 27
. (period), 346
+ combinator, 27, 28
> combinator, 27
* selector, 33
@ (at symbol), 346
@import at-rule technique, 17, 138, 158
1-Click ordering, 113
456bereastreet.com, 316, 322, 336

A

A-grade browsers, 52
A List Apart Magazine, 41, 185, 189, 338
absolute positioning, 134, 161, 165,
    170–171, 274
accessibility, 12–16
    and content-out approach, 62
    and Flash, 245, 247
    and grid-based designs, 187
    guidelines, 12, 16, 60
    how most designers view, 13
    laws, 12, 16
    and multicolumn layouts, 339
    and table-based layouts, 62
    testing, 13
    as usability issue, 12–13
Acebal, César, 345, 351
ad server services, 134
Adams, Cameron, 32, 38, 267
<address> element, 86–88
address lists, 276
Adium, 49
adjacent sibling selectors, 28, 175

Adobe GoLive, 128
Advanced Layout Module, CSS3, 345–357
    defining grids with, 348
    designing with, 351–357
    display-model property, 346, 352
    documentation for, 315
    flexibility of, 353
    and grid-based layouts, 346
    purpose of, 314, 345
    and template-based positioning, 349
advertising billboards, 243
aesthetics, 255
:after pseudo-element, 31, 295
Airbag Industries, 204–205
Ajax, 113, 114, 125, 179, 269
Allsopp, John, 34
ALMCSS, 345, 351
alpha-transparency, 136, 168, 328
alt attribute, 276, 316
alternative text, 276
Amazon, 113, 269
"Anatomy of Web Fonts, The," 243
Andrew, Rachel, 8
annotations, 76, 117. *See also* comments
Apple
    Dashboard Widgets, 49
    iPhoto, 253
    Safari. *See* Safari
AppleScript, 49
Ashai Shimbun, 221
asymmetrical grids, 197, 198, 208, 263
attribute selectors, 25–27, 296, 316, 330
attributes, semantic naming of, 33–39
autisticcuckoo.net, 274, 335

B

background-color property, 136, 166–167,
    279
background-image property, 193, 230, 287,
    341
background images
    for flexible layouts, 230
    naming conventions for, 36
    of rulers/grids, 193
    using multiple, 320, 322, 325–334
Backgrounds and Borders module, CSS3, 314,
    320–324
banners, 304
Barnard, Frederick, 111
Basecamp, 107
baseline grid, 226, 227, 229
BBC Browser Support Standards table, 52
:before pseudo-element, 31, 295
behaviors, 278, 279
best practices, 127, 131. *See also* Web
    standards
billboards, 243
block quotes, 67, 84–85. *See also* quotations
<blockquote> element, 84–85
BlueRobot Layout Reservoir, 41, 345
<body> element, 154, 159–160
Book of Calculating, The, 185
border property, 287
borders, 287, 305, 321, 337
Borders module, CSS3 Backgrounds and, 314,
    320–324
Bowen, Lawrence Llewellyn, 233, 236
Bowman, Douglas, 8, 36, 41
Box Lessons, 41

box model hack, 31
boxes, 321, 322, 332, 336
Boxes and Arrows, 127
branding area, 61–62, 149, 153, 167–168, 304
Briggs, Owen, 41
broadsheet newspapers, 194, 211, 213, 238
browser extensions, 131–132, 134
browser matrixes, 52
browser styles, 65, 158–159
Browser Support Standards table, BBC, 52
BrowserCam, 325, 334
browsers. *See also* specific browsers
  adding measuring tools to, 193
  compatibility concerns, 15, 21, 25, 52, 273
  CSS support, 8, 10, 16, 50–52, 273
  for developing/testing interactive prototypes, 131
  extensions/plug-ins for, 131–132, 134
  and floats, 135
  Gecko-based, 343
  limitations of, 16
  and Multi-column Layout Module, 337
  and multiple background images, 322, 325, 334
  overriding style defaults for, 158–159
  testing Web pages in multiple, 325
  and text shadows, 331
  usage statistics, 17
  Yahoo's "grading" of, 52
Budd, Andy, 34, 193
buggy software, 15
buttons, form, 330

C

C-grade browsers, 52
Camino, 16
Çelik, Tantek, 8, 31, 32, 147
Champeon, Steve, 20

Chandanais, Rob, 41
Chandra, Debra, 20
Changing Rooms, 233, 235
chat clients, 49
child selectors, 27, 296
Chipman, Steve, 251
<cite> element, 149
clagnut.com, 231
Clark, Joe, 13, 198
class attributes, 86, 317
class selectors, 296
clearing elements, 307
CMS integration, 166
code, creating reusable, 127
collaboration tools/techniques, 107, 119, 166
colon combinator, 27
Color Palette Creator, 251
color palettes, 251
color styles, 138, 158, 166–167
colors
  alternating, 318–319
  background, 136, 166–167, 279
  differentiating content with, 227
  emphasizing columns with, 209
column boxes, 336
column-count property, 336
column-gap property, 336
column overlays, 228
column-rule property, 336, 337
column-span property, 338
column-spanning headlines, 213, 217, 338
column-width property, 336
columns. *See also* grids
  allowing content to flow among, 336, 337
  background colors for, 136
  changing width of, 162
  combining, 226
  creating, 134, 161–162
  in newspaper design, 213–223

  placing rules in, 336–337
  readability considerations, 213, 335, 336
  subdividing, 195, 227, 229, 352
  switching position of, 161–162, 351
  using color to emphasize, 209
combinators, 27
combined selectors, 27
comma combinator, 27
comments
  conditional, 32–33, 295
  marking sections in CSS with, 137, 154
compounds, XHTML, 84, 146, 147
comps, 121
computation, 319
conditional comments, 32–33, 295
Constantia font, 308
content. *See also* text
  "above the fold," 227
  approaching markup from, 66
  changing visual layout of, 62
  choosing most appropriate markup for, 65, 76
  defining source order of, 119
  describing meaning of, 76
  gathering, 107
  generated, 31
  highlighting relationships in, 119
  readability of. *See* readability
  removing CSS from, 60
  separating branding area from, 62
  showing hierarchy/structure of, 122
  showing order of, 60
  tracking delivery of, 107
content-based process, 103–105, 121, 131, 141
content briefs, 107
content divisions, 147–148. *See also* **<div>** elements
Content Management System integration, 166
content management systems, 134

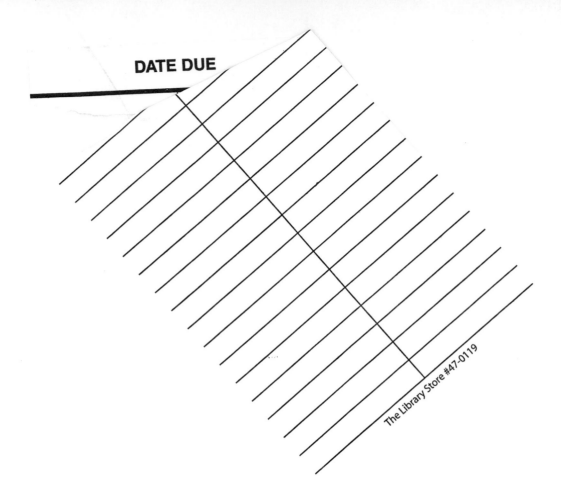

DATE DUE

The Library Store #47-0119